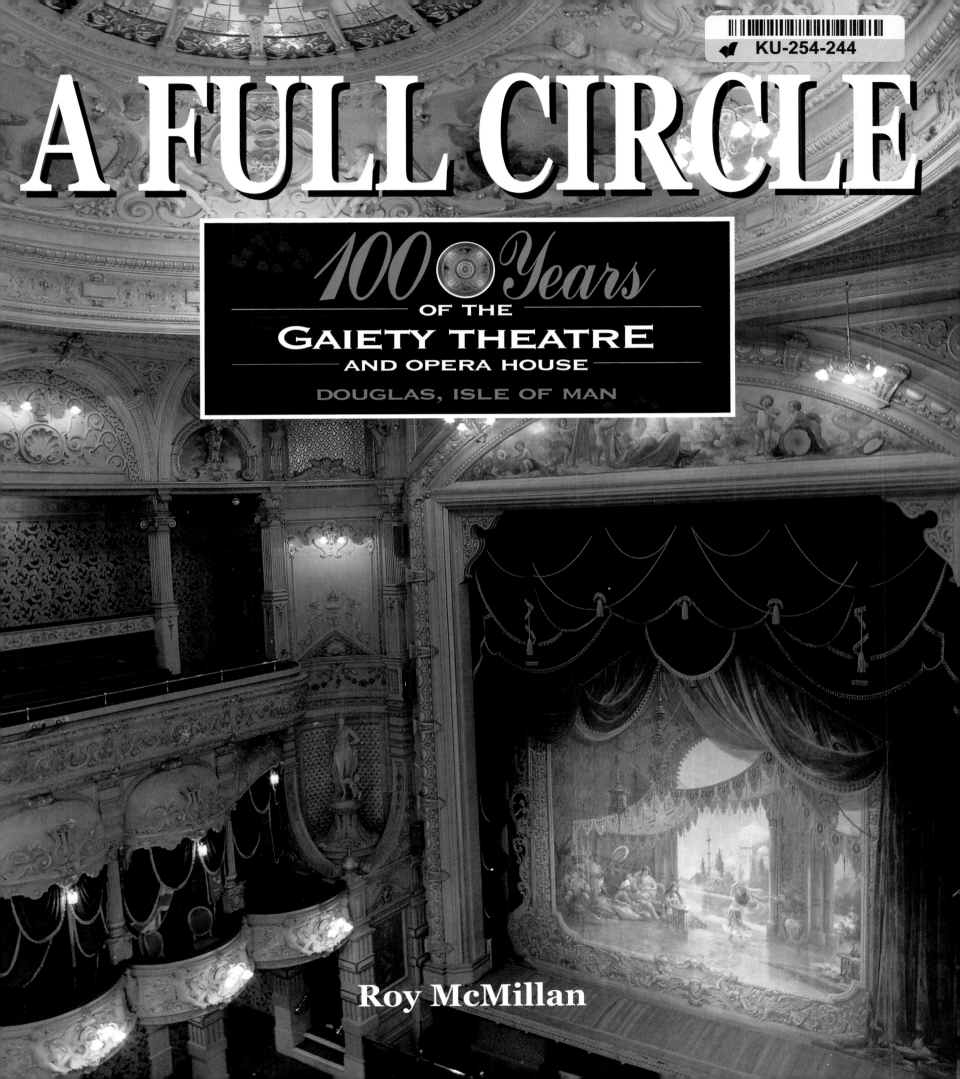

A FULL CIRCLE

100 Years
OF THE
GAIETY THEATRE
AND OPERA HOUSE
DOUGLAS, ISLE OF MAN

Roy McMillan

For Amanda and Catherine

A FULL CIRCLE

100 Years
OF THE
GAIETY THEATRE
AND OPERA HOUSE
DOUGLAS, ISLE OF MAN

Roy McMillan

Published by Keith Uren Publishing
12 Manor Lane, Douglas, Isle of Man, IM2 2NX

Text origination and design by Keith Uren

Printing, reprographics and binding by
The Bath Press, Lower Bristol Road, Bath, BA2 3BL

ISBN 0 - 9538628 - 0 - 1

CONTENTS

Photo by]   Ellis & Walery.
Mr. LEWIS WALLER, as "Brigadier Gerard."

GAIETY THEATRE
DOUGLAS.

MONDAY, AUGUST 6th,
SIX NIGHTS AND ONE MATINEE.

MR. LEWIS WALLER,
MISS EVELYN MILLARD,
AND ENTIRE COMPANY FROM
THE LYRIC THEATRE, LONDON,
IN
"Brigadier Gerard,"
Conan Doyle's Soldier Play.

Preceded by Henry Hamilton's One Act Play,
"FORTUNE'S FOOL."
Philip Challoner - - MR. LEWIS WALLER.

Page ix   Acknowledgements

Page x   Foreword

Page xiii   Preface

Page 15   Introduction

Page 16   The Island and the Architect

Page 29   The Gaiety Theatre

Page 49   Up and Running; Down and Out

Page 61   Stopping the Rot

Page 77   Restoration

Page 93   Completing the Circle

Page 111   A Cast of Thousands

Page 153   Appendices:
(i)   Original programme of
      'The Corsican Brothers'
(ii)   A Century of Performance
(iii)   Technical specification of the Theatre
(iv)   Thanksgiving Service for the
      Restoration of The Gaiety Theatre:
      Order of Service
(v)   Bibliography
(vi)   Publisher's Presentation copies
(vii)   Roll Call

Page 173   Index

ACKNOWLEDGEMENTS

M any people have, occasionally under duress, given generous help in the preparation of this book, principally in providing memories and records of their association with The Gaiety. Those listed here are in no particular order, and some are thanked with fuller explanation in the Preface.

Mervin Stokes, David Wilmore and Séamus Shea know more than anyone about The Gaiety from its construction to the present day. They gave enormous help, and with great patience relayed their stories of the restoration, as well as offering advice on each chapter as it was produced. Other contributors were Alec Smith and Sir Laurence New, who also read early drafts of some of the chapters; Charles Sentance and Lionel Hull of the Friends of The Gaiety; Jimmy Bridson, Alan Pascoe, Ken and Dawn Daly and Arthur Corkill, who were all actively involved in working at the theatre at various times in the last fifty years. For the political side of things, thanks are due to the Chief Minister, Donald Gelling, and to Eddie Lowey, M.L.C.

For many of the photographs, Ian and Monica Clark of Island Photographics and their technical staff were indispensable, as was Andrew Barton who took many of the pictures. Additional research was carried out by Kit Gawne, with the assistance of Roger Sims and the staff of the Manx Museum Library. The Manx Museum, and especially Stephen Harrison, the Director, gave invaluable support. Thanks are also due to Clive Dixon and Moore Stephens for facilitating the research.

Thanks also to Brian Walker, the author of a biographical article in the book 'Frank Matcham: Theatre Architect', which he also edited, and which forms the basis for much of the material about Matcham in this book; John Bethel, who was on the Management Committee in the early 70s; Mr Docherty, for the production of early advertising cards; and Peter Longman of The Theatres Trust, for his corrections and the Foreword.

Doreen Barwell, wife of the second manager of the theatre, possessed a priceless record of events at The Gaiety, which she generously allowed to be used and reproduced. My parents, James and Doreen McMillan, offered their services as early proof-readers. Douglas Corporation Library and Planning Department gave help with archive material; Lynn Copley and Tracy Smith typed some of the Appendices; and thanks also to my wife, Amanda Barton, for all the reasons that authors normally list, and one or two that they don't.

FOREWORD
Peter Longman, Director of The Theatres Trust

Nearly twenty-five years ago in 1976 a small group of enthusiasts sat down to record what was left of the British Isles' stock of Victorian and Edwardian theatres. When eventually they published their book in 1982 it was called 'Curtains!!! or a New Life for Old Theatres', and The Gaiety Theatre had been chosen to illustrate its front cover.

Now The Gaiety has been given a whole book to itself, and I, who as a junior Arts Council officer had encouraged the *Curtains* team to apply for the grant which paid for their research, have been invited to write this foreword. The Theatres Trust, of which I am now Director, was set up by the United Kingdom Parliament in 1976 to protect theatres there. We keep an eye on the four hundred or so - old and new - which are now in use, and on a list of 'sleeping beauties' which are waiting in the wings to come back to life. Whenever I want to encourage someone I tell them the story of The Gaiety and how it was rescued. And, having previously been the UK government's chief adviser on museums for ten years, I also reckon I can recognise an important piece of heritage when I see it.

The story of The Gaiety's first seventy years is not untypical of many seaside theatres, which went from initial boom to a slow and gradual decline, and then faced closure and demolition. But whereas eighty-five percent of those theatres that had stood at the beginning of the First World War were lost, including all the other traditional theatres on the Isle of Man, The Gaiety has been revived, and in a manner which inspires all who care for the theatre and for our heritage.

Credit for this achievement must go first and foremost to the Isle of Man Government, which took the decision in 1971 to buy it, and then brought in one of the world's foremost experts, Victor Glasstone, to advise them. The Gaiety was one of the very first theatres in the British Isles to be rescued by a public authority in this way. It was a remarkable and far-sighted step, which many local authorities in the UK have since followed.

But this book is really the story of what happened next, and of how Mervin Stokes, who had started to work part-time at the theatre in 1969 and became its Manager in 1984, set about completing the restoration. And what a story it is! It is a story of determination and a refusal to take 'no' for an answer; of painstaking detective work; and of an infectious enthusiasm and an amazing ability to charm, browbeat or beg countless people and organisations to join him in his crusade. The image of Mervin piecing together the jigsaw of shattered fragments from the auditorium rose window on a pair of old doors over a table at home will long remain with me. So will the moment in the stage basement when they tested the trolley and the moving opening in the stage above it and rediscovered how the Victorians made a Corsican Trap which didn't risk decapitating one of the stars of the show! Credit for this and for much else must go to Dr David Wilmore, who took Victor Glasstone's dream of a proper restoration and made it a reality.

The Friends of The Gaiety also deserve our applause as an inspiration to similar groups everywhere. Sponsors and individual donors and, of course, the Government have all played their parts in an incredible transformation scene. Mind you, the raw material on which they had to work could hardly have been bettered. As the author says, if you had to choose a theatre which represented the essential elements of the greatest theatre architect of British history, The Gaiety fulfils the criteria almost perfectly. To my mind it's the prettiest theatre in these islands; even on the dull day in February when I last saw it, with the heating off, the drapes removed and the decorators in, it was still a staggering sight. The Gaiety is not Frank Matcham's biggest or grandest theatre or his smallest, and nor is it particularly old, but as now restored it is capable of showing better than anywhere else the opulence and the sense of occasion that we associate with late Victorian and Edwardian theatre-going in its heyday. And of course it now has its complete set of recreated Victorian wooden machinery under the stage to fascinate visitors, and all in working order.

The fact that this theatre *is* in working order is very important. As a heritage attraction it can now stand proud alongside those buildings that are owned and run by the Manx Government under its Museum and National Trust hats. But as a working theatre it also needs to earn its keep and to provide a service to the Island's residents and to their many visitors. There is no other conventional theatre on the Island, and Mervin has ably demonstrated that the heritage and the live theatre uses can complement each other. What's more, the whole job has been done at a fraction of the cost of certain other theatre restoration projects I could mention, and of course without being able to call on the UK's National Lottery.

I am sure some things will need to be finished, and that some things may yet be improved. It will be vital not to let the momentum slip. The worst thing that could happen now would be to relax standards, so that with poor routine maintenance and well intentioned, but inappropriate, alterations the theatre again starts a slide towards unauthentic décor or fittings and to lose its unique character and appeal.

The Gaiety is the sort of theatre that can and will draw performers and publicity to the Island, as well as tourists. It deserves to be better known, and this book by Roy McMillan will help to spread the message that there is a new jewel in the Isle of Man's crown. It also tells the story of how an enlightened Government employed the best advice available to recreate something that is now unique. And it shows how the theatre's Friends and the business community were prepared to join the Government in backing a decision to go for the very best and to refuse to compromise on standards. We all owe it to all who have supported this venture to see that the fruit of their efforts continues to amaze and delight for the next one hundred years.

Peter Longman
Director of The Theatres Trust
22 Charing Cross Road
London WC2

February 2000

PREFACE

This is an anecdotal history, not an academic one. It is built from the memories of those involved with the restoration of an extraordinary building.

The principal contributor has been Mervin Stokes, Manager of the theatre since 1984. While it is true that without him this book would never have needed writing, since he is the prime mover behind the restoration of the building it celebrates, it certainly could not have been written as it is without his recollections. The immense vat of his knowledge of every aspect of the work was comprehensively tapped, and a more willing and helpful provider would be impossible to imagine. Apart from his own profound understanding of The Gaiety and Frank Matcham, he has spent the last decade in conversation or correspondence with everyone associated with the building and the man. He was also in possession of a huge archive of material relating to the theatre, from press cuttings of the recent past to lost programmes and ephemera from a century ago.

A significant contribution also came from Dr David Wilmore, the consultant on the restoration, and a man whose academic and practical qualifications make him the best source possible for much of the history of theatre generally and the mechanics of the understage machinery in particular. His years of patient research have been plundered wholesale as well.

There were many others who told their part of the story, such as Séamus Shea, whose close association with the contemporary features of the building as well as the restoration was invaluable.

Charles Sentance and Lionel Hull supplied essential information about the Friends of The Gaiety. Doreen Barwell provided an outstanding source of archive material from her late husband's collection, and Kit Gawne trawled the Manx Museum for hours searching for apposite cuttings and references.

None of this, however, guarantees absolute accuracy, and while it would be a relief to pass on any blame for mistakes to the many who have offered their experiences, expertise and understanding, the responsibility for any errors rests firmly with me.

Memory is a notoriously fickle thing, and there may be some who remember events differently. As a result, there will be individuals, groups and organisations that will feel offended by their absence or inclusion, and for this the author is truly apologetic. Apologies also for failing to offend those who richly deserve it, but the Isle of Man is a small place and we all have to earn a living.

Some of the sources quoted in the bibliography have not been independently checked, and should perhaps therefore carry as much of a warning as the rest of the book. About the theatre itself, however, its construction and restoration, it is believed the information is accurate.

The bibliography may seem slender stuff for future researchers, and indeed it is. However, it should be remembered that the principal source of the information is the dedicated years of practical and academic research carried out by those who are the main players in The Gaiety's story, which constitutes a primary source of the highest order.

Andrew Barton, the photographer, and Monica and Ian Clark of Island Photographics have been extraordinarily generous, patient and efficient. Their collaboration over many years and especially in the preparation of this book has been exceptional, and the whole project would have been almost impossible without their willing, friendly and professional assistance.

Stephen Harrison of the Manx Museum and National Heritage has also been exemplary in his generosity, as have Roger Sims and all the library staff.

All of this generous assistance has made it possible to produce a work intended to be entertaining but also to stand as a memorial to the finest theatre of its kind in the British Isles, and perhaps the world.

For King and Country.

NEEDING HELP

Grand Concert and Spectacular patriotic Scena.

GAIETY THEATRE, DOUGLAS.

THURSDAY, Nov. 12, 1914.

Mr. ROBERT BURNETT, Baritone.
Miss FLORENCE LAING, Soprano.
Miss CISSIE MILNE, Reciter.
THE DOUGLAS FESTIVAL CHOIR.
THE DOUGLAS MALE CHORISTERS.

GAIETY
THEATRE &
OPERA HOUSE

MONDAY, SEPT. 13th
FOR SIX NIGHTS AT 7-45.

BARRY O'BRIEN

presents the
Vaudeville Theatre, London, Success.

DO YOU REMEMBER

By EDITH SAVILE & JOHN CARLTON

An entirely charming Comedy of youth and youth's extravagant emotions. In Three Acts—with an Epilogue twenty-five years later.

DOROTHY BAIRD
PEGGY PRIMROSE
DENNIS SHAND

Directed by MICHAEL HILLMAN.

"A Breath of Fresh Air in the Theatre." *Daily Herald.*

Talkie Pictures every Sunday at 8-15.

Programme.
Grand Opening Monday, July 16, 1900.
FOR SIX NIGHTS ONLY

MISS ADA BLANCHE,
FROM DRURY LANE THEATRE.

Supported by her Own Company of London Artistes.
Chorus of Telephone Girls and Special Dancers.

The Telephone Girl!

THE YEOMEN OF THE GUARD

GAIETY THEATRE, Douglas, at 7-45.

ST. STEPHEN'S NIGHT, | NEW YEAR'S NIGHT, and
Monday, December 29th. | FRIDAY, JAN. 2nd (last time).

THE ORCHID

THE TELEPHONE GIRL

BY
F. C. BURNAND
ARTHUR STURGESS
and
SIR AUGUSTUS HARRIS

GASTON SERPETTE &
J. M. GLOVER

The Catch of the Season

BY Seymour Hicks

Mr. George Dance's Co.

GAIETY THEATRE,
DOUGLAS.
MONDAY, AUG. 13th, Six Nights.

Mr. GEORGE DANCE'S Company
in the brilliantly successful Musical Comedy

The Catch of the Season,

FROM THE
VAUDEVILLE THEATRE, LONDON.

POST CARD.
THIS ADDRESS ONLY TO BE WRITTEN HERE.
AFFIX HALFPENNY STAMP.

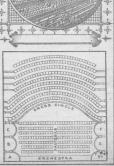

GAIETY
THEATRE
PROGRAMME

DOUGLAS,
Isle of Man.
The PRETTIEST THEATRE
in the Island.

INTRODUCTION

This book is about a building - The Gaiety Theatre and Opera House in Douglas on the Isle of Man. It is also, as a matter of course, about what makes a building - what makes it important, interesting, significant, extraordinary, or representatively ordinary. Since the book covers aspects of the construction and reconstruction as well, it will include an examination of the technology and artistry which literally made it, and which define its significance both in Douglas in 1900, and on a wider scale in 2000. With a theatre by Frank Matcham, all this is relevant, because he was such a significant figure in theatre architecture. His work reflects the role theatre had in the late nineteenth and early twentieth centuries, and exemplifies his capacity to meet the demands of his paymasters and the paying public, whatever their class.

But the story of The Gaiety Theatre also merits telling because of its survival and its restoration, a ten-year-long, dedicated, determined and ultimately triumphant resuscitation. It has reached one hundred years without the grotesque overlaying of fashionable additions which was the fate of so many theatres in Britain; without the indignity of ill-suited conversion which also befell many of its contemporaries; and perhaps most miraculously, without being ripped to shreds and thrown on a bonfire for the valuable land it was built upon. It suffered neglect, certainly, of a grievous kind, and a real threat of demolition. It was only a combination of the amateur theatre companies on the Island, the Manx Government, the first restoration by Victor Glasstone and the creation of The Friends of The Gaiety that allowed its continued existence. It is now recognised as an important part of the architectural heritage of the British Isles, and, by extension, the English-speaking, theatre-loving world.

The word 'heritage' is rather a loaded one, and needs an explanation to stave off the suggestion of a theme-park on an ancient site. History matters, just as science and art do; it is what happened and why. The point about heritage is the idea of something passed down, either deliberately or by chance. As something is inherited, it develops, is re-used, changed. Historical buildings on their own are effectively museums; but The Gaiety Theatre has had to function, to fulfil a continuing need, and maintain a role in a society which changed around it. At the same time, and thanks again to its largely unaltered state, it offers a view of the past that is almost unparalleled in any other theatrical building. So, while there are plays, concerts, recitals, variety shows and the like, there is evidence to even the least curious observer of what such performances must have entailed in the past. There are, for example, visible and tangible signs of the class divisions that buttressed the social requirements of the theatre's original patrons. The different entrances and exits used by the different classes are now simply quick and convenient for everyone. There is a computerised sound and lighting system, and yet beneath the stage are wooden paddles and traps making up one of the most complete examples of Victorian stage machinery in the world. The theatre can be two-thirds empty with a dreary play in endless progress, but a moment's glance at the surroundings indicates what a sensuous (and sensual) experience the audience of 1900 wanted and were provided with.

To the more curious, the place is overflowing with insights into a previous world. That door there, for example, was used by the most fashionable as a means of making an entrance in full view of the audience. The tiles are practical - easy to clean, so the grubby masses didn't erode the valuable wallpaper. But they are in keeping with the colour scheme, as well as indicating the complex hierarchy that controlled the design. The whole stage, in order to accommodate the sections that slide and disappear to bring about the change of scene or dramatic and sudden entrances and exits, wriggles like a flat, wooden snake. The circles are cantilevered, allowing everyone has an uninterrupted view of the performance. They are built around a frame of sufficient elasticity for the structure to give, like a dance floor, by as much as four inches. This flexibility accidentally led to a structural inquiry in the 1970s when one alarmed audience member became convinced that the whole thing was about to collapse.

A theatre does not exist without its context and however much it has an intrinsic value, it is also a party to and part of the society it serves. Although much of the visual evidence of The Gaiety's changing purposes is gone, it was obliged, occasionally without much enthusiasm, to adapt itself to the shifting requirements of popular taste. It has been used as a cinema and the stage has been iced over for one-off shows. As a theatre it has presented opera, drama and variety. It has had to struggle to keep its audience when the town was a thriving entertainment centre, and struggle to survive when it was not. So its history is also that of the people who came here, of why they came, and what they wanted to see. It allows a slight, but vivid, glimpse of the social and economic history of the Isle of Man, from tourist destination - which was the original reason the place was built - to finance centre - which is how it was possible to restore it. Not just the regulars who come to the plays, although their dedication has been essential to its survival, but also the many thousands who have given to make the restoration possible. It is not a triumph of corporate capital, however much that has made specific schemes possible. It has been the willingness of people to put their hands in their pockets and give their loose change. It has been the generosity over a long period, and the ceaseless enthusiasm of the volunteer helpers which has made The Gaiety a work of the people who came, and still come, to watch plays and musicals; and of those who can't stand plays and musicals but wanted to be included in a significant part of the Island's past.

The fact that it exists at all is proof of the money to be had from the visitors, and of the success of an industry which became the staple for many Manx people. The restoration has been made possible by the more recent financial industry which is still struggling in some quarters for acceptance. Equally, The Gaiety's decline reflected the death of the holidaymaker as a source of a guaranteeable income. The fact that it was left alone rather than redeveloped indicates the pace with which that death was recognised. For this neglect there is much to be grateful, although there are enough ghosts of glorious structures around the Island to show how nearly it came to falling into the ground.

The Gaiety's life story, from the glory days of its first two decades, through the changes and decay that nearly destroyed it, to its slow, painstaking rejuvenation, is therefore indirectly the story of its people. This is not remarkable; but the Island's particular situation - politically and historically - makes it more than a tale of regional development, and more one concerning national identity: from a destination for the workers who kept the British Empire in good health to a place with a powerful, and growing, sense of holding a place in the world in its own right.

But this is also a book about reclamation, and the two men responsible. The first was Frank Matcham, without peer in the design and construction of theatres, who was presented with an unprepossessing building and created within its extremely limited frame a gorgeous and ornate setting to satisfy the eyes of his audiences and the expectations of his employers. The second is Mervin Stokes, whose inspired overseeing of the restoration has made the book necessary. Without him, the complex matter of bringing the old theatre into second bloom would never have been achieved.

THE ISLAND AND THE ARCHITECT

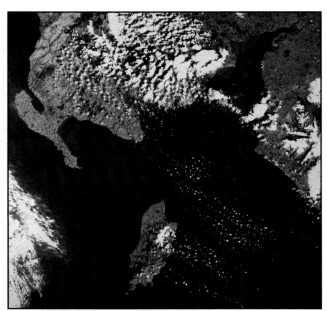

A satellite view of the Isle of Man.

Photo: Courtesy of Island Photographics

Tourism replaced the traditional Island industries, as these arrivals during the late nineteenth century indicate.

Photo: Manx National Heritage

The Isle of Man is thirty-two and a half miles long, thirteen and a half miles wide, and sits in the centre of the British Isles in the Irish Sea. It is a separate place from its neighbours, however similar it may superficially appear. This separateness is geographic at first, but is also more substantial. A defining feature of the Isle of Man is the profound belief in that separateness. The Island is not a part of the United Kingdom, and never has been. It is a Crown Dependency at the moment, although that title could change, which means it is internally self-governing. There are no MPs at Westminster representing the 75,000 inhabitants, and its own elected government decides on matters such as tax rates - which have paved the way for its renewed prosperity in the last thirty years.

The basis of its relationship with the United Kingdom is complex and determined by precedent rather than written constitution. The essential and perpetual issue is that the Island not only believes itself to be separate, but that it also has a distinct social, political, linguistic and economic history. Some one thousand years ago (nominally 979, although the exact date is, unsurprisingly, unknown), the Vikings invaded and established an assembly, in a basic democratic form, called Tynwald. This has continued without interruption ever since, making it the longest continuous Parliament in the world. This allows Manx politicians a certain smugness when dealing with their counterparts from the UK, who like to think of theirs as the Mother of such institutions, although this smugness is tempered by the fact that an element of true democracy only came in during the 1860s.

This is by no means the only first on the Island. The Royal National Lifeboat Institution was created here by Sir William Hillary, who saw too many ships go down in Douglas Bay. He built a little castle on Conister Rock, The Tower of Refuge, for floundering sailors, which still stands. By the end of the Victorian era there were the world's first electric trams, of a design reputedly copied by the City Fathers of San Francisco. The world's biggest water wheel, for pumping water out of the mines, was built in Laxey. There were plans for absurdly grandiose schemes such as a lift to take horses and carriages with their passengers up to a suspension bridge across Douglas Harbour and thence to a headland. The whole thing looked like an unappetising mixture of the Clifton Suspension Bridge and Blackpool Tower and was, thankfully, never built. Despite this particular failure, the Island was a thriving home of invention and investment in invention.

It is also a small island in unforgiving waters, where for many centuries a way of life had to be coaxed out of the sea and the land, where fishing and farming were staple industries until well into the late nineteenth century. The scars are still vivid. The fishing industry is still passionately protected, despite the shrinkage of the fleet to near-extinction, and the farmers are still substantially supported as providers of essentials. This has much to do with not letting go of the past because it is still so close to some communities and a determination to appear self-sufficient - or separate.

The Island has its own language, similar to but different from Scottish and Irish Gaelic, and it is currently enjoying something of a renaissance. It is fundamentally Celtic. Although the Christian denominations of the British Isles are dominant, there remain plenty of reminders of its past, from standing stones and place names (the Isle of Man is said to come from Manannan, the Celtic sea god) to the more quaint, such as the Fairy Bridge, which is conveniently situated on the main road from the airport to the capital, Douglas. This ancient cultural past, however much doctored and tailored, forms an integral part of the Island's uniqueness, and is one of many reasons it became a favourite holiday destination. Another is the scale of the place. In some ways, the Isle of Man's relationship with Britain is similar to that of Britain's to America. For example, it contains in miniature many of the scenic aspects from glens and valleys to rolling hills, sandy beaches to plunging cliffs or bleak moorland, and all so easily accessible; it is profoundly different but reassuringly familiar; there is no language barrier; and there is the same resentment of cultural imperialism. It is, however, much closer. A boat trip of some three or four hours made it seem like abroad, without having to actually *be* abroad, an important quality in any resort for the British who, since the package holiday, have taken to *really* going abroad to somewhere that feels, looks and smells like home.

Tourism replaced the traditional industries during the course of the 1800s, as the industrial revolution in Britain gave mass employment, factories and regular holidays for people eager to get away from the population centres to somewhere scenic and quiet. They came in their hundreds of thousands. Boat after boat filled to frightening capacity brought the visitors to the Island. Photographs show the promenade in Douglas literally black with them, and the quayside loaded with still more ready to spill into the town. Harbours were alive with masts and rigging, steamships and traders. Associated businesses, from the hotels and boarding houses to pubs and entertainment centres, were packed with people eager to spend their money. They wanted to escape the urbanisation of their own country, where seventy per cent of the population had become 'townies' when only three generations before the percentage had been in single figures. On the back of the industrial and urban shift, there were massive increases in public transport by rail and boat. This had several significant knock-on effects - time in Britain was, rather ironically, only standardised to accommodate train timetables. And there was a huge demand for mass entertainment.

It was to satisfy this need of the many visitors that The Gaiety Theatre and Opera House was built. It was not built for the Islanders, but for those who had come to expect a certain quality in their amusement. An ornate sumptuousness was part of the package, adding to the sense of being transported to another world; the kind provided by the theatres and dance halls to be found in places like London, Manchester, Blackpool and Glasgow. This was the competition whose standards the Island had to equal or surpass. And in the matter of theatre design, there was one man who set that standard - Frank Matcham.

Frank Matcham was to theatre design what Brunel was to engineering, Stephenson to trains,

Watt to electricity and Edison to lighting. His output was staggering. He effectively designed at least one hundred and fifty (it is believed there may be more as yet unattributed), either from scratch or as a reconstruction, over a period of thirty years. This amounts to five a year, a statistic which becomes more extraordinary the more it is considered, and is at least twice as many as his nearest rival. He was not only prolific, but inspired, not just elegant, but practical, and not just popular but technically innovative. His works have suffered from the lack of critical attention given to the late Victorian era, which has found them frequently gaudy and vulgar, and many of his buildings have been destroyed for commercial reasons without a second thought for their intrinsic value. This may in part be because there were so many. When almost every major town has at least one Matcham in it, the cause for individual preservation loses its weight; and when theatre becomes less significant as a medium for entertainment, the building's

The London Hippodrome, opened in 1900 and designed by Frank Matcham.

Photo: Faulkner Collection (Crown copyright)

Frank Matcham circa. 1900.

Photo: Mervin Russell Stokes collection

purpose is redundant. At least a stately home keeps a family housed.

Some significant theatres remain, though. In London alone, there are The Lyric, Hammersmith; The Richmond Theatre; The Hackney Empire; Shepherd's Bush Empire; The Coliseum; The Hippodrome; and The Palladium, all in differing states of repair and having undergone varying degrees of internal reconstruction. Throughout the British Isles, there are, however, only about twenty-five which can be considered survivors. Of these, and probably of all the others too, The Gaiety in Douglas is a quite outstanding example.

It was built because the owners knew they needed something like it to keep the public happy. Theatre, in its late Victorian form, was booming, but the building on the site, The Pavilion, was perceived as not pulling its weight. There was a need for something more upmarket in the owners' portfolio. The owners were The Palace and Derby Castle Company Limited. This group was formed by merging the management of several different venues to obviate the potentially ruinous competition between the various entertainment companies in Douglas. This is frequently a problem on the Island. Competition works well for a while, forcing prices down, but generally fails because there isn't sufficient market to allow all the firms involved to make any money. It tends to a quasi-monopolistic system, often bolstered by legislation. In 1898, solid commercial sense saw The Palace and Derby Castle Limited come into being. In ten months it had saved over three thousand pounds in expenses, quite apart from the benefit of not having to compete against itself. The market in the theatre-going public was changing quite quickly, and they needed to supply the demand. If they wanted to supply it with the highest quality, there was really only one man who could fit the bill.

Frank Matcham's journey to the position of the pre-eminent theatre designer of his age seems to have been, if not easy, certainly blessed with good fortune. A large percentage of that fortune he deserved. Professionally, he was renowned for architectural and engineering ingenuity. Personally, he was gregarious, loyal, modest and generous, a man who took evident pleasure in living. He made lasting friendships with colleagues, which extended beyond the work-place. Theatre owners were in turn loyal to him because of the quality of the work he produced and his ability to fill apparently impossibly-shaped sites perfectly and on time. Yet despite his status and achievements, there is remarkably little record of his private life or his working methods. This is in part because a bomb hit his company's London office during the Second

World War. As for his private life - perhaps he simply kept himself to himself, determining to keep his familial life away from the extremely public business of building theatres. Given the boom in theatre construction during his lifetime, he may also have regarded himself as a jobbing architect, who had no need to keep a detailed record of his activities for posterity, an attitude which was shamefully adopted by the establishment, who seemed to ignore his status and value to their world.

He was the second of nine children, born in Newton Abbot, Devon, on November the 22nd in 1854 to Elizabeth and Charles. The family moved to Torquay shortly after Frank's birth, and his father became the Manager of a brewery and a malthouse, both of which belonged to Mary Bridgeman. He went to Babbacombe School, one of the oldest in Torquay, and with an excellent reputation. Then came the first stroke of what seems in retrospect his good fortune. The Bridgeman family evidently took a liking to the Matcham family, and at the age of fourteen, he started work in the office of the local architect and surveyor, George Bridgeman. After a while he left to serve an apprenticeship to a London-based quantity surveyor, then returned to Bridgeman's as a Senior Assistant. Whether his rise to such a position was due to an innate ability or enthusiasm - or just lack of alternative - is unknown, but he was well served in his role because Bridgeman's became extremely successful, and George Bridgeman eventually rose to be Chairman of the Urban District Council of Paignton. Matcham may have left a tiny signature somewhere in the town's design detail; but it was his next move that marked the fundamental turning point in his career. He went to London again, to the offices of Jethro T. Robinson, who was one of the greatest theatre designers of his day, responsible for, among many others, the reconstruction of The Old Vic. There are three aspects of his time with Robinson which, on a professional level, were vital (and one personal one). First, he was immediately involved with a specialist in theatre design, someone who knew how theatres worked, so he would have been exposed to all the complexities and particulars of the job. This would have included negotiating for the contract to build, the discussions with local authorities and owners, working with theatre managers - and actors. Being on a Matcham stage is a thrill in itself for a performer. The audience seems close and intimate, irrespective of its number. The acoustic is perfect and there is no question of whether you will be heard at the back. The knowledge that you can be clearly seen wherever you are and wherever you are being watched from also draws the audience into the show.

The second is the fact that Robinson was an acknowledged expert, and consultant on theatres to the Lord Chamberlain. He was intimately involved in the laws that were passed regarding safety, in particular the fire regulations. Between 1802 and 1896 there were some 140 significant fires in theatres in the United Kingdom, so it is hardly surprising there was felt to be a need for legislation. This close, detailed understanding of the rules regarding what must be done, allied to his inventiveness, allowed him to show what could be done, without compromise.

The third significant professional element of his work with Robinson was the work Robinson did with Circuses, or Grand Cirques. These he built in London and Liverpool for his friend, Charles Hengler. Matcham himself also designed one for Hengler, in Glasgow, as well as one in Bolton and Hippodromes in Brighton, London and Manchester. The great advantage of a Cirque was that ostentation and imaginative fancy are expected. A world of dancing horses and extravagant, daring acrobats suits (indeed requires) something exotic and gorgeous. It allowed a greater freedom from the constraints of the Classical style favoured by his contemporaries for the more upmarket theatres, and appealed to what turned out to be his populist imagination.

On a personal level, his relationship with Jethro Robinson must have been at the very least amicable, because on 9th July 1877, he married his younger daughter, Maria. This happy state of affairs was to be destroyed only a year later, when Jethro died suddenly, at his home in Bloomsbury, which led to Matcham's taking over the business. Immediately, at the age of just twenty-four, he started completing work on the Elephant and Castle Theatre, and negotiating for the modifications to the Cambridge Music Hall. Once again, he seemed to have been catapulted into a position over which he took a natural advantage, and while the death of his father-in-law can hardly be said to be fortunate, it nevertheless placed him at the forefront of his profession. But Matcham was not a man who pushed ambitiously for success. Within a few years, his two daughters (and only children), Eveline and Constance Amy, were born, and although he must have been almost fanatically busy for the next thirty years, what little remains there are of his home life indicate a man who loved and cherished his family, enjoying social activities and putting on plays with his brothers as well as his daughters. He also made a point of bringing the whole family together at his home in Dollis Avenue,

The London Hippodrome, circa 1900

Photo: Theatresearch

Finchley, whenever possible. He himself played the violin - apparently owning a Stradivarius - and loved painting tranquil watercolours, sketching when he travelled.

Almost as soon as he became the Head of the firm, he had to meet a difficult commission. The Royalty in Glasgow was on the first floor of a four-storey building. Matcham successfully managed to build the theatre within this uncompromising framework. Moreover, he incorporated an improved ventilation system, using a vent over the main auditorium gas light to create a movement of air, a scheme he also employed at The Gaiety in Douglas. Ventilation and safety were to become as much a part of his design as the innovative construction methods he used to ensure perfect sightlines for the audience. This was partly because of new laws, which had incorporated advice from Jethro Robinson, but was also because Matcham knew they mattered. In The Gaiety in Douglas, the air vent is above a gas light known as a sun-burner. The intense heat causes the air nearest it to rise and allows fresher air to enter. The Gaiety sat some 2,000 people and has permitted smoking, so there was a lot that needed expelling. In some theatres, he introduced fresh air vents at a height of six feet above the ground to increase air intake without making the audience feel they were sitting in a draught. His work in this area at The Paragon in Mile End Road was considered particularly successful and added to his growing reputation.

The Grand in Islington was completed before The Paragon, and was significant because it (eventually) afforded him inclusion in a standard reference work of the time, Edwin Sachs' *Modern Theatres and Opera Houses*. Originally, Sachs disliked Matcham for what he felt was a rather garish populism, quite at odds with his preferred grandeur. However, The Grand was, in a later volume of his work, included as a prime example of a suburban theatre. Although claiming it has little to recommend it architecturally, Sachs does allow it to be marked by 'good sighting and acoustics ... economy of space and cost, and rapidity of execution.' The purists might not have liked it, but to any potential theatre owners this must have been as high a recommendation as could be imagined.

In 1886, Matcham was asked to alter The Theatre Royal in Blackburn by James F. Elliston. This in itself was only a small commission, but it illustrates again how his genial and professional approach was rewarded with friendship and loyalty from his clients, because this in turn led to a series of connections that would continue the development of his reputation. Within two years of the Blackburn project, Matcham and Elliston were travelling through Europe together, and gossipy press reports at the time indicate they were having a high old time of it (though Elliston was repeatedly very ill on sea-crossings; or, as a newspaper of the time had it: '...[Elliston's] proportions were sensibly diminished by his offerings at the shrine of Neptune.'). Matcham travelled through Europe fairly extensively, and is thought to have visited Holland and Belgium before 1890, and gone much farther afield in later years, to Brindisi, Sicily, Egypt, San Remo and the Riviera in 1912. He clearly enjoyed travelling (which was just as well considering how much of it he had to do for his work) but Maria, his wife, was reluctant and preferred to avoid sea journeys. So his time abroad would probably have been spent alone, sketching and painting, or in the company of friends such as Elliston.

Elliston was a manager and lessee of a number of theatres, and a good friend of the Revill family, who were famous in the north, and were in turn related (by marriage) to the Purcells, another theatrical family. When Purcell's Theatre Royal in Stockport was destroyed by fire, Elliston persuaded Revill to engage Matcham for the rebuild. A similar combination meant that Matcham rebuilt The Opera House in Bury, which belonged to the Purcell family, and Elliston was the lessee. To continue this merry-go-round, Purcell lent his carpenter to lay the stage for the Revill's new

theatre in Stockport (opened 1889) - which Matcham had designed. This was a significant success for Matcham because it became a benchmark for provincial theatres.

During this period, and with the help of his good friends, Matcham was developing a reputation throughout the north of England. The first example of what was to be many attempts to incorporate his name into a prologue came with the opening of The Theatre Royal in Stockport. It was customary to preface the opening of a new theatre with a series of speeches, from owners, managers and the like, and to include a few lines of poetry to bless the new development. This doggerel was no doubt intended to raise the tone and elevate the welcoming speeches beyond the simply corporate, but they must, from 1890 onwards, have been a torment to Matcham. He was not a happy performer on a public stage, and while obliged to be present at such occasions, must have dreaded the moment when the lead actor or actress attempted to pun him into the proceedings: 'Yet few the houses, reared with such Matchless skill / As Matcham's work; his praise the world shall fill'; or 'The Architect's arrangements, if you'll watch 'em / (Like these two rhymes), 'tis hard to match 'em'; or 'No fairy fabric this (some may hatch 'em). / Sterling stuff alone from Master Matcham!' which last was pronounced at The Gaiety in Douglas. Given the number of such events he must have endured, it is slightly less surprising that he stopped working almost completely in 1912.

Interestingly, if slightly bizarrely, these introductory verses sometimes made reference to Matcham's safety features. In Cheltenham, the panic bolts to allow easy egress in case of fire, and the hydrants, were pulverised into a couplet. In Portsmouth the safety feature of a water curtain, included a reference to its cubic capacity: "It seems most simple, but there's volumes in it / 'Twill shed four thousand gallons in a minute". This is significant because of the importance given to precisely such care in the design. Matcham used the combination of fireproofing, easy exit, auxiliary lighting, hydrants and ventilation to allow his audience a combination of safety and comfort, while never compromising the opulence or sightline. It mattered; many of his works were advertised on the basis of these qualities, because without them it could be an extremely uncomfortable business watching a show. Given the advances in almost every other area of technology since his time, it is perhaps surprising that air-conditioning is still promoted as a luxury commodity in some London theatres, and seen as dangerously extravagant elsewhere in Britain.

The spectacular London Coliseum, one of Matcham's more ambitious projects, opened in 1904.

Photo: Theatresearch

Matcham's connections with the Revill and Purcell families, his growing reputation and the continuing demand for new theatres meant that by the late 1880's and early 90's he was involved in projects in London, Brighton, Douglas (The Grand), Bolton, Hanley, Bristol, St Helens, Dewsbury, Stockport, Newcastle and many others. His practice must have been in a perpetual ferment, with himself as the figurehead in constant motion between projects. Not all of them were completed - some never went beyond the drawing board - but the demands on him must have been almost overwhelming. His health did suffer quite badly, and he said in 1888 that the workload nearly killed him. He was reported as looking much older than his thirty-five years in the same interview. Yet his invention never ceased. Theatres sprang up in every style, from the Baroque to the Military, the Oriental to the Louis XVI in practically every corner of the country.

Matcham was also extremely good at adapting. He would frequently be required to alter existing theatres, and where possible (partly because of the commercial restraints on time) would happily use what was extant if he thought it would serve. With The Gaiety he had to incorporate an entirely new theatre within the existing framework. With The Metropolitan Music Hall in Edgware Road, although inheriting a hexagonal auditorium and an effectively triangular stage, he still used some of the original walls and retained the auditorium shell. With The Grand in Islington, despite rebuilding the interior three times, he kept the original façade.

It is unclear just how much he actually did himself. Given how much he had to complete, his style necessarily became recognisably his, and he would take aspects of design from one theatre to the next; but he must also have delegated work to some of his office assistants, as Jethro Robinson must have done to him. He was able to bring out the best in people, certainly, and the mutual loyalty must have made for a great deal of practical shorthand in the limited time and space he had to operate in. But there seems to be no doubt that what were and are regarded as Matcham theatres are the result of his vision and his ability to transform that into bricks and mortar, using craftsmen he trusted and encouraged. This is exemplified in his work with Felix de Jong, known as the "King of Fibrous Plaster Manufacturers", which although a title that hardly rolls off the tongue, indicates his supremacy in a craft that Matcham used a great deal. They became so close, Matcham named him as his executor.

Between 1892 and 1895, two powerful forces in the world of theatre emerged, and both had Matcham as their designer. H. E. (Edward) Moss and Oswald Stoll independently created circuits, which eventually united to become the huge Stoll Moss Theatre Circuit. Matcham started with Moss in Edinburgh, with The Empire in 1892; with Stoll, the first was also an Empire, this time in Cardiff, in 1895. Before long, his work with them and others took his reputation solidly from the provincial to the national. It goes without saying that he became extremely friendly with both men, and between them, they used Matcham on well over twenty projects, from the relatively straightforward (in so far as any of Matcham's works can be so called) to the frankly overwhelming, as with The London Hippodrome and Coliseum. In these, hydraulic lifts enabled the entire stage to be raised or lowered, there were three concentric stages or massive water tanks to create a lake or a cascade. The Coliseum was intended to allow up to four performances daily. The Hippodrome shows included elephants plunging down a slide into a pool. Much of this work seemed over-extravagant even at the time; but Matcham's great pleasure seems to have been the element of spectacle, and he was given a practically limitless canvas with Stoll Moss. In many ways, he was a delightful and delighted man, enjoying the luxuries his success allowed. He had a chauffeur-driven Daimler-Benz in which he would ride while smoking a cigar. But he took a great and unforced pleasure in his family and his many friends.

It must have been difficult for his wife to keep up with him and his constant moving would have made her existence somewhat lonely. She was not a good traveller anyway, but even if she had been, he would have had little time to be alone with her because of the constant demands on his time. The design features, the negotiations, the consultations with the craftsmen and Clerks of Works, the regulations - all had to be completed in such a little time in each place. She was obviously the home-maker, if only by virtue of her being there most of the time. There is, however, a record of at least one occasion when her presence was required elsewhere. In 1894, the construction of The Wakefield Opera House had fallen slightly behind, and there were concerns from the local council that it might be unhealthy for the patrons to find themselves sitting in a theatre that hadn't sufficiently "dried out". For obvious reasons (publicity, cost), the owner tried to persuade them there was nothing to fear, but it seemed no licence was to be given. It was decided to tempt the Committee responsible with an invitation to the prestigious first night. To add weight to the claim

H. E. Moss.

Oswald Stoll.

of complete safety, the owner (one Councillor Sherwood) said he would be there with his wife, and the Matchams would also be in attendance. It was believed the Committee would recognise that the owner and designer wouldn't dream of placing their own or their wives' health at risk by exposing them to even a hint of damp. It worked, and the licence was granted. Whether Maria enjoyed the performance, however, is not recorded.

By 1899, Frank Matcham's position was effectively secure, and anyone building a major

theatre would have considered him as a matter of course. So when the recently-formed Palace and Derby Castle Limited decided they needed someone to develop their site, the choice of Matcham was a statement of intent. Not only did it emphasise that they could afford a major investment, but his name carried a cachet with it, a ring of success. Matcham's position seems to have been something along the lines of a combination of Andrew Lloyd-Webber and Norman Foster - his work was ubiquitous, popular and prestigious. It is hardly surprising that The Palace and Derby Castle in the Isle of Man wanted him to design their theatre. As for his motives for coming, he had been to the Island before, to work on The Grand. He liked travelling, and a sea voyage would be an added incentive. He had built in all the major towns in England, including some at holiday resorts. There might have been a professional pleasure in being responsible for the houses of

The Empire Theatre, Edinburgh, the first theatre owned by H. E. Moss to be designed by Frank Matcham, pictured in 1910.

Photo: Theatresearch

entertainment where people lived and worked, and also designing the one they visited when on holiday. He may also have enjoyed the opportunity to place a more permanent mark on the townscape than his work with The Grand had allowed. There is a romantic possibility that he wanted to reacquaint himself with the circus family he had worked for in his earliest days - there was a Hengler circus immediately beside the docking area in Douglas. The most likely reason - if any reason is needed - is simply that the Isle of Man was another job, and an energetic and capable company was offering him the chance to build another theatre there.

At the time, The Palace and Derby Castle Limited was a powerful force and the principal organisation in the Island's entertainment world, but it was by no means the only provider. In the opening night speeches at The Gaiety, there are several mentions of another theatre, and how The Gaiety, which was the new one just around the block, was not intended to destroy its rival. This may have brought a wry smile to the face of the owner of The Grand, Alfred Hemming. At the time The Gaiety was being built, he was in the process of refurbishing his theatre, and had managed to get it re-opened just before. As it transpired, The Grand was to be bought by The Palace and Derby Castle twenty years later, so any suggestion that it didn't want to damage the audience share became irrelevant. As a company, their statements of goodwill required salt in good measure from those they were aimed at.

The Grand was known as a 'blood and thunder house', and was the only completed part of a much more extensive scheme. Originally, in 1875, the site was to be an aquarium, baths, concert hall, reading room, promenade and theatre. John Robinson, a Manchester magnate behind this grandiose plan, was not attempting the unknown. Such arcades were successful elsewhere, and given the prosperity the Island was enjoying, might have been a reasonable enough project. But his financial acuity seemed to desert him, as he originally projected a total cost of £17,500, but only managed to get the baths completed for a total of £15,031. It will hardly startle the solvent that the company went into liquidation. But the site was bought for £5,000 by Thomas Lightfoot (the man responsible for the horse-drawn trams that ran and still run along Douglas Promenade), who recognised the potential for theatrical development, and set about creating The Grand. The story of that theatre is fairly fraught, and Lightfoot's largesse cost him dear. He reputedly said: "Never mind the brass, let's have a good theatre" and succeeded, although not as he anticipated, for within three years of a renovation in 1888, he had to sell out to stave off bankruptcy. He was perpetually redesigning and seemed to insist on changing his architect midway through any alterations.

In the early 1880's, Douglas had several theatres, including The Grand. The Theatre Royal suffered the unusual fate of becoming part Salvation Army Barracks and part beer store, an uncomfortable alliance all round. There was also an earlier Gaiety which, by the time of the new one, was a picture-framing factory. There was an Empire Theatre, seating 550; and a small Opera House. It was felt by The Palace and Derby Castle Limited, however, that another was needed, not least because a rival entertainment firm of almost any description was anathema - despite the fact that it had practically every other form of amusement in its portfolio. This determination led to one or two curious events in the development of The Gaiety.

The Palace and Derby Castle was formed in 1898 with the express intention of cutting costs and abolishing competition. It was put together by John Archibald Brown, a director of the Derby Castle Company, and who was also the editor and proprietor of two Manx newspapers. This should perhaps be borne in mind when reading any reviews of shows or buildings. The group was made up of The Palace Pavilion, which had floor space for ten thousand dancers, and was a magnificent, ornate and successful building in the middle of the Promenade, with a race-course and sports centre behind it; The Derby Castle at the northern end, a variety hall which also presented the occasional straight play; The Falcon Cliff, also at the north and atop a steep cliff, which was a concert room and dance hall that was eventually turned into a hotel; and The Marina on the Gaiety site, towards the south of the two-mile crescent that is Douglas Bay. Between them they raised some £28,000 a year, and the Directors reckoned they could make an extra £14,000 on the savings in terms of staff and administration, quite apart from being able to arrange artistes without competing. Other benefits included selling tickets that granted admission to several venues during the whole season for a set sum, and similar incentives to encourage the visitor to holiday in The Palace and Derby Castle manner. The battle for control of the tourists' money was a dangerous one in the Island at the time and followed a pattern which is familiar to the Manx. There is demand; someone meets it. Then as the demand grows more people try to join. The demand is limited (the Island's catchment area is defined fairly clearly by the coastline, after all), and businesses feel the pinch. In order to survive, they

try to either cut their costs or decrease their prices as an incentive. Some go out of business, others survive, normally the most powerful, which leads to the problems of monopoly control, which means the prices go up to recoup the losses made. This imbalance may be unsatisfactory for the consumers, who will clamour for greater competition, but who will suffer if there is a total collapse of whatever service is provided. Where there is a thriving market, there will always be room for competitors; but even with a booming tourist industry, in the 1890s the alternatives were proving 'ruinous' according to Brown who, despite being anything but a disinterested voice in the argument, was probably right.

The Palace was the powerhouse of the group, and all the Directors of that concern were included as Directors of the amalgam. One major concern was The Pavilion, the name of which had previously been The Marina. Described by Brown as 'a horror architecturally and a failure financially', it hardly stood as a jewel in their glittering collection, at least in their public estimation. This is somewhat at odds with the public's own estimation, however. It was extremely popular, and seen as a success. It was also described when it opened as the finest building of its sort in the United Kingdom,

An 1896 Programme for a Grand Theatre production, promising "all the latest and greatest London successes".

Photo: Manx National Heritage

although it should be remembered that no building worth its salt was described as anything less in the contemporary papers. Whether this is because of the extraordinarily high quality of building at the time, or because the reports were written by the buildings' owners is, at best, unclear; but it was only when a building was bought and altered that any mention was made of its defects. Similarly, the universally outstanding quality of the entertainment provided at every venue of every description seems to have less to do with objective reporting and more to do with PR.

The site for what became The Pavilion and then The Gaiety was excellent - easily accessible, near the centre, and ripe for development at the time. The first attempt to put a theatre of sorts there was, however, dogged by problems from the outset. Contemporary reports state baldly that the enterprise was attacked with spite, envy and hate by competitors in the market (Brown and his colleagues are not actually named, however), and the whole project doomed by others. A company called The Marina (Douglas, Isle of Man) Limited was determined to ride the storm and construct a place of entertainment to designs by William J. Rennison, who had been one of the many architects and designers involved with The Grand. One hundred workers a day over a ten-week stint put the whole building up, though only after a change in the Directors and an injection of cash. But in July 1893 The Marina opened. It aimed to entertain two thousand people with dancing and variety shows. By September, despite the excellent site, the hard work and some glowing press reports, it had lost £500. It seems the malicious undermining of the public's confidence, or the accurate prediction of the owner's incompetence, had proved correct. The shareholders were asked to provide some £5,000 to save the company but, perhaps not surprisingly, they refused. There is only so much spite, envy and hatred that can be borne, particularly when it succeeds. The Marina was put up for sale. The following January, four hundred people witnessed Mark Carine, a local builder acting for the creditors, buy it for £7,560. By an ironic coincidence, Carine was the builder responsible for the 1900 renovation of The Grand. Given the interconnected nature of the building, business and entertainment worlds in the Island at the time, this is perhaps less of a surprise.

The new owners decided that what Douglas needed on the site was a 'public shelter', and

The Castle Mona Estate purchased by John Archibald Brown and offered to the Government as a potential dwelling for the Isle of Man Governor.
Photo: Manx National Heritage

thought the local council (known as the Commissioners) might like to buy the building from them for £8,500. Quite what a 'public shelter' for 2,000 people might be is unclear. Whatever was planned, it was certainly hoped by some interested parties that no entertainment would take place. The Commissioners were offered £1,000 by the owners of The Palace towards the cost of their 'shelter', in an act that the charitable might describe as a sweetener. It wasn't the first time Mr. Brown had tried to stifle opposition. Some years before he had bought the Castle Mona Estate with a syndicate, a substantial and important piece of the central area of the Promenade. It was offered to Tynwald as an ideal place for the Lieutenant Governor's residence. When this failed, he offered it to the Commissioners suggesting they turn it into a park and museum - anything other than a rival entertainment centre. The Commissioners could not take on the task, however, and he was forced into building The Palace and its associated sites. So it is perhaps not surprising that he should attempt to stop The Marina becoming another place of amusement. But the new owners of The Marina were not to be forced from their intentions and set about preparing the place for the coming season.

Among the preparations was a name change since the possibility of association with a failure was to be avoided. The new name was The Pavilion, which may have been a minor gesture of defiance in the direction of Brown and his group, because their principal attraction was The Palace Pavilion. Alterations were by no means simply cosmetic, and included stand-by gas lighting in case the electricity failed and substantial fire prevention measures. The following year, Edward Forrest was engaged to develop balconies and boxes and improve the seating. He was also asked to build a house for the manager at the back of the building to comply with the licensing regulations. There is still some evidence of it today, although it is now part of the dressing rooms. The change of owner and the interior alterations worked, and not only in the summer season. The owners recognised the need for an all-year entertainment centre, and one that catered for the mass market, not simply the tourists.

The 1890s saw the end of the peak years for the mining industry on the Island, and the ancillary industries that developed around it. Tourism was also at its height, but was seasonal. To keep their tills ringing, managers of places such as The Pavilion had to find a means of entertaining the local population, which included the vast numbers of immigrant workers employed in extraction. Bazaars were extremely profitable, partly because

The Marina, from a music cover of a waltz by Oliver Gaggs written to celebrate its opening in July 1893.

The Pavilion Theatre, Harris Promenade, photographed shortly before it was to re-open as the much grander Gaiety Theatre and Opera House. Its role within the community was no longer reflecting the demand for higher standards and, as such, was inadequate.

Photo: Manx National Heritage

they required limited outlay for the management, but other experiments were also successful. In 1897, the seats in the stalls area of The Pavilion were removed to make way for a roller-skating rink, which operated throughout the winter. The Pavilion was a tremendous success - it even included the showing of cinematographs on selected evenings during the season from 1896 - and was the most popular facility in Douglas.

All of which makes the decision to sell it rather curious. The decision to sell it, including any existing contracts, for just £12,250, to Leonard Broadbent, a solicitor and director of The Palace and Derby Castle, seems more curious still. Mr Broadbent (who was also a Director of two theatres in the west of England) then sold it to The Palace and Derby Castle, along with other properties he owned, for some £205,000. Perhaps the business of running such a venture proved too time-consuming for those creditors who had taken it on. Perhaps it wasn't making enough, as was suggested by the remarks of the new owner. Perhaps they simply didn't want to take on the might of The Palace and Derby Castle and decided it was easier

in the long run to sell to them. It is possible, though scarcely credible, that they did not know who Leonard Broadbent was when they sold it to him. Perhaps The Palace and Derby Castle operated on the axiom 'If you can't beat them, buy them' (as they did with The Grand, twenty years later) and believed it was time they had control of the most successful venue in town.

Even then, the transition to The Gaiety was not entirely smooth. Broadbent sold to The Palace and Derby Castle in September 1898, having bought the building in March. The summer season was lost, with the exception of a fortnight when the space was rented out for a porcelain, china and earthenware sale, hardly an event likely to whet any theatrical appetites. At a statutory meeting in August of 1898, the Chairman, John Brown (whose capacity for promised brevity followed by luxurious verbosity places him in the same league as Polonius), implied that there were busy times for the company ahead, presumably meaning the forthcoming purchase of The Pavilion and its rebuilding. By December, it was clear that they had made the right decision in amalgamating the various companies. In the nine months since the company was formed the estimated savings were over £3,000. This was achieved despite several serious problems to contend with. There was a major site unused; there was overbooking as a result of contracts signed by the separate parts of the company prior to its merging, and it was in a poor season too, when the weather was so fine people couldn't be tempted indoors - a perennial problem for entertainment managers still. Either that or it is too unpleasant and people won't come out.

Negotiations with Frank Matcham had been conducted during 1899, and he presented his plans to Douglas Corporation, as the town Commissioners had now become, in March. They had approved them, but there was to be no work done on the site until after the last summer season of the century. So The Palace and Derby Castle staged a Trades Exhibition. This seems a little disappointing as a turn-of-the-century spectacle. It was a prime site, there were major plans for the area and the Victorians were brimming with self-confidence as the century ended. Even the Press regarded the exhibition as merely 'useful and beneficial', although they did go out of their way to say that 'the general *coup d'oeil* [was] superb'. Among the exhibits were spinning and weaving machines, electro-plating baths, wicker-work, magic cleaners, Indian shawls and china stalls. Worryingly, there was a shooting range with a specially designed target, an incubator with 'a real, live, Manx baby' in it and an X-ray demonstration all in the same room. It should be said the exhibition was not the only thing on display. There was a ten-piece ladies orchestra, character songs from Miss Mona Cookson, and in the evening a group of 'negro minstrels' was greeted each evening 'with applause'. There was also a series of tableaux produced with the aid of 'elaborate scenery and effects'. The article demonstrates the variety of entertainment that might be provided at non-specialist venues and, apart from the Trades Exhibition, is quite like a music hall or variety evening, but it is significantly short on the rhetoric of superlatives that normally greeted an event of almost any kind. It seems the company had decided to ride this summer out, and then reveal its hand the next year.

There was evidently some impatience with the Trades Exhibition, however. When £200 was found to be owed by the Exhibition, and the people responsible had left the Island, The Palace and Derby Castle sent in the Police, seized the assets and locked up the building. The instruments of the ladies orchestra were held until the owners expressed their destitution without them. The whole argument seems to have been rather manufactured. The rent was due weekly, and it was claimed that it had been paid on the Friday. Manx law at the time stipulated that the owners were entitled to all the assets until the owner's dues were paid - which was on the Monday, when a cheque arrived from the chief promoter of the event. All the goods were given back to the owners and the arrest withdrawn. But the bad feeling engendered by calling in the Police, the poor publicity, and the apparent unwillingness to wait for the rent cheque to arrive or offer any warning suggests that The Palace and Derby Castle wanted the Trades Exhibition finished, and would use whatever excuse it could find. This is not that surprising. The question is why, despite the success of bazaars in general, they wanted it on in the first place, given how prestigious the site was considered and how much importance it had for the company.

In mid-December 1899, the company held its annual general meeting. Here the plans for The Gaiety were presented to shareholders for the first time. Brown, as Chairman, had a chance to expand on the company's progress and development, as well as outlining its plans. He started by saying he would not detain his shareholders for many minutes. This was possibly the only element of the presentation that proved a disappointment. Brown went on to explain how satisfactory the accounts were and how much this satisfied him, as the man who had recommended the amalgamation in the first place as early as 1887. Then he went on to

consider the Falcon Cliff and The Pavilion, which had been described by some as 'lame ducks'. Not by Mr. Brown, naturally; he had seen them as places that just needed to be put to their proper use containing 'potential elements of prosperity'. The Falcon Cliff estate was developed, with parts being sold off, and the building refurbished as a hotel before it too was disposed of. Then he turned to The Pavilion, and allowed himself to be carried away into the fantasy realms of contemporary journalism, to which he was to some extent entitled: 'I look upon it myself - to use a simile taken from natural history - as a chrysalis, from which we hope, under the beneficial genius of Mr. Frank Matcham, to evolve a butterfly equal in beauty to anything that Nature herself has turned out (laughter and applause) . . . It is intended, as you know, to make it a theatre . . . recently I had an interview in London with Mr. Matcham, our architect, principally with regard to this Company's business, and he assures me that out of that building he will be able to give us one of the finest theatres in the Kingdom . . . [he could hardly have promised anything less] . . . I think it will be "a thing of beauty" and as we hope "a joy forever"'.

He also mentioned the ensuing competition such a venture would bring to the owner of The Grand. He stated there was no malicious intent in pursuing the dream of The Gaiety, and explained 'the rapid expansion of Douglas should, as the poet says, afford 'ample room and verge enough' for both theatres', and believed there was room for more. He repeated this belief at the opening night of The Gaiety. Finally, he said he was not a well man but was doing his best. It is a matter for unkind conjecture how much more he might have said had he been hale.

But the matter was now official. On the site of The Pavilion, previously The Marina, was to be a Matcham theatre, The Gaiety.

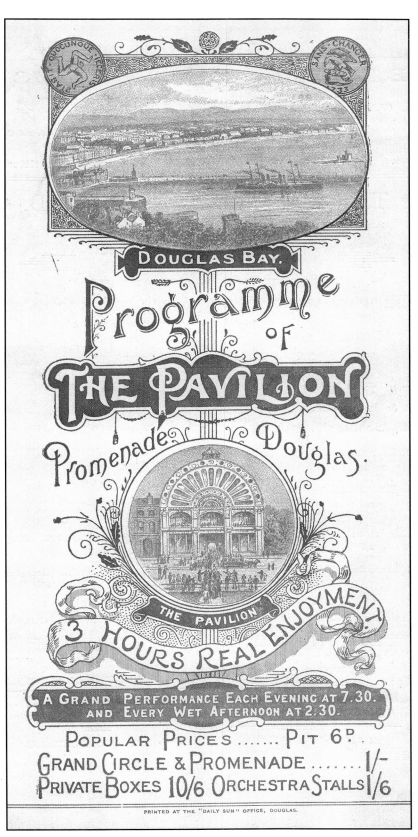

Programme for The Pavilion, 1898 - The House of Non-stop Entertainment.

Photo: Manx National Heritage

Clockwise from top left: The Funicular Railway proceeds towards Douglas Head; a crowded beach - guaranteed at the turn of the last century; a roller coaster ride erected at the top of Douglas Head.

Photos: Manx National Heritage

THE GAIETY THEATRE

Between 1878 and 1912, Frank Matcham was responsible for more than one hundred and fifty theatres in 44 towns and cities in England and Wales. Ten per cent were at seaside towns, which were booming during that period. One of his greatest strengths was the adaptability to location he brought to any job. Two of his surviving works testify to this. In Richmond, an attractive London suburb, he brought richness and sedate plushness, with red velvets and a dark elegance. The Gaiety, on the other hand, is light, playful and refreshing as well as sufficiently grandiose to appeal to the upper end of the market. Both, however, are superb theatres; visually rewarding and perfectly designed to accommodate the masses who would go there and provide them with a temple of illusory luxury (not just illusory; it is real gold leaf on The Gaiety's ceiling), which had the added advantage of having perfect sightlines, acoustics and safety precautions.

This unity of form and function should be a given in any building, but a brief glance at many civic centres, shopping arcades or private houses shows how rarely it is achieved. One of the problems any theatre architect faced was knowing precisely what function the building had to fulfil. Was it a Variety Hall? Music Hall? Theatre? Opera House? All of the above and more? Obviously, the latter was ideal, and since the theatres (to use the generic term) were frequently changing what they offered to the public, a certain amount of adaptability was required with the décor contriving to suit whatever was offered. Too vulgar, and the cream of society wouldn't come - not publicly anyway; too forbidding, and the heaving masses would go elsewhere for their fun. And there were plenty of options for people on holiday in a town such as Douglas - and on the whole island - that had its livelihood dependant on providing amusement. There were bicycle rides and concert rooms. There was a revolving tower on Douglas Head. There was bathing in outdoor pools and funicular railways among whole areas built for and dedicated to pleasuring the public. There was the Exhibition of Industry, Science and Art erected in a Winter Garden on the site now occupied by the National Sports Centre. There were trains (the first to employ electric lighting), trams, electric railways, boat trips and racecourses (the Isle of Man is where the first Derby was run, sometime between 1627 and 1651, instigated by James, the Seventh Earl of Derby). There were pubs a-plenty and, of course, the seaside itself. There were outdoor stalls and illuminated gardens, and all manner of street entertainment. There were circuses, bowling alleys, swimming baths, almost innumerable dance halls; waxworks, aquaria, and a skating rink. All were desperate for a share of the tourist spend. So a theatre, while unquestionably benefiting from the huge potential audience looking for a good night out, had a fair amount of competition to fight, and fighting competition is a bloody business at the best of times - which these were.

The nature of the content in the theatre was a matter of swiftly changing tastes, too. Despite its tremendous popularity, theatre as a profession and as a spectacle was still struggling to rid itself of the 'rogues and vagabonds' label that had been applied to actors almost three centuries before The Gaiety was built. As a form of entertainment it was still stuck between the rowdy, raucous and disreputable on the one hand and the genteel higher art on the other. That The Gaiety was called a Theatre and Opera House indicates this dichotomy; that the words 'Opera House' are more prominent on the posters indicates its aspirations. Opera was regarded as a thoroughly respectable and socially acceptable evening out. At the turn of the century, opera was hugely enjoyed by millions of people of all classes. Nevertheless, it was considered a more respectable and elevating experience. It may be this attitude that has lingered in the British imagination, and explains why even now it is seen as élitist, patronised by people with money to burn and evening dress to wear, while remaining unattainable for the uninitiated; a cultural Lodge.

It is difficult now to distinguish between Music Hall and Variety. One sprang from the other, but the name changed to allay the suspicions of the morally careful, who found the material at Music Halls unacceptable. To a large extent women were excluded from the audience until a time when they believed their delicate sensibilities would not be offended by the content of the entertainment. They were right to worry, but the form developed during the nineteenth century at great speed to become more inclusive. It didn't take too long before the shift from outrageous satire for men only to outrageously spectacular for all the family was completed. At the same time, melodramas and serious plays found as much favour as the light comedy and operetta. This latter is a fine example of the compromise in form at which the British are supreme. Opera was too specialised, but a modification would satisfy the social demands of the audience as well as the Manager's returns. It was also a form at which the catchy but less challenging music could be married to the kind of wordplay for which the language is so fitted with seamless and spectacular quality. This, however, was to come later.

The Music Hall had its beginnings in taverns, where food and drink were part of the staple entertainment. To keep their customers satisfied some kind of performance was also on tap. There was singing, dancing, serious recitations and scabrous satire. To some extent this variety was forced on the taverns by the law because, in 1662, two theatres alone had been given the right to perform straight drama - The Royal Opera House, Covent Garden and The Theatre Royal, Drury Lane, known as the Patent Theatres. Application had to be made to them to perform straight drama, otherwise you could only obtain a licence for entertainment with music. Naturally, there were ways round this - placing songs in the middle of plays and so on; hence 'melodrama', which translates (roughly) as 'acting with music'. The public liked plays, but the law made presenting them on their own illegal in certain circumstances. But the demand for drama led to one or two curious means of allowing it to be shown, although none were entirely satisfactory. A musical chord every five minutes loud enough to be heard at the back of the theatre was sufficient to fit the legal obligation. Charity showings were also exempt from the need to have a licence granted by the Patent Theatres. Some places attempted to sing Shakespeare just to get him played. There are stories of halls being raided for producing 'Othello' without the requisite musical additions, with the audience and performers being taken into custody. The idea of a Shakespeare play being subversive, or being an underground pleasure in the urban back-streets seems quite startling nowadays, and any teacher of English would be only too glad if normally reluctant students thought it 'cool'.

However, this legal restriction remained until 1843, and is partly the reason so many theatres were built to accommodate any number of functions, not just theatrical ones. The 1843 change was to some extent brought about because the Patent Theatres weren't getting their audience, as people crowded to other halls. In an attempt to recapture their public, they went as far as asking stars from the East End variety bills to appear, or putting lions on the stage. The new legislation, however, had a twist in it for the lovers of straight theatre. It required any drama to be performed without eating and drinking in the auditorium. This led to a kind of split personality developing. Theatres solely as places for drama were built, but taverns wanting to provide entertainment couldn't just put on a show - they had to be essentially musical in nature. Since they were providing a good night out mainly for men, the acts were rarely entirely discreet, but they were very popular. Managers of thriving taverns, therefore, built huge rooms with stages at one end, and even balconies, to accommodate diners who wanted a laugh and a song. Some were more respectable than others, naturally; and a less salubrious generation of back-street halls developed as well as the more sumptuous surroundings of the well-heeled sort.

But as such buildings were proving successful, and as demand for theatrical presentations increased, other entrepreneurs set about catering for a market which didn't wish to feel it was being pushed quietly out of sight for some illicit thrill. The Music Hall was essentially that. The Palaces of Varieties had far more worthy pretensions. Variety was essentially the same thing as Music Hall, only cleaner, lusher, more intended for a man and wife to come for a night of sober if pleasurable amusement. Variety it certainly provided. Songs, playlets, recitations, sketches, monologues, impersonations and bizarre animal acts (always a favourite with the Victorians, who had a slightly higher regard for a dog walking on its hind legs than Dr. Johnson) would form one night's fare. It wasn't theatre or drama by any means. Yet it was so popular that theatres had to be able to turn themselves into Variety or Music Halls at almost a moment's notice. Far more Music Halls were built than theatres during the golden era of the form (1880 - 1910), and very few theatres could hope for mass appeal without being able to offer this sort of show.

In short order, Music Halls developed along not dissimilar lines, and became palatial, separate entities from their public house roots. Venues such as churches were taken over and renovated, their function turned over to feed the ever-growing demand for music. The distinction between a music and a concert hall became blurred, and they both became vast and socially acceptable. One in Southwark - the Surrey Zoological Gardens - could seat ten thousand people and accommodate a thousand musicians. Architecturally, they, along with the Palaces of Variety, took the restraint of the Georgian period by the scruff of its neck and threw it bouncing down a back alley, replacing it with a relish for the exotic that bordered on the debauched. It also bordered on the insane in terms of what diversions were on offer. There is an illustration of The Alhambra in central London (it was demolished to build the Odeon, Leicester Square), with a proscenium at one end, the audience seated at tables, eating and drinking, while a troupe of cavalier gentlemen in swimming trunks fly on trapezes, juggling and performing acrobatics. More than just a fly in the soup was a distinct possibility, and this lavish superabundance of entertainment was mirrored in the building's decoration. It had been adapted from a Panopticon of Science and Art, but this high-minded venture had failed, despite offering the first ever 'Ascending Carriage' - or lift - to be installed in any public place. It was furnished with a rotunda some 97 feet in diameter and height, with a fountain, which shot a jet at least as high as the third balcony would have been. The design was fabulous, if rather over-rich for modern tastes. There were Moorish domes and minarets, a theme used with slightly more restraint in the Turkish kiosks, which adorned the Southwark enterprise. Orientalism was very 'in', adding spice to the luxurious decorations of these popular palaces, and suggesting that even if the audience could never travel to the places implied by the design, it was the designers' duty to bring its flavour - however much doctored by their own perceptions - to the audience. This habit is evident in The Gaiety's act drop, with its images of a sultan being entertained by dancing girls. As an indication of the social standing of such exuberances, Queen Victoria herself never visited The Panopticon; but she brought her children along to The Alhambra when it was a circus. By a happy coincidence, Matcham was later involved in minor alterations to The Alhambra in 1912.

In the poorer areas, particularly city centres, the Music Halls grew in a fashion more in keeping with their origins. While many were developed inside old churches or mission halls, they still offered the working class an evening of riotous thrills and fun, to some extent evident in their design. They were not, by and large, exciting places to look at, but only in comparison with their rivals. They still had a genuine charm, and a rather wistful grandeur, which was somewhat at odds with the behaviour of their audiences. Frequently dangerous and overcrowded, much plainer and accommodating every level of the society in their area, they were heaving pits of popular entertainment and believed to be extremely disreputable, an accusation which carried considerable justification.

This sense that theatres were places of not entirely satisfactory human communion was a feature of the time. It was reckoned that prostitutes could find themselves a patch within the promenade areas of the bigger theatres with a ready market at hand, and the foyers around the auditorium were known as Fops' Alley. The opportunity to mingle and show off gave new occasions for vanity and brought about changes in fashion, too. When electric light was introduced, diamonds came back at the expense of rubies and sapphires because they sparkled so well in the light. Some ladies were profoundly affected by the novel brilliance of the illumination, however, because it showed their make-up in a less than favourable light. Theatres sensitive to such delicate concerns maintained gaslight in the public areas. In the auditoria, the very present threat of fire was compounded by the overwhelming stuffiness and discomfort. A survey by Dr. Angus Smith in 1884 found the quality of air in the dress circles of theatres to be worse than that in sewers. Drink was usually available and availed of. The moralists of the time had several sins to clamour about. Drunkenness was a very real concern; the average spend per person on drink almost doubled between 1860 and 1876 and theatres made a lot of extra revenue on drink. This meant that the managers had to do everything they could to get the people in and is another reason why theatre-going was so popular and so divisive. There was also hygiene and sexual mores to concern the guardians of popular good, quite apart from the content of the plays and varieties being offered, which meant the theatre had to change its image in the latter third of the century if it wasn't to be completely condemned.

A combination of events brought about the necessary shifts, and Frank Matcham took advantage of them all. While no doubt despairing at the improprieties either committed in or implied by the theatres, local authorities were by no means blind to their value. They were often seen as useful symbols of civic pride, and competitions were held to design them. At the same time the Continental influence began to make its presence felt in the design. Towns could find their cosmopolitan attitude - or Imperialism - reflected in styles from French to Baroque, Rococo, Viennese, Oriental, Indian, Bavarian or Gothic. Music Halls, being by their nature less discriminatory, tended to take a buffet attitude to the overall look. Everything went into them. But by the 1880s the 'straight' theatre was being seen as 'legitimate' (another distinction still prevalent within the British psyche), and the opulent excesses of the Halls were becoming a kind of parody of the more consistent architecture of the theatres. This didn't stop the theatres being opulent; it merely

meant they weren't perceived as excessive.

Industrial innovation was also having an effect on the buildings and their safety as well as comfort. Electric light (first used in The Savoy Theatre in 1881) reduced the need for gas, which was notorious for its oxygen consumption as well as its flammability, although it was retained as a stand-by in case of electricity failure. Steel construction techniques allowed balconies to be built that didn't require pillars to hold them up. This benefited the spectators' view, of course, and also reduced the obstructions that might hamper easy escape. Fire killed many, but smoke and panic killed far more. C. J. Phipps, one of the pre-eminent theatre designers of the time, admitted after a blaze killed 140 people in Exeter in 1887 that he had designed against fire but 'did not allow for smoke'. The average life of a theatre was about 23 years before something destroyed it, and fire was too often the culprit.

As a result, legislation was introduced regarding fire escapes, fire curtains, staircases, stages, equipment, door-widths, even the siting of the place. This meant a theatre had to have sufficient access to public highways, and explains why so many built after 1878, when the legislation came in, were on corners, rather than packed into profitable but dangerous smaller streets. It also meant they were obligated to become prominent, which added to the pride the owners would have to take in their construction. This led, indirectly, to the erosion of the difference between a Music Hall, a Palace of Variety and a Theatre. Theatres generally were aiming at the more sophisticated audience, and would include the title Opera House to indicate this. This pretension was largely superficial, however, since they were frequently obliged to offer much more populist fare.

Opera had always had a cosmopolitan, alien feel to it for the British, who have traditionally adapted to and embraced (if not invaded) the foreign while insisting that they can't stand it and aren't affected by it. Because the whole thing is sung, almost always in an unfamiliar language, it is necessarily more difficult to follow and enjoy than a play or a song. It is much more demanding in terms of time and the effort required from the audience to appreciate it. A brief look at the relative lengths of 'Burlington Bertie from Bow' and 'Götterdämmerung' indicated the distinction. One is a catchy, light piece satirising the lifestyles of the rich and care free that could easily be picked up and sung by the crowds. The other is a four hour epic dealing with mythic heroes, sung in German. For those looking for an evening's light relief, the choice was not difficult, especially if they were several rungs below the care free social ladder, and would not have been able to afford the Wagner even if they had the mental stamina to enjoy it. This is an exaggerated polarisation and probably more accurate now than it was in the late nineteenth century.

It was not generally until after the First World War that opera was hijacked by the middle class into an exclusive form. Nevertheless, Opera House was a term intending to appeal to the upper classes and, although they liked to go to the Halls too, the traffic in the other direction was less valuable socially, even if it was profitable. The distinction was naturally reflected in the buildings intended to house the different spectacles. Opera was associated with the rigours of Classical architecture; Music Hall was an escape from the rigours of every-day life, and provided a fantasy in which to be lost. Straight theatre sat squarely between the two, and maintained a presence at both ends of the social scale. The classics were performed, but there was a great deal of contemporary work eagerly consumed, which ranged from the penny-dreadful style of melodramatic moralising to the sharp, Shavian, intellectual essay-as-drama, and the sweetly subversive wit of Oscar Wilde. It is not too far-fetched to see the provision of theatrical entertainment in all its forms as the equivalent of today's television schedules. The same arguments about the quality of what is provided, the same need for decent audiences and the same concerns about amusing but bettering those who watched were all debated.

The almost exponential growth in the number of the buildings indicated very persuasively how popular the form was, whether theatrical, musical or variety, and was very good news for those who actually performed. The number of professional actors of one form or another grew by sixty per cent in the 1890s, and a further seventy per cent in the next decade, assisted by the development of travel which allowed relatively speedy connection between the various towns and cities. Performers were able to take their act on the road for years without needing to change it because the chances were it hadn't been seen or heard before. Some survived on only one popular 'turn', taking it round and round the country, without ever needing to adapt it or develop new material. Contemporary comics and singers must occasionally yearn for such a luxury. Instant stardom on the television may be glamorous, but the chances are you can only use a joke once because it will be seen everywhere at the same time. The audience is just as voracious, and just as determined to have more spectacular provision as it has ever been, and it is only the manner of sating that appetite that has changed.

Matcham was essentially a popularist. His first theatre was The Elephant and Castle (1878) in South London, one which was caricatured in press at the time as the kind of venue where Dickensian good-timers went for their fun. Twenty-six years later, he designed The London Coliseum (1904), as brash and as showbiz as was conceivable. In between he manufactured circuses, which are hardly models of restraint, and it is possible he was never given the formal recognition his overflowing talent merited because of precisely this mass appeal. There is a suggestion he was offered a knighthood; and another rumour he rejected it. Whether he was or not, he was never considered 'one of us' by those to whom such distinctions mattered, although he provided houses for the classics as well as the spectacular. Certainly audiences loved spectacle, and would rush for it in precisely the way people do for the latest special-effects film now. In Matcham's day, there was the added thrill of real danger. Having horses do a mock-up of The Derby is exciting enough if imagined actually taking place on special running-boards in a live theatre; when the possibility of the jockey being thrown is added to the mix, it becomes almost irresistible, precisely because of the genuine danger to the rider. Just how dangerous it could be is illustrated by what happened to Fred Dent at The London Coliseum in 1905. His horse caught two sections of the stage, one of which was moving, and missed its stride. The horse went over the footlights and into the orchestra pit; Dent was sent head-first into the side of the proscenium, and died. The Coliseum closed for 18 months soon after. There was unquestionably something rather Roman about the late Victorian delight in - or hunger for - the spectacular. Their appetite for the seemingly impossible and questionably tasteful, suggests the excesses of the earlier Empire. The technical proficiency of the engineers who created the stages to accommodate such extravagance is astounding, and as peoples' expectations rose, so did the expertise of the showmen. On the other hand, the appetite of the people seems to have grown for the more

extravagant, novel, gorgeous and seemingly impossible rather than, necessarily, the better. The popular taste seems to have gorged rather than feasted, and there is an uncomfortably gluttonous feel to the orgy of spectacle. This tendency is neither new nor remarkable, but remains perpetually surprising, and can be seen as evidence of a society at a point of change or decline. That can only be said in retrospect, of course, because there are always people saying "It's gone too far!", and one person's fun night out is another's canker of debauchery. For the mid- to late-Victorian audience, the range of effects grew very fast indeed. From simple trap doors, through effective lighting and complex scenery, then to storms at sea and eventually, as with The London Hippodrome, to elephants sliding into pools.

What the audience also loved was the sense of occasion that the new designers brought to the business of going to the theatre. Going to the theatre itself had been and remains a fairly fundamental part of British cultural life. While Music Hall, Variety and Opera were developing in their different places and styles, the presentation of plays had continued to be hugely popular. Whatever buildings were provided for them, people wanted to go. Again, the television comparison is apt. Not everyone enjoys it, and certainly there is division over what is worth seeing. However, a look at the percentage of the population that owns a TV set indicates how many want to be able to watch. In the same way, plays of one form or another were a staple of the entertainment world. As the audience grew, architects and designers worked to make the experience more than just an aural and oral one. They created a world of opulence and escape in a manner that contrived to appeal to those who might normally find it rather vulgar on such a scale, as well as those for whom it was a doorway into an environment of the imagination and the senses. The plush and gilt were for universal enjoyment, even if the upper class had separate seating, walking and drinking areas. But every level of society expected a theatre to be this luxurious. Theatre was one of the few ways in which the classes mingled. They were kept apart, but housed together to see the same shows. The significance of

The London Coliseum, circa 1904, showing the act drop.
Photo: Theatresearch

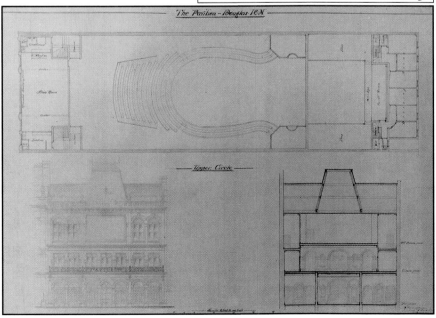

What The Gaiety might have been. Plans drawn by William Rennison in 1897 showing a Grand Theatre in the French style which was never executed.
Photo: Manx National Heritage

The interior of The Pavilion Theatre set up for a Trades Exhibition circa 1895.

these superficialities, including the as imposing, luxurious, ornate decoration - as well as the underlying skills in technology and architecture, and the implicit tensions between the different sections of the audience, made the Victorian theatres microcosms of their society.

The Gaiety was such a microcosm, but in rather special circumstances. It was to be a beautiful addition to the Island's building stock, but it was trying to appeal to a large cross-section of a mobile population. Its commercial obligations meant it had to be filled with nearly two thousand people most nights, and at the same time had to be seen as a more classy option to The Grand. The Pavilion site around 1897 was due to be renovated and there

were plans by Rennison showing a rather imposing, French style work, but there is no evidence of any further work being carried out. It is possible these plans were associated with the eventual sale of the building. It is also possible the early attempt to redevelop the area indicated how much demand there was for another theatre.

The Pavilion itself was constructed on the Belfast Roof Principle. This involved hoops of iron forming the basic barrel-vault shape of the building's skin - effectively a sturdy Nissen hut. These hoops rise from below dress circle level, with their foundations essentially in the side walls. Each main beam was comprised of three metal plates blocked out for strength and stability with laminated wood, which followed the curve of the beam rather like a ship's hull. On either side of the middle of each beam there are two metal rings, which suggest the possibility of the kind of acrobatic excess The Alhambra was famous for. These did take place in The Pavilion, but, more prosaically, the rings may have been for construction purposes, or used simply as general suspension points throughout the building. There were dressing rooms at either side of the stage, and the Manager's house at the back. In the auditorium, it was pretty plain fare. There was a gallery that ran all the way round and abutted the proscenium arch, perhaps slightly lower than the present Dress Circle level, and this, added to the sparse seating, gave the impression of a large Methodist Hall. The stalls area probably had no seats at all, or if it did they were removable; the gallery may have had benches for those wanting to watch from above. The stage was little more than a concert platform, although it had an act drop depicting Laxey Glen Gardens, which, apart from being a fairly prominent local attraction a few miles up the road (or a short trip in an electric tram), was not owned by The Palace and Derby Castle Limited. Looking up from the plain wooden floor, the vault of the roof had a flat, curved ceiling with ribs of ornamental plasterwork. At each intersection was a four-leafed boss with a finial at the centre.

There length of the central axis of the roof was glass, and there were windows under this in the ceiling, which allowed daylight in. These could be blotted out with roller blinds. The walls were divided into sections with plinths supporting pilasters that had ornamental heads for decoration, all probably painted cream and rose. Above the stage, the proscenium was painted with swag curtains, which included the Three Legs of Man, the Isle of Man's national emblem.

From the outside, The Pavilion did not look particularly appealing. In fact, it looks like a man-made cave with a frankly stern façade of red, Ruabon brick and sandstone decoration. Perhaps the photographs do it little justice, but it has a rather severe functionality to it. At the centre of the front is a large entrance, and above is a balustraded walkway that ran the whole width of the building, with three fairly flat arches. On either side were shops, one selling chocolate, the other the sort of beachside ephemera that would nowadays include "Kiss Me Kwik" hats. Immediately behind the frontage was the barrel-vault, with the end facing the Promenade being a very large, semi-circular window. It was divided into segments of coloured glass in raspberry and citrine. The Pavilion had little to cheer the spirits in its external form, and is reminiscent more of a terminus than an

The Three Legs of Man

The symbol of the three legs appears to be the result of one of the Island's periodic changes of ownership. The Island was bought for 4,000 marks in 1265. A Scottish king, Alexander III, who ruled the Isle of Man from 1266 until 1285, brought the symbol from Sicily via the English court, where Henry III was preparing his son to be the king of the Mediterranean island.

An alternative explanation is that its roots are in the Norse-Irish tradition, and go back a good deal further than the thirteenth century. In either case, the device is a development of a sun-symbol. There are echoes of sun-symbols in many other forms, such as the Greek cross, or 'gammadion', the Indian swastika - the one later used by the Nazis - and there are some Roman finds that also have it inscribed. Its roots may also trace a line to the Christian cross.

In the Isle of Man, the legs are armoured, and generally run, as it were, from left to right, following the sun. The motto is: 'Quocunque jeceris stabit', which can be roughly translated as 'Whichever way you throw it, it will stand'.

For many Manx, the most important aspect of the three legs is that whichever way you throw it, it doesn't kneel to England.

Sketches by Frank Matcham of the proposed new Gaiety Theatre and Opera House.

Photo: Mervin Russell Stokes collection.

The construction of The Gaiety Theatre in early 1900 showing
Matcham's cantilever construction of the amphitheatre and gallery.
Photo: Manx National Heritage

amusement centre. Inside, there were entertainment rooms, and the cellar area offered a buffet. There was no division of the audience - whoever came along joined in the throng on the dance floor, or watched the performances with whoever else was there. The class divisions that are such a feature of The Gaiety mark an important decision in the development of the site. They show how the owners saw their audience and the nature of the entertainment they were to provide. It was to be a building of distinction, as well as one that made them.

Matcham's basic plans were ready well in advance of the work being constructed, and although he visited the site, he would not have been in regular attendance. There is very little mention made of the building in his diaries - so far as is known - except to say that he enjoyed himself and ate well; but in his defence he was working on six others at the time. Given the importance now attached to the building, this neglect may at first sight seem a bit of a disappointment; but in fact it gives The Gaiety a greater significance. It is likely most of the design work came from his stock supply. The theatre was not to be the biggest one he ever built, nor the smallest. It incorporates elements of engineering which he pioneered and which affected theatre building as a whole. He was at the very height of his skill. In short, if you were to choose a theatre that represented the essential elements of the greatest theatre architect of British history, The Gaiety fulfils the criteria almost perfectly.

When Matcham arrived to start the work, in 1900, Alex Gill was engaged as overseer. Alex Gill was a Director of The Palace and Derby Castle, so his appointment may not have been in Matcham's gift. His Clerk of Works, Mr. Philips, however, probably was. This position is roughly equivalent to that of a Site Foreman, responsible for organising materials and the quality of work. Matcham only used a handful of people as his Clerks of Works throughout his career, and regarded them as the significant link between the plan and the reality. He trusted those he used, and the fact that they would have shared a great deal of experience together meant much would have been understood without the need for detailed explanation. It would have made the matter of constructing a new design much simpler if both parties were comfortable with the working methods and manners of the other.

When building work began, the first thing that was done was to cover the interior with scaffolding, and effectively create a completely new building. The stage had to be extended by some 42 feet in order to make it a proper theatre. This led to the reduction of the seating capacity, for which Matcham compensated by enlarging the circle and building the gallery. This required substantial redevelopment of the existing interior, namely, building a third floor with sufficient exits and staircases. To do this, the two shops outside what was The Pavilion were removed, and the two entrances to the walkway were closed off. He added a third level, staircases in concrete and the exterior in rendered brick, to the two sides of the building, which incorporated stairwells leading to the upper part of the auditorium. Practically everything under the barrel-vault roof was demolished, with the unusual exception of some decorative plasterwork above the gallery. This was presumably an expeditious measure, but it means the gallery in The Gaiety is one of the few with any ornament at all, as the fashion was to reduce the decoration in accordance with the level on the social scale.

Having created a third storey, the builders moved on to the structure of the interior. The gallery and amphitheatre are held in place on a cantilever system - one that Matcham patented - and a similarly designed circle meant there were no supporting columns visible anywhere. There are fairly substantial columns in the fauteuil section, which support the range of boxes, but no-one's view is blocked. These columns are to some extent symbolic as much as necessary, since they also serve to divide, visually, the fauteuils section of the auditorium from the pit. This visual distinction is apparent in the pit itself, too, where the line of the rear barrier is carried through to the tiling and thence to the Fauteuil barrier, which creates a sense of a penned area. Which, of course, it was.

The proscenium arch is likely to have been built at the same time as the circle, and the boxes. The boxes are constructed out of the side wall, rather than resting on the frame of the Circle. The magnificently decorated ceiling was probably the last part to be added to the basic interior shell, and was positioned so the people in the expensive seats could admire it, while the poor could hardly see it at all, which shows just how complicated sightlines could be for the socially aware architect. The ceiling sits some eighteen feet under the original roof, and is basically a square, with a large, shallow dome set into it, which reaches its outer boundary. It is decorated to enhance the depth of the dome, leading the eye to its centre, where a spectacular window is lit from above, and holds a gas-powered Sun-burner to draw the hot, smoky air out of the building.

As with most nineteenth century theatres, the under-stage machinery was the work of specialists, rather than designed by the architect. Normally, the plan had a blank at this point with a note saying 'Area for Stage Machinery', in much the same way early cartographers inscribed 'Here be Monsters' on the uncharted regions. In the case of The Gaiety, this machinery was put in place by the firm of J. L. Killip and Collister of Tynwald Street, Douglas. Although the firm was not registered as a specialist in this field, they may have been involved with the work at other theatres on the Island, or directed by an unknown expert from the United Kingdom. There was nothing remarkable about what was installed. As with much in this theatre, what is remarkable is its survival. In essence, the stage was wooden, with a series of holes cunningly disguised to allow the quick removal of scenery or actors on stage, or their equally sudden appearance. These devices were operated by substantial manpower and a collection of winches and windlasses, counterweights and ropes which made the underside of a late Victorian stage rather like a large, elaborate clock mechanism - or Heath Robinson invention - to produce the effects which happened in front of the audience. There was a carpet cut at the very front, which allowed the swift removal of painted stage cloths or carpets. This was simply a pulley attached to whatever was on stage, in a manner not unlike a horizontal roller blind with the mechanism under the stage. Centre stage, there was a grave trap, so-called because of its use in the grave scene in 'Hamlet'. It was a six feet by two feet platform, which could be raised or lowered from a

A word about the seating arrangements.

Nowadays there are fewer designated areas in theatres. The stalls are the downstairs, the circle (or dress circle) the upstairs, and the upper circle is above that. There may still be reference to the gods, which are the farthest from the stage and highest in the building. In The Gaiety, as in many other theatres of the time, it was more complicated. At the front, downstairs, were the fauteuils - comfortable and expensive, very much for the better sort. Behind them, separated by a solid barrier at seat height, which also ran across the aisles, was the pit, which was for the significantly less good sort. Up one level, and on the sides, are the boxes.

In some earlier theatres (up to the late Georgian period), these were at right angles to and almost on the stage so much were they a display area for the socially elevated. The fashion for angling the Boxes more and more towards the audience was continued to its ultimately uncomfortable and frankly foolish extreme in some theatres after about 1910, when they became an ornamental irrelevance. It would be impossible for all but the osteopathically challenged to see the show at all.

In The Gaiety, it is still possible to watch a performance from them, although it's sometimes necessary to sit at a rather uncomfortable angle to see everything. Immediately facing the stage on this first floor is the Governor's circle, which was the first five rows of what is now called the circle. The name is particular to the Island because it has a Lieutenant Governor, the Queen's (or King's) representative, who has few powers now, but many symbolic roles still. In 1900, he was a very significant person in the political life of the Island. Behind these first five rows was the family circle.

Up another level, and above the boxes were the slips, which were at right angles to the stage, and the amphitheatre. To the very back and the very top was the gallery. The prices for the programmes of 1900 show how much they were for different social classes; but they were no reflection on the visibility or audibility of a play presented at The Gaiety. Everyone could see and hear perfectly, unlike some other theatres, where, for example, the overhang of the circle would limit the view from the pit.

Private Boxes - £1 1s (a Guinea); Circle - 3s;
Fauteuils - 3s; Amphitheatre - 1s 6d;
Pit 1s; Gallery - 6d.

The total number of seats was 2,000.

Sheet music for the Corsican Brothers circa. 1860.
Photo: Mervin Russell Stokes collection

floor beneath the stage. Adjustable counterweights assisted the movement of actors and scenery. On either side of the grave trap was a corner trap. These are the most basic sort - a square which opens up to allow an actor to burst through the stage on a platform raised by virtue of muscle-power and counterweights, still a favourite at pantomimes when the mechanism is usually disguised by a flash of magnesium.

Further upstage was the number one bridge. This was a large platform about three feet wide that ran the full width of the stage. It could accommodate a chorus or a substantial piece of scenery, and formed a major part of the transformation scenes in large-scale productions. Immediately upstage from this was cut number one, also running the whole width of the performing area. This was fifteen inches wide, and accommodated scenery rather than people when used in conjunction with 'sloats', which were wooden boxes inside which was a timber tongue that guided the scenery up to stage level by way of pulleys and ropes. There was a second cut and another bridge further upstage.

The basic design for the stage was at least a century old by the time The Gaiety was built, and the techniques had become refined and almost standard equipment at the turn of the twentieth century, with the result that stagehands and actors were completely at ease with the technical and physical demands it made. In order for the stage to allow the major deformations of the bridges, for example, it had to be made of a tongue-and-groove design which allowed it to snake and ripple, to distort enough for parts of it to be dropped down an inch or so. Under the floorboards, a paddle would be drawn back to release a section. There was a maze of runners, into which the dropped section would fall. This was at an angle, allowing the section that fell to disappear and be taken away to the sides. Then the levers, pulleys and ropes were hauled and the bridge, loaded with whatever was required, pulled up into place. With the simpler traps, a platform was sited far enough under the stage for an actor to stand on it. As with the bridges, the trap door would be opened, the stage section would fall into its runners away from the stagehands who would haul on the lever system to propel the actor onto the stage. With the assistance of counterweights, this took only moments to achieve. It sounds laborious, and was certainly labour intensive, but when practised, and used in conjunction with the other effects available, all timed to coincide precisely, it was sufficient to create an illusion of absolute immediacy.

Between cuts one and two was a Corsican trap, a method of showing a ghostly illusion, which only

had specific relevance to one play, 'The Corsican Brothers'. This was first performed in 1851 when it was directed by Charles Kean. By the time The Gaiety was built, the Corsican trap was an almost mandatory feature in every theatre, because the play was still extremely popular. In it, a twin who has been killed has to appear as if rising up and gliding across the floor of the stage. It was not the only special effect called for by the ambitious script. Careful lighting was also needed for some of the transformation work (such as revealing a forest clearing as imagined by one of the brothers while he is in his house). But it is an example of the kind of refinement the stage had undergone in its growth as a medium of spectacle as well as drama. The Corsican trap was two feet wide, and ran the width of the stage. The effect is achieved by having a square platform under the stage on which the actor stands. Immediately above him is another square at stage level, with a hole in it large enough to accommodate his body. These two must move at the same speed, with the actor's platform being on an inclined plane, rising from six feet under the stage on one side to level with the stage on the other. As his platform moves along and up the inclined plane, the section of the stage with an aperture in it moves at the same time, which requires the whole, two-feet wide section of the stage to be able to move as well, rather like the action of a roll-top desk. To add to the illusion, the aperture is covered with fairly thick bristles, like a chimney-sweep's brush, so the actor seems to be pulling the earth with him as he rises. It was a complicated piece of mechanical theatricality, which caused a sensation whenever it was used. It probably also caused a few injuries in its time.

Elsewhere in the British Isles such features are almost completely lost, and certainly there is nowhere else - with the exception of The Tyne Theatre and Opera House in Newcastle - which provides so comprehensive a view of a working Victorian under-stage. There are few enough stages with traps at all, which means that the operating skills have become almost extinct, and the more testing effects have faded into something approaching mythic status. There is no need to mourn this in itself. It was new technological advances that made it all necessary and desirable in the first place, so it's hardly rough justice that it died because of cinema and television. But the fact it has survived in The Gaiety allows what is otherwise an exercise in imagination to be realised a little more fully, quite apart from the benefit to historians and social chroniclers who would otherwise have to estimate such matters on the basis of piecemeal evidence. The Gaiety places a completed mosaic in the hands of those who would otherwise have to struggle with fragments.

In most theatres where plays are to be shown there is usually evidence of a 'fly-tower'. This usually looks like a large, square section built on top of the main part of the building, and is used to house those pieces of scenery which are dropped into place on stage from above. It is normally at least as high again as the visible height of the stage from the audience's point of view, to enable scenery to be flown out of sight. Around the outer edge of the fly-tower runs a gallery on which the operators stand to pull the lines that are attached to the scenery. In modern theatres, these lines are counterweighted, but in 1900, the majority of flown scenery was raised and lowered on hemp lines with nothing but the strength of the operator to control them. Above the gallery is the grid, where guides and pulleys keep the hemp ropes in place as they run above the stage, 48 different lines in all, and 48 feet above the stage. On The Gaiety, however, there is no external sign of the fly-tower, because Matcham set the stage further into the ground, and the height of the whole building accommodates all the flying room required. This is beneficial for two reasons. The first is aesthetic. It would not have suited the building to have had a huge, square construction atop its semicircular outer frame, especially given the care to make the front look, if anything, rather less imposing than its neighbours. The second reason no fly-tower was of benefit concerns survival. In many other theatres, the join between the main part of the roof and the tower was a weak link. Gutters at that point would inevitably fail, allowing water in all around the area where the proscenium arch met the auditorium walls. Plaster would fall around the orchestra pit, and local authorities would deem the theatre unsafe. It would be shut down, pending repairs that would always be too expensive and lead eventually to its closure. With The Gaiety, although water managed to penetrate during many an unloved year, it dampened the interior of corridor walls, and left practically all the ornamental parts alone. Those who hoped to knock it down in the 1960's must have cursed the construction which cocooned the important sections in a shell of rather more resilient material than anyone would have anticipated.

There is one area where Matcham's usual eye for combining the necessary with the pleasing failed. This is the area from the back of the stage to street level, where companies bring in their scenery and their costume and prop baskets. Nowadays, there are usually large doors leading out to the street at the back of the theatre, with the stage level at the

height of a lorry's loading gate, and all the equipment can be unloaded with relative ease. At The Gaiety there is a fairly steep, and by no means straight, flight of steps, which is difficult enough to negotiate without carrying a heavy weight that obstructs your view. Why such an inconvenience was allowed remains a matter for some conjecture. It may simply be the lie of the land on which the place was built - the stage had to be sunk, so bad luck if you needed to manhandle stuff down onto it. It could be that the number of stagehands was sufficient for it not to matter, and labour was cheap, so it was felt it required no special attention from the architect. Certainly the theatre expected companies to tour their shows, despite possessing a paint-frame to create its own scenery, bringing all their equipment with them, so this inconvenient entrance for the stage furnishings is striking. The fact that other theatres suffer in a similar way suggests Matcham simply didn't regard it as a problem; or possibly he never got round to solving it. On the other hand, not everything done by the great is automatically great (Shakespeare's jokes are just one example). Frank Matcham had a genius for designing theatres, but not all those he was responsible for are testament to the wealth of his ability. Some worked far better than others. The stage access problem, which stands out so much to modern eyes, was clearly not of any importance to Matcham. Perhaps it's because such high standards are expected of him that this apparent oversight jars at all.

Other features which have survived on the stage itself include 'wing forks', The wings are the areas

The hemp flying gallery prior to the installation of counterweighting.
Photo: Island Photographics

The exterior of The Gaiety Theatre and Opera House, 1901.
Photo: Mervin Russell Stokes Collection

immediately to the side of the stage, which are invisible to the audience. Forks are literally that. Imagine a simple rake with stubby, sparse but regularly spaced teeth, standing on its handle-end. Make it a good eight feet tall, and that's pretty much a wing fork. Its use was to hold the flats securely in position without, necessarily, the need for a stage-brace behind to keep it upright. Flats are tall, usually thin, pieces of scenery with a simple timber surround, which form such things as the walls of a room on the stage. They were placed near the wings to prevent the off-stage area being seen by the audience. The Gaiety's forks are adjustable in height, and are believed - again - to be the only ones still of operational quality, and certainly the most complete.

There is also the paint frame. This was for the scenic designers in the theatre to be able to paint on a canvas without having to be up and down ladders all the time. The frame runs the width and height of the stage, and is a wooden square with internal timbers to strengthen it. Flats could be attached to it, and flown upwards. Above and behind the stage was a studio - known as the paint floor - with a gap where one wall should be. Into this gap the paint frame was raised, and the flats could then be painted. One of the benefits of having a raised area off the stage where such work could be done was the fact that it was built in a space with large windows, so much less artificial light was needed, and the stage and backstage areas were kept clear. This was good news for everyone - the owners, the artists and the actors. As you will no doubt have guessed, an authentic paint frame in any condition is rare in any theatre, but one in such a fine state is extraordinary. It was raised and lowered using counterweights and a drum and shaft mechanism on the grid, and controlled by a windlass on the fly tower's gallery.

For the outside of the building, the look changed dramatically. From the functional, two-storey exterior, he created a facade of cheerful but understated elegance in keeping with its role as a seaside theatre. First, there was the matter of the entrances. In the previous building, there had been one. The Gaiety had five. A different door led to each of the amphitheatre, the gallery, the early doors, the foyer and the pit. The last entrance had been the opening for the original, but was given new mahogany doors. Then on the first floor level, where there had been a walkway across the whole of the front, Matcham filled in the two side-arches as part of the scheme to build the staircases up to the amphitheatre and gallery. Where there had been just two large entrances to the open walkway with arches above, now there were walls decorated with four windows on each side. There were two stained-glass *oeil de boeuf* on the side, and two square, one above and one below a central decorated section. The upper window had a slightly rounded top, which matched the still-evident shape of the archway. Above these two arches he built a third tier to house the uppermost parts of the staircases, and decorated these with three long, thin windows with curved tops, and above that a decorated gabled roof topped with flagpoles. This immediately lifted the height of the building and, apart from changing the overall look from being somewhat squat to something far more elegant, it also helped disguise the huge, looming barrel-vault behind it. To carry on this good work, Matcham designed a decorative arch to sit between the towers on this third level, on which was placed a statue of Progress holding a torch illuminating the way into the next century. Whether this was entirely Matcham's idea or one planted by the owners - who were far more likely to see such an investment in these terms - is unknown. His next move was to block off the raspberry and citrine windows with rendered brickwork decorated with the new name of the building, add a plinth with a pediment and top the whole off with a flambeau. This exterior was lit by two electric lanterns, hanging between the *oeil de boeuf* windows, and four more large lanterns on the canopy. This was a *porte-cochère*, a canopy able to allow horse-drawn carriages to fit underneath. Its stained glass and wrought iron protection meant the wealthy patrons could alight and enter without being soaked by the rain or battered by the wind off the Irish Sea, which was only a few yards away.

If Matcham had done nothing but this external renovation, the Isle of Man would have owed him a century of debt. It is a magnificent transformation, fresh where it had been dull, approachable where it had been almost forbidding, exquisitely in keeping with its surroundings. It is easy (and, given the nature of this book, almost compulsory) to fall headlong into hyperbole and pretension about The Gaiety, but it really does work extremely well. Its decoration seems less fussy than its immediate neighbour, The Sefton Hotel, which predates the theatre. The theatre also appears a little set back, which makes it seem slightly self-effacing. It contrives to be both light-hearted and rather august, which is precisely what was required when it was built, with the *joie de vivre* of its light colours and friendly face matched by its symmetry and hints at Italian Renaissance style (or 'lively, debased classical', to use the jargon). The friendliness of the front might not have been entirely apparent at first, because the exterior was not painted when it opened. This might explain Matcham's (typically) little speech on opening night, when he apologised

for the state of the theatre and hoped it would all be in 'apple-pie order' in a few days. He may also have been referring to the tiles along the pit wall. Apparently, Thomas Quayle of Douglas, responsible for the tiles in the theatre, expressed his concerns that they would not be finished by the first night. He was told it would be better to get them up any way he could in advance of the occasion, and not worry if they weren't perfect. This he duly did, and as is the way of such things, they have never been altered since, despite the fact that it is quite easy to trace the speed at which they had to be put in place, since the tiles become less and less straight as Quayle and his men increased their speed.

The much-vaunted safety of the audience had not been forgotten in this rapid rebuilding programme. The gallery had two stone staircases by which to exit, both of which could branch on to another one that became available at the amphitheatre level. The amphitheatre itself had four exits, again down stone stairs. The circle had exits down to the foyer, by way of the grand staircases, or by two exit doors that took you down the side of the stage and out. The pit was, unsurprisingly, less well-accommodated - two exits straight out. Yet Matcham was a master of continuity. The fire escapes were an essential feature, but hardly showpieces. Nevertheless, he decorated them in a manner in keeping with the rest of the building, if slightly less ornately, in two-tone pinks.

In the fauteuils, the patrons could go up and out by the boxes or take the safety exits that ran along

The auditorium on opening night, 16 July, 1900.

the side of the stage. A by-product of this class stratification was that the building could be evacuated extremely efficiently because the audience was streamed to different exits as a matter of course. There was no chance of blocking an exit with too many people, and as a result less chance of suffocation or crushing - and no uncomfortable social trauma.

There was a safety curtain, which may have been used as an advertising space, or possibly had some other designs painted on it. Briggs' Patent Panic Bolts were on the exit doors (brass handles for those likely to be used by the manicured and kid-gloved, iron for the rest), and there were water buckets and sand buckets, hydrants and hose-reels throughout. As expected, there was gas back-up for the electric lighting system. The electricity was provided by the two on-site generators, which were Otto gas engines that had been there in the building's Pavilion days, and the electric lights were provided by Blackburn and Starling from Nottingham. On the stage, there were footlights - a row of lights along the very front edge of the stage, set into a small trough, which sends light up onto the actors' faces - and these were gas, although electric was also available. The gas may have been for the softer light they would cast on the performers, but they certainly weren't a safety feature; there had to be a length of wire in front of them to stop actresses' dresses catching fire and turning a light comedienne into a lit one. Ventilation was principally provided by the sun-burner at the centre of the ceiling. This intense heat at the top of the building caused air to circulate around the whole of it, and fresh air was drawn in from two ducts in the ceilings of the pit and circle, as well as from the circle promenade area. This was a corridor-cum-lounge behind the circle where the better sort could be seen and allowed to mingle. There was, however, practically no heating, with only four radiators in the whole building - two in the circle promenade area and two

in the foyer - supplied by a boiler. All other heat was generated by the ample warmth of the audience.

The audience arrived following the class system, a moving social scale that started with the early doors. These opened an hour before the curtain went up, and were specifically for the pit, gallery and amphitheatre. Half an hour later, most of the cheaper seats would be filled, the theatre would have warmed up a bit, and the pavement outside could be swept for the next tranche to come and take their seats. The taking of the seats was again determined by the place you held, and marked by a series of divisions that varied from the Austen-like understatement of the Governor's circle and family circle boundary to the brutal simplicity that distinguished the Fauteuils from the pit. The fifth row of the Governor's circle ran from wall to wall with no side aisles. Those in these five rows entered to their seats by way of the two doors beside the boxes, and which had similar, tented decoration, and meant everyone in the circle could see you as you took your place. The other people in the circle, who sat in seats of the same style and decoration, entered from the rear, where no-one could see you at all. To get into the fauteuils you walked up the grand staircase and down a corridor at box level before entering by a door effectively at the side of the stage, which allowed everyone in the theatre to see you, and prevented one having to walk through the pit area. At the back of the fauteuils, running the entire width of the stalls area, was a wooden barrier some six inches higher than the seats and as impregnable as the Iron Curtain, with a broadly similar purpose. The Governor's circle division from the family circle was significant but essentially nominal (although the current occasional practice of clambering over a seat to attain your rightful place was unlikely to be much in evidence); the division between the comfortable armchairs in their carpeted seclusion and the benched seats behind was an invisible though impenetrable wall through which would be no communion.

Buying tickets was equally the province of the class system. Each section had its own box-office window, as well as entrance, to prevent any danger of social compromise. It should not be imagined there was a clutch of top-hatted theatre-goers queuing at the window at a quarter to eight, though; it's likely the maids of the gentry would have been the ones to actually buy the tickets, rather than allow their lords and masters to sully their hands with trade.

This compartmentalisation was mirrored in the décor, too. In the pit, the underside of the circle was bare, the walls were tiled up to waist level, with a straightforward pink wash on the wall above. The floor would have been wood block - plain pine - but with some lengths of thin carpet running down the aisles. Lest it be imagined the designer had suddenly been overcome with a social conscience in allocating such a luxury as carpeting to the lower classes, it was in all likelihood to keep the noise down rather than provide comfort. This paucity of decoration had a practical purpose as well as a political one. The clothes of the working men and women would have been, not to put too fine a point on it, filthy. Heavy duty clothes, worn for a long time and rarely cleaned, allied to heavy shoes which would have been tramping along roads that were principally for the use of horses, contained a good deal of dirt and as such could be deposited on the pit, gallery and amphitheatre walls. But tiles could be cleaned easily, especially the highly varnished type Matcham used. As for the seats themselves (supplied by A. R. Dean and Company of Birmingham, almost certainly from their stock supply), the pit was normally a benched area, the wooden benches themselves simple, raised on iron legs and with padded backs. For the amphitheatre and the slips - which ran along the section immediately above the boxes - there would still have been no carpet. The amphitheatre had tiers on which were wooden benches. Between each tier, running down the middle, and on either side, was a half-step, almost as if the staircase had been carved out of the amphitheatre itself. The amphitheatre and slips were blessed with the same wallpaper as the fauteuils, but again this was not a nod of generosity towards the faithful in the cheaper seats, but because those in the more costly ones could see it. Further up, and the gallery was even more Spartan. Wooden, uncarpeted floors again (it's rather tempting to imagine the owners saying: "Should consider themselves lucky to have a floor at all!") and the crowd simply sat on the wooden tiers. Above the gallery was the section of the ornamental ceiling that survived from The Pavilion, allowing someone in the cheapest part of the house an unexpected bonus, since under normal circumstances it would have been as plain as the area above the pit.

For the fauteuils and the circle, there was wallpaper, cushioned tip-up seats and carpeting. In the fauteuils, it was wall-to-wall carpeting. To add to the separation of identities within the auditorium, there were pillars placed at the front and back of the fauteuil section, on the aisles. In conjunction with the barrier, they create a sense of rather intimate isolation from the rest of the house, and that is no doubt precisely their point. When people went for refreshment, they were kept distinct as well. The poor had to make do with a temperance bar (the threat of drunkenness among them still held) in the void under the amphitheatre. The circle level had its promenade area with sofas and refreshments, and a retiring room with a bar, which overlooked the Promenade outside. At the back of the pit was another bar, inside the auditorium, a remnant of Music Hall days, when it was fairly common to allow the performance to be enjoyed - or at least witnessed and heard - while drinking. Once refreshed, the audience could take advantage of one toilet at gallery, circle and amphitheatre level for each sex. Clearly, people did not anticipate taking in too much liquid during the evening. There were larger facilities in the cellar for the masses - the Pavilion buffet had been removed.

Inside the theatre, the architecture was a brilliant mixture. Italian Renaissance is the general feel, with a Baroque ceiling and Elizabethan strapwork under the circle. But Matcham's achievement is in the fluidity of the whole design, and its seamless continuity. There is (or was) an argument that suggested the ornamentation was unnecessary given the structural freedom granted by the new technologies of the time. These should, it can be claimed, be a force for greater functionality. There is another argument that posits the interior design can "bring the audience closer" to the stage, include them more. These both seem specious, or at least misleading. When the lights are out the decoration is effectively irrelevant, and the play should be the thing. When the house lights are on it hardly matters if the audience is brought closer to the stage, since there's nothing there to be closer to. During a performance, the reflected light does mean the interior is never completely black, the way a cinema can be. It is also true that the environment in which a play is presented has an effect on the state of mind of the audience member, whether that environment itself is visible during the play or not. With a Matcham theatre, the ornamentation, the rich plasterwork and colours, are part of the occasion as a whole. Matcham's decorations *are* functional because they satisfy that part of the experience, and the grinning cherubim are not unnecessary additions but essential artefacts with as much right to be in the theatre as the audience in all their separate areas. The sense of opulent escapism, of lavish unreality, is made by the detail of the stained-glass panels and gilded flourishes as much as by the more intellectual amusement of the stage presentation. And everything in the design contributed to this pleasure.

The foyer hardly prepared people for what was to come. It was lit by gas, rather small, and understated - a common practice at the time. It was also rather dark - mahogany prevailed - which again was a feature of Matcham's designs. The audience would be led through various sequences of ever-lighter shades, such as the promenade area in a light pine, until arriving at the auditorium where they would be greeted with an explosion of vibrant colour. In the foyer, a dark green, patterned wallpaper echoed the colours on the marble columns of the staircase. The staircase itself was white marble, but only at the sides, because under the central carpet it was concrete. Time and money were saved, with no loss of apparent luxury. The carpet was turquoise, with a strong marine feel to it, echoed elsewhere in the overall design. The foyer floor was covered with brown and cream tiles - hard-wearing, but by no means the most spectacular floor in the world. The box office windows that faced the interior of the foyer were decorated with stained glass and the one on the right had a large sash section because it was also the gentlemen's cloakroom.

In the auditorium, the ceiling is set well below the original roof. This is because the design plan required an essentially flat ceiling for The Gaiety, so its ceiling had to start as near as possible to where the old Pavilion vault was still vertical, before it curved too much. As a result, the central rose window had to be falsely lit. Originally this was with a circle of lights at the centre, above the window and out of sight, which allowed the light to decrease as it reached the outer perimeter.

The glass panels of the window are richly coloured, and outside the glass area, the circle in the heart of the ceiling has four picture-panels showing the seasons (Nature's seasons, not the Island's tourist ones). Beyond the central circle, the ceiling is smothered in plasterwork which was provided by Matcham's good friend, Felix de Jong

of the Plastic Decoration and Papier Machè Company, Wellington Street, Strand. Sometimes, the plasterwork gives way to *trompe l'oeil* painting where it cannot be examined too closely, although this expedient was considered unnecessary for the ceiling. It is used, however, in the upper areas of the niches beside the proscenium. Gold leaf of 232/3 carats smothers every frill and putti. The warmth and exuberance of the whole came from the colour scheme - old rose, ochre and cream. The three boxes are bow-fronted and have an elaborate, half-domed, tented look to them, quasi-Eastern in keeping with the act drop, and similar to Matcham's Birmingham Empire. The curtains around the boxes (supplied by Turner, Son and Walker in Liverpool, who were also responsible for the upholstery) were an essential part of the design, but are frequently neglected in restoration work. The curtains were patterned mohair, the valences crushed mohair in the same viridian shade. Tassels of dark blue, flecked with gold, hung from the centre. Within the boxes, the wallpaper was ochre, with a fern design in gold. Each one could accommodate four people sitting on bentwood chairs. The proscenium was segmented, with a tympanum at the top holding a fresco of the Muses. On each side of the proscenium are plaster copies of Canova statues set into ornamental niches. At stage and circle level are paintings, designed to look like mosaics, representing Comedy and Tragedy. On the box on stage left, there is an ornamental cherub with a purpose other than decoration. There is a little hole in his stomach that allowed the projection of slides or the numbers of the acts if a variety show was on. Throughout the theatre, there are pictures of mythical creatures in Classical style, which were all carried out by Messrs. Jonas Binns and Sons from Halifax.

In the slips there was extensive stencil work. Stencilling was also in evidence up the grand staircase, and into the coffee-bar, with a simplified version of the design carried down the corridors to the boxes and into the fauteuil entrances. There was also stencil work from the back of the pit to the pavement exit, which really does look like extravagant excess, given the tendency to leave all decoration for the well-heeled. To light the auditorium there were four chandeliers in the ceiling, in gilded brass. Above the proscenium were another three chandeliers, two double-lights hung above the slips and electroliers were fixed to the front of the circle and the amphitheatre. Each box was fitted with a single light diffused by a beaded shade, and electroliers on the front. There were no shades on the other original lights, which must therefore have been rather stark. In the corridors and other areas there were gas burners to illuminate the darkness.

The stage curtains were of patterned mohair with a heavy fringe and were of the tableau variety. This means that they were gathered about two-thirds of the way down and drawn up. The material matched the viridian velvet of the boxes, which in turn matched the upholstery on the fauteuils, the sills on the boxes, circle, gallery and slips, and was patterned velour with a heavy fringe. No pictures or plans remain of the curtains when down, so it's uncertain precisely what the design was, but it was standard practice to embroider them, perhaps with a monogram and a border. Once they rose, they stayed up until the end of the show. This allowed the act drop to come into play (as it were) at the end of each act. This was an essential part of any Victorian theatre, and it hardly needs saying how extraordinary it is that The Gaiety still has one. However, as it was usual to repaint it - and even advertise the change as an attraction for the public - to have one completely untouched after a century is approaching the miraculous. It is the only working one of its age in any public theatre in the British Isles and was painted, almost certainly in London, by the acknowledged master of the craft, William Thompson Hemsley. Its tone and colour are consistent with the decoration throughout the auditorium, but with an Oriental theme, as with the domed box fronts. It shows a Sultan in a lavish tented palace being entertained by a dancing girl while being fanned and in the company of two other ladies. The view behind is of a domed mosque and minaret, in glorious, light, golden sunshine, while the interior of the palace is hung with lamps and perhaps incense burners. Around it all is what appears to be a frame, mirroring the decoration throughout the auditorium. It is reminiscent of some of the designs in "Hay's Views of Cairo", a large folio volume Hemsley is known to have possessed. An act drop was basically something to look at during the scene changes; the audience at The Gaiety had something as lavish as the best of their surroundings to lose themselves in, wherever they sat.

William T. Hemsley (he always used the middle initial to distinguish him from another William Hemsley, an artist of the time) was born in Newcastle in 1850. There was artistry in the family - his great-uncle was John Graham Lough, the sculptor. He originally trained as an engineer, in Swindon, but in his spare time went to a local art school, a combination of interests which is surprisingly useful in the theatre, and particularly in his chosen line of work. He was evidently gifted, because at just sixteen he had a First Class certificate and a teacher's certificate. He went on to London where he continued studying at Lambeth School of Art, and made some extremely useful friends at Covent Garden, Haymarket and Drury Lane theatres. In 1873, he married Fanny Harriet May, three years younger than him, the sister of the Punch cartoonist Phil May, and spent the next several years at Margate as a scenic painter. This was an important position, especially in the more expensive shows; indeed, for London productions, a different artist might be employed for different scenes, and the name of each artist mentioned in the programme. In the 1903 production of Richard II, produced by Herbert Beerbohm Tree, there were fourteen scenes, and Hemsley painted four of them. Joseph Harker and Walter Hann took the others between them. There are early Gaiety programmes that make mention of different people being responsible for the scenery in different acts of a play, so such large-scale productions would have toured as well, frequently with reproductions of the original works.

Hemsley was also a caricaturist, with work appearing in the Margate Free Press, and this speed of eye and accuracy remained with him throughout his later career. From 1886 until at least 1912 he painted the scenery for the annual Cambridge University Greek plays. He opened a "scene factory" with Charles Wilmot, but the partnership only lasted a few years, and in 1892 he set up on his own in Felix Street, Westminster Bridge Road, London. His studio was built especially for him, and he was hugely in demand. His engineering skills were recognised as much as his artistic ones, and he was noted for his 'mechanical ingenuities' as much as his scenic effects. Outside the theatrical world, he apparently designed a free-standing tree supported by hoops, which was said to be very popular. His output was prodigious and prestigious, including work at practically every major London theatre. Other work included fifteen years painting the massive backdrops to the Military Tournament and the Horse Show. He naturally came into contact with H. E. Moss of Stoll Moss, and worked on over sixty productions with him. It is not too much to speculate that this is how he came to know Matcham, although their paralleled success made their meeting almost inevitable. He naturally had apprentices, who called him 'Guv'nor' or 'The Captain' (or said they did). His favourite play, according to one such apprentice, was 'A Midsummer Night's Dream'. He was regarded as one of the best scenic artists in Britain, and possibly the Continent, and his act drop for the London Opera House was described as the finest in the West End. Such encomiums should be taken with the

Jonas Kenyon Binns

Jonas Kenyon Binns was born in 1837, and by the time of his death in May 1904 had become an extremely successful businessman in Halifax. He was apprenticed at his father's firm of fresco painters, and the calibre of his work, in particular the decorative side, was recognised throughout the country. He worked on major buildings in London and most of the major cities in Britain, as well as his home town, and, of course, Douglas. In Halifax itself he was involved with many of the churches and chapels, the Town Hall, the Victoria Hall and the Palace Theatre (not a Matcham). He seems to have been extremely amiable, retiring but dutiful, not one to take a leading role in any particular aspect of his social, professional or political life, but to have a role there anyway. He was a well-known member of the St. John's Lodge of Freemasons, and there is a suggestion of some Masonic influence in his work at The Gaiety. Above the proscenium is a cherub holding the Compasses. Whether this is because Binns or Matcham wanted it is unknown; the cherub might simply represent mathematics. At the time, in the Island at least, membership of the Masons was not considered to be such a secretive matter as it is seen by some to be today, because the papers published lists of recent initiates.

Binns was also an Oddfellow, vice-president of a Constitutional Club, a member of St Paul's Church in Halifax, a member and promoter of an amateur drama group in his younger days and a known Conservative in his later ones. In none of these fields was he active, in the sense of seeking to push himself forward or attain power. Clearly, though, he was fully involved in all aspects of them, being responsible, for instance, for the scenery used by his drama group over a period of some dozen years. He played the cello in the band formed out of this dramatic group, was married and had three sons and three daughters, all of whom - along with his wife - outlived him. His death came rather suddenly, thought to be of heart disease, after a short illness from which he seemed for a brief while to have recovered. His funeral was quite an event, attended by representatives of several Lodges and Master Painters' Associations, Oddfellows, churchmen, Conservative groups, as well as family, friends and members of his Constitutional Club. It should be noted, too, that workers and employees were also at the graveside, with six of them acting as bearers. The blinds of the houses near his home were drawn as a mark of respect for an unassuming but popular and successful member of the business community, and a large crowd lined the street between the home and the church.

same reverence as the descriptions of new buildings, of course, but his CV alone testifies to the quality he must have brought to his work.

The work itself could be a mammoth operation. Even for a theatre such as The Gaiety, the size of the work alone is daunting. The act drop needed to fill a space some 30 by 28½ feet. It has to be detailed enough to withstand close inspection and bold enough to be seen clearly from some distance. This is painting on a scale only usually imagined on frescoes or Vatican chapels, and The Gaiety example used appropriate colour schemes and *trompe l'oeil* to draw the viewer into its fantasy. Matcham presumably told him the colour scheme, gave him the dimensions and let his fellow professional get on with it. There is an attractive theory that he came over and did it on site, but it is more likely he conducted such business from his own studio. Once completed and dried, the canvas would have been carefully rolled and transported to the Island to be re-hung just behind the house curtains. When it dropped down, the painted, heavy swag of the curtains at the corners added to the illusion. In all, he painted over fifty act drops for provincial theatres.

He had seven children, although one died as an infant. His second son, George, followed in his brushstrokes, and took the skill to India, prior to his early death at just 47, when he was killed at Vauxhall Station. William Hemsley himself died in 1918, five years before his wife.

Below the stage was an orchestra pit, which could hold about twenty musicians, with a valence to match the rest of the theatre's curtains. There was a conductor's chair, a tip-up one with a highly ornamented back (which cost 18 shillings and sixpence from Dean's). A brass rail with a curtain separated the orchestra from the audience. The stage itself overhangs the orchestra pit, to bring the stage forward and prevent the actors getting lost behind the gulf, and there was a pitch-pine sounding-board to bounce the music out into the house.

All of these elements, from the sweep of the circle to the boxes to the proscenium, from the ceiling to the fire escapes, from the foyer through the stages of gradual illumination to the explosion of colour further inside, fit and function together. They are not added as separate extras, but built into the whole with a continual movement and consistent theme. This is why Matcham was considered so exceptional an architect. It was very particular, specialised work, but he succeeded in avoiding the formality of the Classical style, which could be cold and forbidding (quite apart from unsuccessful when it separated the stage and

Conductor's chair, as supplied by
A. R. Dean Limited.
Photo: Theatresearch

audience too much) while having enough restraint and fundamental architectural technique to ensure the proportions are correct. He was exuberant and popular, but combined this with a completeness in both intention and realisation, and his training gave him the basics to design buildings. His career allowed him - or forced him - to develop those skills in pursuance of what the public wanted.

There is one thing that The Gaiety emphatically is not, and that is avant-garde. At a time when architecture, design and style were developing into new forms and with a different manner, The Gaiety was old-fashioned. After all, it made complex provision for the underpinning of the class system, taking full advantage of cheap labour and the industrial processes so hated by great social and artistic reformers like William Morris and Thomas Ruskin (although the latter was in some degree responsible for the Gothic revival which is so much a part of Victorian architecture; to his credit, even he grew tired of it). It served the working, urban comm-unity on its paid holidays and those who paid them, but was not made to be anything but a glamorous hint of the high-life that might be lived if one had enough money. There was no suggestion the theatre was a place for communicating with a familiar world - it was supposed to be exotic, distant, a dream world. It

celebrated the Imperial, rather than the local, despite being made to suit its location. It was as if the works of Charles Rennie Mackintosh or - more pertinently, since he was living on the Island - McKay Hugh Baillie Scott didn't exist. Their work would go on to influence the American and European world of the future; Matcham's celebrated the vigour and potency of his contemporaries'. The Art Nouveau movement, although reflected in details of The Gaiety's design (such as the stained glass, light shades in the boxes, and door handles) is evident in other Matcham theatres. But The Gaiety almost refers to a previous generation, which may reflect the inherent conservatism of its owners. The derivative nature of the work he did may offer another reason why his accomplishments, and that of others like him, is not given its due credit in the architectural world. He was not a revolutionary, he was a functionary; he didn't change the way people saw the manufactured world, he reflected its desires.

Throughout The Gaiety's interior there is evidence of work which was typical of Matcham, if not directly copied from elsewhere. The two statues on either side of the proscenium could also be found in The Queen's Theatre in Keighley until its demolition in 1961. The decoration at the back of the Circle is also evident at Cranbourne Mansions, originally a part of the London Hippodrome. The plasterwork under the amphitheatre is similar to that in the same place at Richmond in London, which was being built at the same time. For the original, this shows how he was working from his stock books, using tried, efficient and successful methods to fulfil a brief from his employers. For the restoration, it meant there were precedents that could be followed, and examples to copy from when the original was lost. For the audience and the owners in 1900, it meant they had what they wanted - a Frank Matcham theatre.

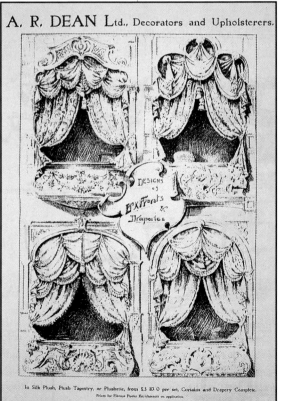

A page from A. R. Dean's catalogue, showing designs for box
drapes, circa. 1900.
Photo: Theatresearch

UP AND RUNNING; DOWN AND OUT

In the 110 or so years prior to The Gaiety's opening, there had been some eighteen theatres in the Island. Precisely how many is difficult to determine partly because there is confusion over different names that seem to refer to the same building. The first two, however, were built in 1788. One was called Banks' Dining Rooms and Playhouse, as concise a description as could be desired. The other took concision to its limit, being known simply as The Theatre, although its full title was Captain Barton Tennison's Assembly Rooms, a name which somehow failed to catch the public imagination. Of these two, the latter has the best claim to being the Island's first theatre, since it existed solely for the purpose of entertaining people, whereas the former seems likely to have been a music hall of some description, serving food while the performance was carried out on a small stage.

Both were situated near the quayside in Douglas, and although little is known about their different styles of production, it is possible Banks' was for the wealthier, merchant class and The Theatre for lovers of fairly raw melodrama. It presented such plays as 'The Road to Ruin', 'The Surrender of Calais' and 'Wild Oats'. This last was performed in 1797, the same year as the Duke of Rutland visited the Island, and who mentioned the theatre, but not whether he saw this play. This is a shame, simply because it would have been interesting to know whether he agreed with a report on the production that said it was performed by 'a most miserable set of actors'. It is not clear from this whether they were generally miserable at being in what was probably a draughty hut on a busy quayside near the Irish Sea, or whether it is particular to their acting.

Captain Tennison's venture foundered after sixteen years, in 1804, when a local paper reported, with no apparent irony: 'The Theatre is to be converted into an Auction Room, because fishermen blame the bad fish season on holding such vain amusements.' The fishing lobby obviously had powerful friends. Either that or this explanation seemed entirely plausible given the quality of the acting.

Banks' lasted longer, until 1824 - or at least, this seems to be the case. But the next two theatres in Douglas, The Royal Theatre (1807) and The Coffee Palace (1809, a somewhat enigmatic title for a playhouse) could just as easily be the same places with different names. However, theatres were clearly

becoming more popular in the early nineteenth century, as trade began to impact on the general wealth and growth of the population. As well as the two in Douglas, there was another Theatre Royal in the Court House at Ramsey in the north of the Island, and in the south, in Castletown, another 'The Theatre'. A third 'The Theatre' seems to have been built in Douglas, with possibly a fourth although, again, records are ambiguous. From 1819 the confusion this must have caused overwhelmed the population and no playhouse was ever called The Theatre again, although there were two Royals and, at one point, there was another Gaiety. The habit of adding the word "Royal" was even more common in the United Kingdom. It carried almost universally spurious notions of patronage, and was intended to imply approval. A similar rationale today informs, for example, the use of the word 'traditional' on mass-produced food. But more theatres were built - The Victoria, The Waterloo, The New Theatre, Dixon's Assembly Rooms, The Livery Yard Theatre, The Prince of Wales Theatre, the Royal Theatres and The Grand.

The real boom came with the tourists, of course. Until the 1830s there was no regular ferry service between the Island and Britain; by the end of the century hundreds of thousands were regularly holidaying on the Isle of Man. This speed of development was seen in every aspect of Manx life, and the theatres and amusements rose quickly. Before the 1860s or so, the theatrical fare was considered pretty poor stuff. *The Stage* newspaper, reporting on the opening of The Gaiety, said performers in the past were treated to 'scanty, ill-suited accommodation, quite unworthy of their great art', and suggested those who came to the Isle of Man to perform did so briefly. There were major acts that toured to the Island, but it was considered something of a backwater. With the development of cheap, reliable steam travel, it was transformed and, one after another, theatres were built as the actors came over to play. While the plans

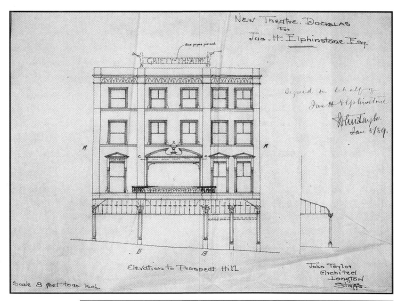

Plans for another Gaiety Theatre, on Prospect Hill in Douglas, in 1889.
Photo: Douglas Corporation

Holidaymakers on Douglas Head at the end of the 19th century
Photo: Manx National Heritage

for The Gaiety were being laid, however, the only purpose-built theatre was The Grand which, twelve years previously, Matcham had been involved in redesigning. Once The Palace and Derby Castle Limited decided there was more than enough room for another, The Grand began a process of refurbishment to ensure it was up to the challenge, and upstaged the arriviste by re-opening before it.

It was originally intended to open The Gaiety on July 5, according to a February preview in *The Manxman* (which included the mandatory rodomontade that it would become 'one of the most luxuriant, comfortable and best equipped theatres in the United Kingdom'). There hardly needs to be a reason for a delay of so short a time on a work of this size (it opened a week later than hoped), but February 1900 saw the collapse of Dumbell's Bank. This was a local institution, and one that financed many Manx businesses. Its fall was a disaster and damaged many Island firms and families. 1900 was about as good a time to lose everything as you can get. Industry was thriving, there were visitors aplenty and employment was high as a result. There was investment in the Island and a good living to be made if luck favoured you. But the collapse of Dumbell's was a substantial blow to confidence just as much as businesses. It is just possible its effects had a minor impact on the construction work taking place on Harris Promenade. If it did, it is testament to the resilience of the workforce (or the demands of the employers) that the work was completed so close to the original deadline.

When the opening night - Monday, 16 July, 1900 - came, it was a grand occasion. Among the invited guests were the Mayor, Mr Alderman Webb, and his wife, the Mayoress; Deemster Kneen ('Deemster' is the title of senior judges on the Island), his wife and daughter; the Attorney General and his wife, Mrs. Ring; J. A. Brown and his wife with their party; and other Directors of The Palace and Derby Castle Limited, as well as any number of other dignitaries. At seven-thirty, under the baton of F.C. Poulter, the theatre's musical director, a choir of eight members of the Douglas Choral Union stood in front of the curtains and sang the National Anthem, during which the audience joined in 'most heartily' (the adverb is used in three contemporary reports, so it must be true). At the conclusion of the singing, John Brown stepped on stage and said:

"Ladies and gentlemen, I must ask you to excuse any trepidation that may appear in me, but you can easily understand that it would try the nerves of most people, and especially one so utterly unaccustomed to public speaking as I am, to stand up before and speak to such an audience as this; but

I have been asked by the Directors of The Palace and Derby Castle Company Limited, the owners of this lovely theatre, to bid you a hearty welcome, to extend to you a most cordial greeting to this new temple to the drama, and as their Chairman, I feel myself called upon to obey their request (Loud applause). I therefore greet you one and all; and hope that your presence here this evening may be the happy and pleasant precursor of many evenings in the happier times to come (Applause). [This may have been a reference to the Dumbells collapse, although on a larger stage altogether the Boer War was continuing.]

"I shall not detain you from the legitimate entertainment of the evening for more than a moment or two; but you will agree with me that the opening of our new theatre affords the directors a desirable opportunity of explaining their ideas, their intentions, their objects in regard to this undertaking (Hear, hear). But, firstly, I would voice our regret and, I am sure, yours also, that his Excellency the Governor, who had graciously granted his patronage, has not been able to add the graciousness of his presence this evening. His genial face would have added to the pleasure of us all (Hear, hear) [The correspondent who wrote a piece for *The Stage*, the newspaper of the theatrical profession, was clearly not present at the occasion, since he claimed it took place in the presence of the Lieutenant Governor at the time, Lord Henniker. He may simply have taken a transcript of the original speech and added some of his own colour, because he also describes the applause that greeted Brown as 'hearty'. On the other hand, perhaps he had heard Brown speak before and decided to miss that part of the proceedings].

"Those of you who knew the Douglas of some three or four years ago will know that a company was formed to bring under one management the principal places of amusement in Douglas, and thus end the ruinous competition which had been indulged in. Amongst the buildings acquired by that company was The Pavilion. You will remember what that building was like. It was a horror architecturally and a failure financially. The question was what was the best purpose to which to devote this unprofitable property. Well, after due consideration, we decided that the best thing to do with it was to make it into a theatre. In the olden days, when Douglas was a much more insignificant place than it is now, it had two theatres, and at one time three. Why should it not be well able to properly support two now? We have no desire to enter into undue competition with any existing institution. I assure you that, while wishing to do well for the Company, we also wish every success to

Mr. Hemming (Applause) - and I think I put myself beyond successful contradiction when I assert that Douglas, in having the Grand and Gaiety Theatres, is to be congratulated on the possession of two of the handsomest theatres in Great Britain - theatres of which any watering-place may well be proud (Renewed applause). Here, indeed, we have a theatre which for beauty and comfort cannot be surpassed - indeed, I doubt if it can be equalled - either in or out of London (Prolonged applause).

"So much for our past. So much for our present. And now a few words as to our future. On that I shall not trouble you with details, beyond informing you that our arrangements comprise engagements with many of the best London companies obtainable. Our aim will be to keep our prices popular, and to give our patrons every consideration and comfort. The metamorphosis we have effected here has been a very costly operation, but may I venture to hope that, in return for our generosity to the public, we shall have ample reward and in the generous appreciation and in the patronage of the public (Applause). And now I have only one other thing to do. I wish to introduce to you our architect, Mr Frank Matcham. You have all heard of the inscription in the great cathedral at St. Paul's, close by the tomb of Sir Christopher Wren - 'Si monumentum requiris, circumspice'. Freely translated, that means, 'If you would see his monument, look ye around'. I can apply that, truthfully, to Mr. Matcham. Cast your eyes around, and from stage to foyer, from pit to sunlight, see a monument to his genius (Applause). Foremost amongst the Moderns as a theatre architect, he has, with the fairy wand of inventive genius, transformed a hideous structure into a building which is a marvellous sample of construction, which is singularly harmonious in design and which, being a 'thing of beauty' may, we hope, also be 'a joy forever' (Applause). Ladies and gentlemen, I introduce to you Mr Frank Matcham."

There was a generous round of applause as Matcham walked on stage. He read the audience perfectly, and said:

"Ladies and gentlemen, after the eloquent speech of Mr. Brown, I am sure you don't want any lengthy remarks from me; but I must apologise for the theatre not being completed. I am very sorry it is not finished; but I hope in a few days everything will be in what we call 'apple-pie order'. I must thank Mr. Brown for his kind remarks, and I thank you, ladies and gentlemen, for your very kind appreciation and I, with you, join in wishing every success to the new theatre."

This bashful reply was followed by the Opening Address, written by G. A. McCammon and spoken by a Mr. C. J. Morton, a 'well-known elocutionist':

'Greet ye, fair dames, salute ye, gallant sirs,
This bright array a happy feeling stirs,
Joy to our hearts a genial glow doth give,
For in your good opinion we would live;
Old friends, old faces, drama's laity,
A meet assemblage for the Gaiety.

Another play house, some one quick may cry!
Well, not exactly! And I'll tell you why.
One theatre you have, a Grand one reckoned;
The town long since did fairly boast a second:
Rivalry we'd scout, but this want e'en supply,
And friendly contest in the issue try.
Our motto, "Onward". Take and give.
The good old maxim ever, "Live, let live."

This temple new, to drama dedicate
Befitting shrine (if we may predicate);
No fairy fabric this (some may hatch 'em),
Sterling stuff alone from Master Matcham.
Fertile of resource, rich in rare design,
His plans in perfect harmony combine;
Expense not stinted to a meagre dole,
The building stands, in truth, a splendid whole.
Solid and safe work, carried out with skill,
Proud tribute to our townsman, Alec Gill.

Celestials all, ye boxes, stalls and pit,
Pray glance around, facts most folk admit;
If ye approve, applause should quickly grow,
Then raise your hands, and justly it bestow.

Our menu will be choice - arranged with care,
Suiting each taste with its dramatic fare:
Classic and comic muse will point the page
And Opera (London's latest) fill the stage.
Music - sweet song (a dainty mental dish)
Shall charm, and leave but little else to wish.
Mirth and wit ne'er will cause satiety,
Gaiety springing from variety.

The prompter's bell! Now must I say adieu!
Once more then, welcome, one and all of you.'

They don't write 'em like that any more. Mr. McCammon, author of the piece, was a man who had been for many years the Chief Clerk of the Customs at Douglas. He was described as 'a veteran drama critic' in one report, and as a man whose 'taste for, and acquaintance with, dramatic, musical and literary matters is well known'.

The play chosen to open this new theatre was 'The Telephone Girl'. This was a light musical, popular and successful in Britain, written by quite

The programme for the opening night.
Photo: Mervin Russell Stokes collection.

a substantial team. There was Sir Augustus Harris, a theatrical entrepreneur of some note at the time; Arthur Sturgess, a librettist; and Frank Burnand.

Sir Francis Cowley Burnand (1836 - 1917) was educated at Eton and Trinity College, Cambridge. He was called to the bar in 1862, but the success of works such as 'Black-Eyed Susan' and, most famously, 'Cox and Box' which he co-wrote with Arthur Sullivan in 1867, meant he could follow his theatrical and literary bent. He started a magazine called *Fun*, but left that to contribute to *Punch*, from 1863, with a regular and successful column called 'Happy Thoughts', and edited the magazine from 1880 until 1906. He was knighted in 1902. It is just within the realms of possibility he had a Manx connection, because his middle name is very common on the Island. This, however, is pure conjecture.

These three worthies only wrote the words; the music was by Gaston Serpette and J. M. Glover. The star, however, was Ada Blanche. She sang, she danced, she kept the play alive with her interpretation of the jolly Lottie. Her performance was lauded for its 'arch by-play' and being 'ever in evidence without being intrusive'; she "never allowed the fun to flag"; and quite clearly stole the show comprehensively. The production was by her own company, and she was responsible for the set and costume design as well. The tenor of the drama can be gleaned from the names and descriptions of some of the cast - Prince Imatoff, a Russian nobleman; Bartholomew Pilchard, a

farmer from Cornwall; and Dolly Dobbs, 'known in London as 'Belle Bell', the unrivalled variety sparkler'. The Gaiety was clearly looking for its namesake in entertainment, and while it may be tempting to mock, there is a time and a place for the likes of Ibsen's 'When We Dead Awaken' (written the year before), and this wasn't it. A holiday Island during a war and after a banking collapse is a place calling for the brittle, painted face of unrestrained 'frivolling', a point made by one contemporary critic:

'There is nothing gained by taking 'The Telephone Girl' seriously. All the combined intelligence of Clement Scott, plus Bernard Shaw and that cockscomb of criticism, Max Beerbohm, could tell you, the morrow after witnessing the performance is, that the audience laughed and were pleased . . . they were lifted for two hours from a pence-counting environment into the realms of pure fantasy, where King Misrule reigns supreme. And this, nowadays, is a great boon . . . The world who today plays in Douglas wants light, and life, and colour. These things are to be found in 'The Telephone Girl', as staged in the beautiful playhouse . . . No-one can be dree if he has paid for his seat in the new Gaiety Theatre.'

Later in the same review, it is mentioned that a future production was to be 'The Christian', from the novel by the phenomenally successful Manx author, Hall Caine. Another of Hall Caine's novels had been adapted and produced in London five years earlier ('The Manxman'), and reviewed by Bernard Shaw. Mr Shaw, frankly, did not think much of the play, nor of the Manx as a result. He wrote a scathing piece on its production in The Shaftesbury Theatre, complaining of 'intolerably copious and intolerably common imagination . . . I have not read the celebrated novel, and am prepared to go to the stake rather than face the last chapter of it . . .'

If the reviewer of 'The Telephone Girl' had seen this, it is hardly surprising he named Bernard Shaw as a man incapable of properly appreciating the necessary and welcome levity of The Gaiety's production.

The Island didn't feel the need for Shaw's approval. It had a new theatre with a sparkling musical and a satisfied first-night crowd to take the good news with them.

The Gaiety was recognised as a fine example of its kind, and a first-class addition to the Palace and Derby Castle Company's stock. The stage was big enough to accommodate opera, and all the spectacular scenery that went with it. In 1900, the Moody Manners Opera Company came to the Island. The name was nothing to do with prima donnas, but referred to the married couple Fanny Moody and Charles Manners, who brought with them a chorus of fifty and a further twenty-five musicians, as well as the principals and other staff, a company totalling 110. In one week, they presented 'Faust', 'Lohengrin', 'Tannhäuser', 'Carmen' and, for light relief, 'The Bohemian Girl'. In one week in a seaside holiday town, five operas were presented. It is extraordinary that they should think it would be worth it, and it was not particularly successful. It also demonstrates how much The Gaiety could cope with. It also managed to deal with the occasional special production such as 'The Corsican Brothers' since the appetite for special effects was undimmed, as the success of 'The Messenger Boy' showed. It had a cast of 65, and the play required as one of its scenes a recreation of the Paris Exhibition and a ballet featuring 'exquisitely dressed representatives of Germany, America, England and France'.

One play carried its own offstage drama with it. 'La Poupée' ('The Doll') was an English opera, panned by invited critics (and the cast and orchestra) at a preview. Despite this, the London public absolutely adored it, and it was a huge success. However, the Producer, Henry Lowenfeld, had given away the provincial rights to his Acting Manager, Peter Levilly, believing them, after the preview, to be of no value. Following its enormous success in the capital, it toured the country, and was a sell-out wherever it went. Levilly cast Stella Gastelle, a renowned beauty, as the female lead. Levilly, however, had more than just the talent of his leading lady in mind when casting her. At every performance, wherever it went, he would reserve a box for himself. This box never appeared to be occupied, but the curtains were always drawn. This led to some speculation, naturally; almost as much as why it was that Levilly kept on changing the person playing the romantic male lead. Almost as soon as one actor took on the role and made a success of it, he would be fired. The cause of these mysteries was resolved when a provincial Manager, having heard the stories, watched Levilly closely when the play was on. During the love scenes and duets, Levilly would creep into the box and secretly watch the performance with fuming jealousy. Levilly's passion was such that if the lovers appeared to kiss with too much ardour, the male lead would be summarily dismissed. In the end, Levilly worked his way through most of the available actors of the time in an attempt to have the ugliest one in all the profession take the part. 'La Poupée' travelled to The Gaiety in July 1906, with Levilly and his reserved box in watchful attendance.

There was serious drama on-stage, too; or at least self-important drama. Hall Caine was born in Runcorn in 1853, but had Manx blood in him, lived on the Island and became the Island's Dickens. He died in 1931. The popularity of his works throughout the English-speaking world was quite staggering, although he seems to be all but forgotten now. Alfred Hitchcock's last silent film was of a Hall Caine story, his works were as fervently awaited in America as anything Dickens wrote, and his plays were received there with greedy rapture. When his play 'The Christian' was presented at The Gaiety, with his sister in the lead role of Glory Quayle, the house was packed. Despite these obvious selling points, the play was received rather grudgingly, both as a work of literature and as a piece of drama, with even Caine's sister coming in for some criticism.

The Gaiety was also from its earliest days the home of locally produced shows, one of the biggest in the first years being 'King Gobnageay'. It was described as 'The New and Original Manx Fairy Extravaganza' and featured 150 school-children performing choruses and dances.

But for most of its profitable life it was a house for frivolling, in comfort and elegance. For the best part of the next century, The Gaiety was the Island's light-hearted specialist. The overwhelming majority of productions were comedies or musicals, revues and variety, presented to capitalise on the holidaying masses' appetite for levity and offer a venue for local companies in quieter times, principally the winter. The summer was always a busy time, and made all the more so by the arrival in 1907 of the Tourist Trophy races. These are exclusively for motorbikes now, and came about because the Island was, and is, able to close public roads to allow racing on them, which had become increasingly difficult in Britain. It is no marketing sophism to call the Isle of Man the road racing capital of the world, and it guards that title with a jealousy some might call reckless. However, it has created a whole new market for travellers and is now one of the most recognisable features of the Island. Mention The Gaiety throughout Europe, and a blank stare is the only response. Mention the TT, especially in Germany, and faces light up in recognition of the glorious racing that can be had, and not just by the competitors. George Formby, the ukulele-playing, buck-toothed, grinning comedian of massive popularity in the 30s and 40s, made a film, 'No Limit', with the TT as its subject. It was made on the Island, and the population is still fiercely proud of it, with some of the older members able to point themselves out as extras in the crowd scenes.

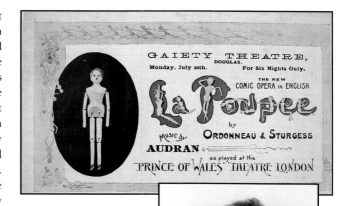

A poster advertising 'La Poupée and, right, its star, Miss Stella Gastell.
Photo: Mervin Russell Stokes collection

The programme for 'King Gobnageay', performed in 1902.
Photo: Mervin Russell Stokes collection

Another Royal occasion is marked at The Gaiety, two years after Queen Victoria's death.

Photo: Mervin Russell Stokes collection

Matcham's grave in Highgate Cemetary, simple in design, marked with a Latin Cross.

Photo: Mervin Russell Stokes collection

The TT was another major cause of the continuing success of the Island as a tourist destination, and was naturally an additional source of income for The Gaiety. For its first thirty years or so, the theatre was extremely successful. A stream of troupes arrived for their weekly show, filled the theatre and left again. Some became regulars, and occasionally a major hit would stay on at The Gaiety for months. A poster for February 19 proclaims of 'Leah Kleschna': 'A triumph for Douglas! 14th Week and Going Stronger Than Ever!'. This 'Famous Crook Play from The New Theatre, London, by C.M. McClellan' was produced by Denville's Famous Stock Company. The Gaiety's name remained the signifier of its purpose, and its fortunes reflected those of the parent company, and therefore the Island. By the fifties, there were serious problems; by the sixties it was evident action and overhaul were necessary; in the seventies, there was some evidence of revival; and by the end of the nineties, it was alive and in rude health.

It also reflected the preoccupations of its audiences. After only seven months in operation, the promoters of a concert at The Gaiety had to determine how to deal with Queen Victoria's death in January of 1901. The Queen had been ill, quite apart from being over ninety years old and, as always happens in such circumstances, there were desperate concerns about what to do should she pass away, and how to reorganise things satisfactorily while she was still alive. For The Gaiety, there was a concert planned in association with St. Thomas's Church. The organisers found themselves in the kind of confusion that strikes television and radio stations still. Should the normal programme proceed, or be modified, or dropped completely? It seemed to the promoters of the concert in 1901 that many people had bought tickets in the weeks leading up to the event and it would be wrong to disappoint them. After all, the Queen's health was not considered so precarious until nearer the time of the show. Once it was discovered that Victoria was indeed extremely unwell, on the morning of the performance, Canon Ernest Savage, Vicar of St Thomas's, and the other promoters thought it necessary to remove all humorous items from the concert to 'bring it more into keeping with the distressed state of people's minds'.

On the other hand, why were people going to a concert at all if their minds were so gripped in fear of Victoria's passing? They weren't to know the funny bits had been excised. One reason was in order to be part of the national mourning. According to *The Isle of Man Times*, there was only one topic of conversation among the gaily-dressed people at the theatre, and there must have been quite a *frisson* through the bustles when the rumour that Her Majesty had died was whispered around the theatre doors at quarter to eight. By this time, there was a substantial house already in, and when confirmation of the sad news came through, Canon Savage ordered the doors to be closed, and announced to the waiting audience their Queen, Lord of Mann, was dead (The news had arrived via the new telephonic system. The Gaiety was one of the first public buildings on the Isle of Man to have the device - the number was 191). Canon Savage was sure they would agree that, under the circumstances, it would be impossible to present the concert, since the universal sorrow at Her Majesty's death would be quite out of harmony with such an event. He also made it clear that everyone would get their money back or could redeem their tickets whenever the concert was re-presented.

There was one other passing that the audience should have recognised, nineteen years later, although there is no evidence it did. Frank Matcham died at the age of 65 on May 17, 1920, from heart failure. This was caused by blood poisoning brought about by over-trimming his nails. It had been eight years since he last did any major architectural work and less than two years after the Great War had finished. By the time of his death, the taste in design had shifted far from his ornate palaces of opulence and gilt, and the self-confident manner of his hey-day had been replaced with the social and moral uncertainty that marked most of the rest of the century. The nature of his death seems oddly banal. Dying quietly in his sleep after a meal at his favourite restaurant (Rules, in London, which is still running after more than 200 years) would have been altogether more satisfactory, but life is rarely so tidy and fitting as art. His wife, Maria, died nearly six months later, on November 13. She was interred beside him at Highgate Cemetery, under a simple Latin cross made of granite. There was no lowering of flags at his remaining theatres at his death, or at least there is no record of it. It was perhaps in keeping with the regard in which he was held for most of the next sixty years.

During the two wars, there was a halt to touring productions coming to the theatre, partly for the obvious reasons concerning the danger of sea travel and the need for able bodies to be occupied elsewhere. The Island made at least one significant musical contribution to the First World War. In 1913, Florrie Forde, a popular and successful star of her age, was singing at The Derby Castle. Among her songs was 'It's a Long Way to

Tipperary', which proved extremely successful. The following year, she repeated the song, and among the audience was a regiment of the Liverpool Scottish Territorials, encamped briefly on the Island. They loved the song, and when the War eventually took them to France, they used its chorus as a marching song. There it was picked up by almost everyone and became a kind of cheerful signature tune for all those wanting to return to their loved ones. Douglas in the pre-War period was known, at least by locals, as the birthplace of popular songs, and Florrie Forde was one of the most popular singers. She was such a regular on the Island, and liked it so much, she bought a tiny cottage on the quiet beach at Niarbyl.

The Isle of Man was also an internment camp for foreign nationals resident in Britain during both conflicts. As a result, there was barbed wire threaded down the centre of the Promenade in Douglas (the sites of the post-holes are still evident) with the boarding houses in use as hostels for the aliens. This did not put an end to all activity at The Gaiety, or in other parts of the Island. The Amadeus String Quartet was created by four musicians who found themselves confined on the Island during the Second World War. Those locals who were spared active service still put on productions at the theatre, and the internees were able to see films and shows there. They were also able to put on their own productions.

The first real threat to The Gaiety as a place of entertainment came from the silver screen. Between the wars, cinema had become the dominant force in entertainment, and The Gaiety was nearly a victim of the explosion in cinema-going. Douglas became crammed with picture palaces - The Regal, The Strand, The Picture House, The Crescent and The Royalty. The Gaiety had always been able to accommodate cinema, and moving-pictures had been shown on the Island since 1896. In The Gaiety, the projection box for the 'bioscopic' pictures was originally sited at the back of the stage, with the projection portholes set a foot above the stage, in an area now occupied by toilets. As the 30s progressed, more and more people wanted to see more and more films. Redevelopment of parts of Douglas to accommodate the swelling demand for cinema was seriously considered, and only the Depression at the end of the decade - and the Second World War - prevented it.

The War once again placed foreign internees on the Island, but also many servicemen. The Island provided a training ground for naval, army and RAF personnel. The building that now houses Manx Radio on Douglas Head was used as a radar training centre (Douglas was to be the first commercial port to use radar permanently), and among the servicemen was a young Jon Pertwee. He went on to become an extremely successful actor, particularly in 'The Navy Lark' on radio, and as Doctor Who and Worzel Gummidge on television. While stationed on the Island, he established The Service Players in 1942 simply because, as a hopeful young actor, the availability of such a wonderful theatre was a chance too good to miss. He brought together other actors in the services and local amateurs to form a company that is still running and still performing at The Gaiety.

After the Second World War, during which there were shows and films for the internees to watch - under guard - cinema became The Gaiety's principal form. The old routine of professional shows through the busiest times had all but ceased, and although there were amateur shows on during the winter, and occasional attempts to revive regular theatrical events, it was film that took over the building for the next twenty years or so. This was not a great success, but was significantly cheaper and sufficiently profitable for The Palace and Derby Castle Company to keep it on. Realising the old projection box was unable to satisfy the requirements of the medium, the box was moved to the very rear of the very highest part of the building. Originally it was made of wood. Film stock was an extremely flammable substance at the time and almost impossible to extinguish, so when this box was damaged by fire, it was a miracle it took nothing else with it. The new box was made of concrete, with fire shutters to prevent any further damage. Despite the number of cinemas, the Island only had access to a limited number of Pathé or Movietone newsreels. This meant that someone had to take them round to the various cinemas. Jimmy Bridson, who was a projectionist at The Gaiety, remembers in his youth cycling furiously between the cinemas with his precious cargo on a schedule so tight that if he so much as fell from his bike, the whole elaborate timetable was ruined. The Gaiety's presentation of the films was not much more

Even cinema-going lost its appeal as indicated by the demolition of The Royalty Cinema, Walpole Avenue, Douglas.
Photo: Mervin Russell Stokes collection

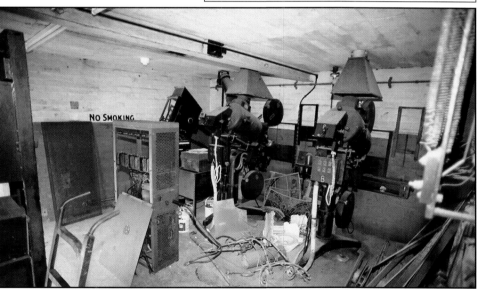

The projection suite of The Gaiety Theatre and below, the rewind room, both currently awaiting restoration.
Photo: Island Photographics

professional. In general, it showed B films rather than blockbusters, because they were cheap. The power system was provided by generators that needed to be switched on a good 45 minutes before the show started, and even then the supply was insufficient. Films were shown on reels that lasted about ten minutes and, when one ran out, the next needed to be cued up and ready on a second projector so the switch from one to the other was invisible. There are little marks on the film itself to indicate a reel is running out, and the two projectors can then be synchronised to make the change as smooth as possible. Alan Pascoe, who worked at The Gaiety from the late 40s, remembers the power supply being unable to cope with the two projectors running at the same time, and the film on the screen would dim perceptibly at the change of reel, something for which The Gaiety became rather renowned. Evening showings were the norm, but if the weather looked or became unpleasant, a matinee would be shown. It was worth the effort for the company, because staff requirements were so low that any quickly gathered trade was money in the bank. It was never money for the building. The Palace and Derby Castle never invested in The Gaiety and the fact that practically nothing remains of The Palace, The Derby Castle, or any of the other cinemas, rather suggests that maintenance was a notion foreign to them.

On the Isle of Man, 'longtails', or 'queer fellows' or 'joeys' are names given to rats, as a result of a maritime superstition. If the 'R' word is used, a whistle is required to prevent bad luck. The state of The Regal cinema was such that the doorman, Harry Campbell, used to spend some time with two dogs and a stick killing rats after the show in the auditorium each night. He would normally manage to do away with 20 or 30. However, even this vigorous action was not enough. One of them managed to get into the workings of the cinema's Compton organ. Around the console of this instrument was a hollow, shaped frame made of a frosted glass and called a jelly-mould, that could be illuminated with different colours as part of the act provided by the organist. One night, while Lenny Uren was keeping the audience entertained at the keyboard, a rodent became the unwitting centre of attention. He or she had found a way into the mould, but could not get out. As the organist played on, the shape of the trapped animal was silhouetted in the illuminated organ surround as the furry pest struggled to get out. The audience was hooting and laughing, except those near enough to the organist, who were screaming in terror, but the poor performer had no idea why.

Finally, the rat found its way out and disappeared, leaving the audience in hysterics of both sorts. Harry Campbell and his dogs had one more to chase that night.

The 50s saw scandal and decay at The Gaiety. The first was in a revue called 'Soldiers in Skirts'. The title explains a good deal. It was a variety drag act. By all accounts it was an extremely impressive performance - professional, funny, well produced and directed. And it packed the theatre. The British attitude towards cross-dressing and the associated issue of sexuality is so bizarre in its contradictions that it merits its own encyclopaedia. The matter is not any easier on the Isle of Man where, notoriously, homosexuality was illegal until 1992 when, under considerable pressure and unwelcome foreign attention, the law banning it was repealed. In 1951, such displays were regarded with something approaching hysteria by the authorities. The owners of The Gaiety were appalled, but the Manager bluntly asked them whether they wanted a full theatre or not. Any lingering doubts over the moral legitimacy of the show were overwhelmed by this financial expedient, and it came back the following year. However, the issue was moved beyond even Mammon's persuasion when one of the actors was discovered in compromising circumstances with a sailor in an alley in Douglas, a matter that reached the newspapers. The show never came back.

A similar controversy arose many years later in the 80s when Mervin Stokes was Manager. The play 'Steaming' had been a huge success in the West End, and Mervin thought it would be a popular choice for the summer crowd on the Island. However, the Island's High Bailiff had other ideas, and banned the play on the grounds that it contained nudity. This caused a bit of a stir at the time, but the law was the law, and Mervin had to find another show. He found 'Funny Peculiar'. While it lacked the subtlety and wit of the original play, it did contain suggestive scenes that Mervin thought would suit the audiences rather well. So he booked it. In the play, there is a moment when the lead actor is supposed to have run from a bedroom naked, to arrive on stage just as a privet hedge glides into place to protect his modesty. Unfortunately, when the play opened in Douglas to a full house all of whom knew exactly the circumstances under which it was being performed, there was no privet hedge. There had not been room on the container for it. The actor, Peter Duncan who had made his name in the television programme 'Blue Peter', was as aware of the circumstances surrounding the production, and arrived for the scene with his clothes bundled in front of his waist and groin. The audience were absolutely silent as the question flashed in neon signs through the head of everyone in the house - will he or won't he? Peter Duncan walked to the centre of the stage; and dropped his clothes to the floor. There was a pause. "Is anyone here embarrassed?" he asked. Someone, somewhere, sniggered - and then the whole audience roared with laughter. The play was a sell-out. Mervin, however, was in a state of nervous exhaustion. He seemed to have unwittingly defied the High Bailiff, and spent the next weeks awaiting a summons. There was no word from the High Bailiff's office.

The Second World War saw The Gaiety begin a long, slow decline. During the 50s, there was a brief attempt to reintroduce the regular repertory season, including local actors, but it never took off. Cinema was the biggest draw, and there were plenty of them. Douglas had one cinema seat for every 75 visitors, compared to the one for every 1,538 in Blackpool. It was hardly surprising The

Palace and Derby Castle decided to keep films on at The Gaiety. But the lack of maintenance led to further dilapidation, and as early as 1957 to an attempt by Douglas Corporation to lease the building. They wanted to encourage its use for live theatre, but for The Palace and Derby Castle there was more money to be made in packing the house with the avid film-goers, and they declined. It is remarkable that the Company did not decide to renovate the building at all, to turn it completely over to the movies. Perhaps by this time, for them, it was just a building which could house people and make money, although it may be there was a vestigial pride in possessing what had become the Island's only theatre. In the mid 50s, The Company owned buildings capable of accommodating some 23,000 people in total, and the business of entertaining them was changing. Television was beginning to take its toll on the numbers of people who wanted to come out, but a more substantial and subtle shift in what people wanted and where they wanted to get it was taking place, and leaving the Island behind.

The auditorium in 1950. Already the original wallpaper has been covered and the curtains above the stage and the boxes have been replaced with a simpler design. Original glass lightshades have been replaced with celluloid versions.

Photo: Kissack collection

In fact it had been leaving it behind for at least twenty years, possibly even longer, but the Second World War had hidden the problem. With the War had come construction activity and military personnel, as well as over 20,000 internees, who were housed all over the Island, rather than just at Knockaloe as was the case in the First World War. This halted what had been quite a steep decline in the economic fortunes of the Manx. The mining industries had all finished, fishing had virtually disappeared, manufacturing was reduced as a result and tourism was in decline. There were limited powers for the Manx Government to do anything about it. Winter unemployment began to require intervention to stave off disaster, but the problem of emigration typified the danger the Island was facing. Between 1951 and 1961 the population of the Island fell by nearly seven thousand, or almost thirteen percent. At the same time, fertility rates were declining, and since the young were leaving the Island as soon as they could afford a ticket, the Island's population was becoming increasingly old. The inherent problems facing a small island with limited natural resources were exacerbated by its constitutional and political position. It was facing all the problems that are typical in a marginal region without the same recourse to the larger body that has assisted other regions facing similar problems. It was effectively on its own, although not sufficiently so to bring about radical economic change. It was also afflicted by a tendency to shore things up rather than invest in different strategies, and offer money to the existing industries without developing new ones. The decline in tourist numbers was evident from the early 30s, but it was to take a good fifty years before the Island's recession was turned around, with the development of the financial sector and the Isle of Man's progression as an offshore centre.

The interlude of the Second World War served to hide the threat to the economy of the changing world order, and the continuing success of the TT provided just about enough for many businesses to struggle by. The changing tastes in the holiday market were not properly recognised and acted upon until late in the century and policies to suit the Island's changing nature took too long to introduce. As an example, planning regulations intended to maintain the symmetry and beauty of Douglas Promenade's famous frontage stipulated buildings must be hotels well after the time when no-one but an insane nostalgist would dream of opening one up. The result was that when a new business wanted to take over a derelict hotel, the application would be refused even if the business were prepared to keep the front of the existing building. This then left the building untenanted until it fell down, thus destroying precisely what the regulations were supposed to protect. The Island stopped being a resort for a whole family to come to for its annual holiday many years ago, but initiatives to develop a more specialised and higher-spending market only started coming into being in the latter part of the 1990s, and even in 2000 the Director of Tourism was suggesting that certain aspects of the tourist industry are still focussing on the two weeks of the TT as their principal earning time.

The major change in the Isle of Man's fortunes took place in the late 50s and early 60s, although it would be some years before the effect was felt. The new industry - the financial services - would provide sufficient growth for the woefully underfunded infrastructure to be renewed, for the Island's economy to grow substantially, for the unemployment level to be essentially zero, and for The Gaiety to be able to call upon business to be part of its restoration. The shift to a low-tax jurisdiction attracting billions of pounds in international funds and investments happened by accident. In 1961, Income Tax was reduced, Surtax was abolished, and there were incentives created to attract manufacturing industries to the Island. The capacity to change the taxation autonomously was the result of prolonged negotiations between the British and Manx Governments in the 50s, and is a change the British might now be rather regretting. Originally, the tax alterations were intended to attract wealthy retired people to the Island, and had nothing to do with trying to become a major player in a global financial market. The result, however, was the development of an industry that allowed an influx of lawyers (advocates is the term in Manx law), accountants, bankers, fund managers, insurers, marine administrators and the like. The knock-on effect is that practically every area of the Manx economy has grown, especially since the conscious work undertaken by Government since the mid 70s to encourage the sector. There are some people who come to live on the Island because of its lower taxes (the upper rate for individuals is 20%), but there are far fewer 'taxiles', as Stephen Fry called them, than is popularly imagined. The Island has succeeded in the financial world because it is able to offer political stability, accessibility, regulation and expertise, not because hundreds of millionaires run to the Island to save on their income tax. Lower taxes don't hurt, naturally, and the right to set them internally is jealously guarded by the

Treasury in the face of growing calls from international organisations for such an advantage to be taken away. The real benefit is that the rates attract businesses, and therefore employ people, who will be on the Island to spend their money building houses, buying food and enjoying a night out. There is, of course, a very real danger the finance world will dominate the Island as agriculture, fishing, smuggling and tourism has in the past, and leave it open to decline and recession should it collapse. It is hoped the broad economic expansion it has engendered throughout the Island will give it a much stronger base to grow independently of the financial world itself. There is as yet no way of knowing whether this is anything more than a heady fantasy, but the success of the sector has unquestionably led to the Island regarding itself as a more mature democracy than before.

These initially gradual developments in the Island's political and economic state were reflected in The Gaiety. As the tourism trade stagnated, and the whole Island needed an overhaul, so the theatre sat neglected on the Promenade, presenting shows that properly belonged to another era. For many years from the late 50s, there was a regular summer season presented by Stella Hartley. This would be a variety show, including accordionists, contortionists, singers and sketches. It ran for some sixteen weeks, from May to September, a family show of the end-of-the-pier variety, with a different programme for the second half of the week and a special Sunday concert that would be a one-man show by the likes of Ronnie Corbett or Frankie Howerd. During the rest of the year, the stage was used for films or for amateur societies. As an example of what was offered, in the 1968 season, the *What's On* promised: 'The Holiday Show', a merry whirligig of fun, music and laughter, with Dave and Jo O'Duffy, Stella Hartley and strong supporting cast. Every night is Gift Night at "Stella's Party" This is one of Douglas' gayest and most intimate shows, and is a must for every visitor.' Stella Hartley was married to Sid Myers, who managed the theatre during the summer for The Palace and Derby Castle Company. He had been unlucky in certain aspects of his professional life. He had at one time been a business partner of Paul Raymond, but when Raymond started introducing nudes to his shows, Sid returned his share of the business on principle. It was just before Raymond became hugely successful. Sid was also the man who discovered Gerry Dorsey, a singer who won a talent contest at The Villa Marina in Douglas. Sid, however, found he was not in a position to become

the young man's manager, and the entertainer was picked up by another agency, who changed his name to Englebert Humperdinck.

Sid died one evening putting his socks on while preparing to go to the theatre for that night's performance. His wife, a professional to her fingertips, still went on that evening.

The Palace and Derby Castle were running out of whatever slight enthusiasm they had had for the building by the mid 60s, and were looking to sell it off. The problem with this plan was the genuine prospect of the theatre being sold off to another private concern that might have less scruple about transforming it into, for example, a bingo hall. This was happening with great success in the United Kingdom. In fact the pencils for the bingo cards had already been imported for the change of use. The pencils themselves were marked 'Reject', and the lead fell out of them every time they were sharpened. The prospect of bingo being played in theatres did not necessarily mean they would be pulled down; it could serve as a holding operation for the building while maintaining its use. This happened at The Wakefield Opera House, The Hulme Hippodrome and The Longton Empire, amongst many others, allowing some to return to life as theatres later. A more pressing concern was that it might be knocked down and turned into offices.

The Gaiety came within one signature of being demolished, and would have been a heap of rubble before Government had said 'Public service!' had it not been for the defiance of Arthur Corkill. Arthur Corkill was the Accountant and Secretary for The Palace and Derby Castle Company, the majority of whose shares were owned by a London gaming and leisure firm, Crockfords. Crockfords had brought their own man over to the Island to run their concerns, Sir Dudley Cunliffe Owen. Sir Dudley was a generous and chivalrous man, but he could occasionally be rather autocratic, and having

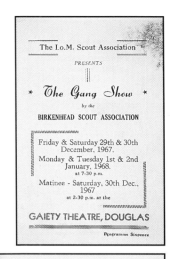

Not everyone thought that live theatre was dead, as this seasonal 'Gang Show' demonstrated.

Photo: John and Celia Slark

replaced the existing Board of Directors with his own appointees, there was little to stop him being so. The Gaiety was losing money during the 60s, and Sir Dudley reacted with a typically firm decision after seeing the appalling returns for 'The Minstrels From Amsterdam' in June 1968. The show itself promised to be 'really different', and starred 'the great Eurovision success, The Happy Holland Minstrels and a host of first-class Continental Variety Artistes.' It is difficult to imagine how Sir Dudley could have expected anything better than appalling returns from such a production, but his anger was such that he asked Arthur to write to a firm in the United Kingdom called Sieferts to organise the demolition. This was not the first time Sir Dudley had decided enough was enough. He had in a similar fashion ordered the immediate destruction of the Palace Coliseum. On that occasion, he got his way. On this, he had Arthur to contend with.

Arthur's father had worked shifting scenery at The Gaiety and as a child Arthur had sat in the wings watching the shows. He had been working at the theatre since 1937 selling programmes, and in his role as Secretary had his offices in the building, in what had been and now is the dress circle bar. He simply refused to sign the necessary paperwork. Sir Dudley, unsurprisingly, was not mollified by this insubordination but Arthur stood firm. He did two things. He went to see Sir Ralph Stevenson, a Director, and told him what was being threatened. Sir Ralph agreed that this was entirely unacceptable, in particular given the concerns voiced over the ease with which The Coliseum was demolished. Sir Ralph agreed to call a Board meeting. The other thing Arthur did was tell the Tourist Board (later the Department of Tourism) in the person of Len Bond, the then Director of Tourism. This effectively primed the Government for what the Board decided. They met and discussed the issue fully. In the end, they decided to approach the Island's Government and suggest the theatre be purchased for the nation. As an indication of Sir Dudley's generous nature, even after the Government purchased the building for far less than the sum Sir Dudley would have expected, he kept Arthur in post. As for Arthur, he said he felt his reward for such a principled stand was to walk past the building and see it still there and functioning.

Having had the matter brought to its attention in such an urgent manner, Government now had to act. The prospect of the Island's only theatre being lost to performance was considered by some as unacceptable. Not everyone was in agreement, but the work of Jack Nivison, Alf Devereaux, Katie Cowin, Geoff Crellin, Percy Radcliffe and Eddie Lowey in Government carried the vote. The significance of the theatre was brought home to some members when on a visit to Pitlochry, where a brand new one was being built. Surely, they thought, if the Highlands can manage it and see it as necessary, it must be possible on the Island. In 1971, Tynwald approved the purchase from The Palace and Derby Castle Company of The Gaiety Theatre for £41,000, and granted permission for a further £9,000 to be spent on essential repairs. Jack Nivison was instrumental in making this possible, and is one of the unsung heroes of The Gaiety's story. Eddie Lowey, who was still involved with the building thirty years later, placed such value on what was achieved with this action that he said he would like his political epitaph to read: 'He was associated with The Gaiety'. Outside Government itself, John Bethel became a significant figure in the rebirth of the building as a member of the Management Committee. Realising that they were in no position to run such a venture, they decided to lease the building to Ken Daly, who ran a company called Mannin Entertainments, responsible for several other venues around the Island. Among the conditions of the lease was a clause allowing Mannin Entertainments to free themselves from the contract every five years. This they did in 1976 when it became clear that the cost of maintenance would be astronomical and quite out of reach of the minor profits the theatre could generate, even with a successful summer season. Having bought the building in an act of tremendous foresight and community provision, the Government then had the unenviable task of running it, something they had clearly wanted to avoid by offering it as a lease. The Manager under Mannin Entertainments had been Bob Wilkinson, who had been involved with The Palace and Derby Castle Company for more than three decades, and it seemed obvious to let him carry on. With this development, the management structure of The Gaiety that still operates today was instigated. The theatre is the Government's responsibility in the body of the Department of Tourism and Leisure who pay for its upkeep, maintenance and staff, and for a Manager, whose job is the booking of acts and the provision of live theatre for the Isle of Man. Bob Wilkinson held the post until 1983, when he retired, and was replaced by Duggie Chapman, a man who used to present a summer season at The Gaiety. His tenure was brief, however, and in 1984 the post was taken by a man who had been working at the theatre in various capacities since 1970, Mervin Russell Stokes.

STOPPING THE ROT

Mervin Russell Stokes was born in 1950 in Peterborough. His story and that of The Gaiety are inextricably linked but, unlike Frank Matcham's development into a theatre architect, there is nothing in Mervin's earlier life to show a beneficent fate directing him towards his ultimate position. Indeed, a cursory glance at his youthful career suggests that he would end up doing practically anything *other* than run a theatre. With the exception of an early, abiding love and understanding of antiques (and the fact that his favourite toy was a Pollock's Theatre), there is little in his background to suggest he would become the man responsible for saving the most perfect example of Victorian theatre-going in the British Isles. He was educated at Westward House School, Peterborough; St Hughes' near Oxford; Bredon School near Tewkesbury and trained to become a teacher at St Paul's, Cheltenham. He confounded his parents' desires and hopes by training to become an undertaker, a move solely entered upon in a moment of pique to frustrate his father.

This brief career plan lasted only a matter of weeks, until he realised his father was probably right about what he should do for a living. Mervin joined the staff of Peterborough City Libraries, and then went on to Collett's in London. The Stokes family was well-known in their home town. The family business was established in 1782, and began as the surgeon-barbers and blood-letters to the Feoffes of Peterborough. Throughout their lives, Mr and Mrs Stokes worked at a startling array of occupations, including hairdressing (maintaining the surgeon-barber inheritance), dog-breeding, supplying angling provisions, promoting boxing matches (a more modern version of blood-letting), owning a tobacconist, toy shop and a sweet shop, and running a mail-order company. In 1969 Mr Stokes senior decided a holiday was due. This was principally for Mrs Stokes who was unwell and he insisted she and Mervin go immediately. He sent his wife and only son ahead to reconnoitre the Isle of Man, a place chosen at random because it was the only destination available at such short notice. Mervin has lived on the Island ever since.

After his arrival on the Island, Mr Stokes grew rather disenchanted with his son's being unemployed and insisted he find himself a job. There were no teaching posts available to a recent arrival (a work permit is still required for people coming to the Island), so Mervin took a job with hardware merchants Clough and Shepherd. This proved unsatisfactory so he moved to Gordon Marsden and Company Estate Agents in Athol Street. He had visited The Gaiety soon after arriving on the Island and his impression was that it was not long to remain. When he first saw it, his immediate thought was: "I wonder what idiot would take on the job of running this." Within six weeks, that idiot had been found, although he wouldn't take over the running of it for another fifteen years. One day, an actor appearing at The Gaiety but finding himself without digs called into Marsden's to see if somewhere cheap was available immediately. Mervin managed to find him a flat, and in gratitude the actor offered a pair of tickets to see the show. The tickets were declined, but Mervin was not completely fulfilled in his work and wondered if there might be a post available at the theatre itself. This was not a result of a philanthropic desire to restore the neglected building seen a few weeks before; he just wanted something else to do and to earn some more money. The actor, not wanting to disappoint, said there was a job as it happened, and he would ring back before 5.30. He did not. This might have deterred a lesser mortal, but Mervin has inherited a stubbornness and determination which, if better known, would make mules redundant in metaphor. So he went to the theatre and found the Manager, demanding the job he had been offered (by someone, it should be remembered, who had no right to offer it). The Manager, Bob Wilkinson, was surprised at being approached by a young estate agent demanding a non-existent job, but Mervin persisted. Mr Wilkinson persisted in his denial that such a post existed. However, since the theatre was still in the ownership of the Palace and Derby Castle Limited, it was allied to various other entertainment centres in town, and there was a vacancy at the Crescent Cinema. Quite what possessed Mr Wilkinson to suggest it - desperation seems the best bet - but he offered Mervin the job.

Mervin Russell Stokes.   Photo: Island Photographics

The Crescent Cinema, pictured in 1979.
Photo: Mervin Russell Stokes collection

This suited Mervin perfectly. He only needed to be at the cinema in the evenings, so the day job was unaffected. However, the cinema was a seasonal business, something that Mervin had not counted on when accepting the job. At the end of the summer season, Bob Wilkinson effectively said he was happy with Mervin's work and looked forward to re-engaging him next year. This wasn't at all what Mervin had in mind. He said he couldn't live on fresh air and promises (he forbore to mention his estate agent's wages) and reminded his employer that even if the cinema closed in the winter, there was still a theatre. Presumably not wanting a re-run of their earlier encounter, Bob Wilkinson took on Mervin Stokes at The Gaiety Theatre in the maintenance and general upkeep of the building.

Over the next eight years or so, he became increasingly involved with The Gaiety, from tearing tickets to taking on the role of unofficial House Manager whenever Bob Wilkinson was away. He kept his job at Marsden's for another two years, and worked at the Co-Operative Stores as Office Manager, a job he sincerely did not want. He only went to the interview because the dole office obliged him. Having been forced to go, he took pains to appear incompetent during the interview, but the panel saw through him immediately and hired him on the basis that he must be terribly clever to attempt such a deception, and therefore worth employing. He then had a managerial role within the Government's lottery, all the while continuing to run The Crescent Cinema in the summer, until his work at the theatre became completely full-time.

At The Crescent, he found himself working in what must have seemed like a parallel universe, one transported from the genteel world of Ealing comedies. For a start, there was a uniformed commissionaire at the door shouting "Seats at popular prices!" Then there were the couple of charming ladies running the box office, who would alternate between ornate politeness ("After you" "No, after you!" "No, I insist . . .") and quivering tearfulness at any suspected slight. And there was a projectionist who could occasionally fall foul of a bout of what might charitably be called drowsiness, and fall asleep on the projector. This caused film to churn remorselessly from the reel to the floor and gradually fill the room with snakes of whirling celluloid. He would also lean against the projector as he slept, which tilted the film off the screen and up against a side wall of the auditorium. The audience, rather than demanding their money back - or at the least for the film to be repositioned - simply shifted in their seats to watch it as it careered from screen to wall.

The house curtains seemed to be operated by an unseen hand (or a ghostly censor) and would descend, unbidden during the middle of a film. In cinemas built before the 1950s, there were footlights to throw coloured light onto the curtains in front of the screen for decorative effect. The ones in The Crescent had a startling design fault that meant that when the dimmer switch was engaged it would explode in flame, requiring the use of gauntlets to operate it. Meanwhile on the stage area, the roof above the proscenium had long since failed, which let in water and meant the Manager would regularly be obliged to lay towels on the stage floor during the performance in an attempt to stop the dripping preventing the audience's enjoyment. The audience's enjoyment was not always the result of the entertainment on offer. At a 'midnight matinee', the late-night showings of X-rated films shown during the Island's busiest period, one couple were taking full advantage of the darkened cinema and the nature of the film. Mervin, a young man and perhaps a little naive, seeing two pairs of legs lying on the floor between two rows of seats in an unpopulated part of the upper circle, was convinced they had fainted. He approached, all tender concern and with an extremely strong torch, to be greeted with a pair of naked buttocks and an angry "What's your game, mate?" The upper circle remained outside his regular rounds at midnight matinees thereafter.

The heating was no less idiosyncratic. On one occasion, when obliged to start up the boiler for the first time in years, Mervin could find only kipper-boxes to use as fuel. They worked perfectly well, but the main flue that ran up the back of the auditorium was cracked, and he effectively cured the audience - the crowd left the cinema reeking of smoked herring. When the building closed as a cinema, it was gutted and turned into an exhibition centre, comprising Louis Tussaud's Waxworks (he was a cousin of the famous Madame, apparently), the Manx Motor Museum, and the Gilbey Horse Carriages. Mervin worked there as Manager until 1980, when it became an amusement arcade, and he became House Manager of The Gaiety. He held that position until 1984, when he took over as General Manager.

Although the Government bought The Gaiety in 1971 for £41,000, with provision for a further £9,000 to cover legal fees and immediate decorations, and although the sums involved seem ludicrously small, Tynwald's decision was remarkable and should be recognised as such. At the time, theatres all over the United Kingdom were being pulled down or remade as bingo halls and a similar fate was feared for the Island's only remaining playhouse. Some would become multi-screen cinemas and a bored audience member might catch a glimpse of the original décor peeping out from behind a partition wall. The prospects for The Gaiety in 1971 were even less appealing. For The Palace and Derby Castle it had become a waste of valuable space, so they considered demolishing it and placing a development of offices, shops and flats in its place. This may have been something of a bluff, however valuable the space was for real estate. It is possible the company knew perfectly well such a scheme would be considered unacceptable and might lead to an offer of purchase. To remove the possibility of any delay, it might have been worth suggesting destruction to concentrate the political mind and lubricate the notoriously slow wheels of Government. Even if it were an empty threat, the options for Tynwald were limited if they wanted to keep a theatre. It could subsidise The Palace and Derby Castle Company with over £10,000 a year; it could buy the theatre and lease it to the company; or it could buy it and lease it to someone who had been working for The Palace and Derby Castle Company - and was now an established entrepreneur - Ken Daly.

The Manx Government was among the first local authorities to take on the freehold of such a building. The reason it was done was an act of extraordinary far-sightedness, and the product of the Island's separateness. It needed a theatre. This need was voiced powerfully by local amateur dramatic societies. These campaigned vigorously for the theatre's survival - or at least the survival of a theatre. A performance space was demanded by the public who had for over a century got used to one, and local societies couldn't just nip to the next county or merge with another group to keep themselves alive as drama or musical groups. They required a space to perform in and, for the Isle of Man as a whole, there was a need for National Theatre. This had nothing to do with the value of the existing one, which was in a desperate state and largely unappreciated. It was simply considered important the Island had a proper theatre. So while the drama societies lobbied for the retention of the theatre or the building of a new one, there was genuine political support for their claim. It is easy to see the attraction of knocking The Gaiety down, but the expense would have been even more demanding on the coffers of a Government by no means rolling in cash. So it was decided to keep it.

Anyone finding themselves examining The Gaiety as a prospective business would have been thoroughly depressed by the state of it. Only necessity or love could offer any argument for its retention, and even then with grave reservations and little hope. The Gaiety Theatre looked thoroughly ready for redevelopment and almost as

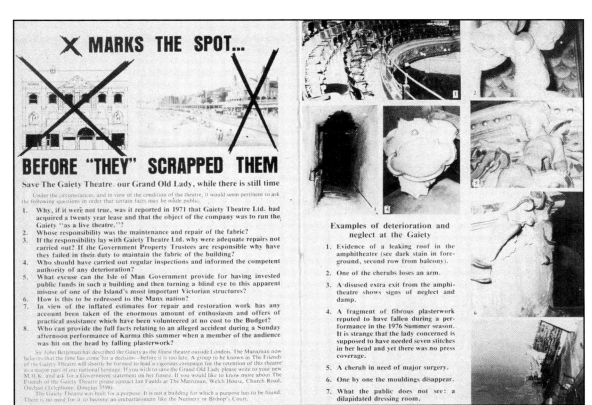

Public concern about the potential fate of The Gaiety Theatre in the late 1960s reaches crisis point as shown by this article in The Manxman .
Photo: 'The Manxman'

Above: Damage to the auditorium ceiling. Above right: the façade. Opposite left: heavily coroded canopy iron work. Opposite right: the rose window boarded up.

Photos: Mervin Russell Stokes collection / Island Photographics

if the demolition would be an act of mercy. The auditorium, once a warm blaze of vibrant colour and light, was so unkempt as to be almost seedy. There were no box curtains, which meant the Boxes looked cavernous and uninviting rather than lush and secluded. The proscenium valence was simply a flat piece of blue material, and the house curtains were torn and patched. The carpet between the seating and stalls and in the dress circle was worn through to the boards. The seating itself was worn and the velour shiny with wear. The foam padding of the seats had dried and shrunk like a sponge left in the sun, making it uncomfortable and ill-fitting on the seat arms. As for the purely aesthetic elements of the design, they were effectively non-existent. There was no wallpaper, only a brown emulsioned anaglypta on the walls. The interior of the boxes and the walls of the gallery slips were painted yellow but, as if that was insufficiently insulting to the original design, incorporated purple glitter. Above, the ceiling had holes in it, but was otherwise intact. It was, however, covered with a seventy years' worth of nicotine, dust and dirt, sucked up to the top by the sun-burner's action. This somewhat destroyed the delicacy of the ochre and *vieux rose* colour scheme. The whole auditorium looked heavy, dark and lumpen without the backlit stained glass of the rose window. The golds, reds, blues and greens of that magnificent centrepiece had been broken, and it was blocked in with plain green hardboard, without any illumination, since the remains of the sun-burner were covered with a 1930s celluloid luminaire. This amounted to a five-feet-wide upturned bell-jar, and was as elegant and suitable as it sounds. Elsewhere in the auditorium, the light fittings were still intact, although they had lost their frilly opaline shades. These had been replaced with heavy, celluloid shades that lacked the lightness and sparkle of the original. There was some good news in that the plasterwork was in fair condition. This is a relative matter of course; it was dirty, chipped and there were pieces missing from many of the cherubs, puttis and scrollwork. All the frescoes were obscured by the accumulated filth and two were overpainted. It was the architectural equivalent of the picture in Dorian Gray's attic.

Outside, the situation was no better. The wrought iron canopy was almost unrecognisable. Heavily corroded, all the fine detail had gone after years of repainting. The stained glass, incorporating the colours of the rose window, was

completely missing, as was the glass roof. This was boarded with light blue corrugated plastic sheeting. The ornamental ironwork on the canopy roof had disappeared as had any sign of the four, large lanterns. In place of the stained glass were boards which were covered in fluorescent advertising hoardings. The whole of the exterior was painted in a bluish grey, with architectural detail picked out in white. All of the doors, which were of mahogany, were painted in purple, white and green. The glass on the two sets of doors either side of the main entrance were used as advertising hoardings, as was the central area around the two front doors. Higher up on the façade, obscuring any architectural detail, was a red neon sign saying 'Gaiety'. Many of the original stained glass windows on the theatre's frontage had lost their glass, with the hole being filled by the domestic frosted variety. The statue of Progress, rather poignantly, had lost an arm, and the sign saying 'Gaiety Theatre and Opera House' in front of what had been the semi-circular vitrine was picked out in Day-Glo orange. Debased classical indeed.

Throughout the interior, the decoration was a combination of grotesques. The foyer was decorated in the same buff emulsioned anaglypta that graced the auditorium, but at least there was some wallpaper. It hardly provided a relief, though, since it was metallic silver with a large, turquoise flock pattern. The box offices had not escaped. The stained glass on both had been obscured by panels of 'Beauty-board', one of the most inapt titles imaginable for a material. It was a cheap print trying to look like wood, and when placed in a context where it was covering an uglier undercoat serves a valuable purpose. However, here it was routinely used to cover up more attractive surfaces, presumably for ease of decoration and low cost. The floor was left alone. The carpet that ran up the grand staircase had a swirly, blue marbled pattern. The grand staircase itself was spoiled because at the foot of each staircase was a large set of green baize doors. This attempt to keep the chill out seems rather pointless given the holes in the roof. The passages leading to the stalls and all the stone staircases, given such simple care in the original design, were painted in arctic blue-grey Portafleck which, when the weather warmed up and because

Woodwork being stripped of white gloss paint in the coffee promenade.
Photos: Mervin Russell Stokes collection / Island Photographics

they were painted in gloss, led to condensation.

The Grand Circle Promenade had a kiosk in one corner about the size of three phone boxes finished in Beauty-board, with a shiny, orange Formica counter, white gloss shelves stocked with sweets, and a tea-urn which sent condensation up to the ceiling leaving orange tannin stains. Whatever demon visited those who contrived these kiosks hardly bears imagining, but some vestige of its spirit can be found amongst the home improvement experts on television. The grand circle was also emulsioned in the omnipresent brownish yellow paint and paper and with the same carpet as the staircase. The stained glass in the doors was cracked, broken or missing and was replaced by the bathroom variety. All the woodwork was painted white gloss.

The corridors down the side of the auditorium had a similar colour scheme. The corridor at gallery slips level was some two feet deep in sawdust to soak up the water dripping from the roof. There were more substantial problems in the gallery and amphitheatre which was all one space. The rake had been altered in the 1930s and the area fitted with seats from different cinemas and theatres from around the Island, with different colours ranging from red to old gold. The changes in seating were because of the cinema audiences. At The Gaiety, the angle of throw from the projection box meant that the screen set on the stage had to be angled backwards. This meant that the stalls were hardly a comfortable place to watch films from because the angle took the film almost out of sight of those in the front. If Management were to make their money, they would need to put patrons in the upper areas of the house. So they decided to put tip-up seating in the amphitheatre and destroy the differentiation between it and the gallery. The new seats required more space and legroom, which in turn meant the rake, so carefully planned and executed by Matcham, had to change. This process was completed but with neither elegance nor great effect. The risers on the stairs between the seats were so irregular as to be a safety hazard and it became a part of a night out in Douglas to watch the usherettes tumble.

The upper part of the theatre had not been cleaned out for decades, and Dawn Daly, wife of Ken Daly who leased the theatre from the Government in the early 70s, well remembers the first major attempt to tidy it up. Sackloads of cigarette ends, discarded ice-cream cartons, sweet papers and much else besides were removed. At about the same time it was decided to try to wash the old box curtains that had been discovered. They were put into a washing machine, but had to be taken out with a ladle as they had disintegrated into a dirty, viridian sludge. The area now occupied by the dress circle bar was divided into four small rooms to house offices for Mannin Entertainments. The offices were for Ken Daly, John Marsland who was a partner in the business, Bob Wilkinson and the smallest accommodated the secretary, Iris Armison, and the ice-cream fridge. There was no alcohol in the theatre as the licence had expired and not been renewed for many years. The pit bar at the rear of the stalls area was still there with mahogany, marble and mirrored back but was shortly to be destroyed and replaced with a replica of the kiosks from upstairs. This particular decision was taken because it was cheaper to change them than install security shutters. The gallery and amphitheatre bar had been divided straight down the width of the room to provide a connecting corridor from the left and right of the auditorium, but the area behind the division was a dumping ground for old business records, costumes and broken furniture.

The toilets were largely unaltered structurally, but cosmetically they were butchered. Those below the foyer had been complete in their Victorian splendour, so naturally they were modernised and changed. Modern tiles were placed over the originals (presumably because it was impossible to remove them), partitions and sanitary ware were removed. To replace them, dividers in white Formica were installed, with orange doors, and the walls were tiled in brown.

The area around the stage itself was by no means free from this neglect. The orchestra rail had disappeared completely as had its original hangings, and it was in effect a low hardboard barrier between the orchestra pit and the stalls. On the stage itself, the floor was the original pitch pine boards but after so many years treading, in very poor condition and given to unexpected splintering. It was also hopelessly clogged with paint, which made any attempt at using, or just finding, the stage machinery impossible. Around the perimeters of the stage was a great deal of rubbish, including scenery and costumes. Above the stage, the flying system was the original. The ropes were an unusual combination of replacement and conservation. When they became old, rather

than be removed, the old rope was simply tied to the end of the new. This new rope would be fed through the pulleys to put it in place, but the old ropes would be left in untidy heaps on the floor of the flying gallery. Even without this hempen superabundance, the flying of scenery was a very untrustworthy affair. In a well-equipped theatre, the flying bars are plumb-straight rods with

strength enough to carry a weight with no distortion, held on secure and reliable lines running through a series of well-maintained pulleys to guide them. Those at The Gaiety in the 70s (and into the late 80s) were old lengths of timber nailed together, which defied anyone to hang a cloth on them correctly. They sagged in the middle, and waggled at the side as well.

The amphitheatre and gallery without the barrier, showing different types of cast-off seating taken from cinemas. It also shows the changes in the tiering, the 1930s decoration, the fibreboard ceiling and the raised safety rail. The central heating pipes are also evident. The lighting, hanging from the front of the gallery, obscures the architectural detail.

Photo: Island Photographics

Rubbish cleared from just one side of the stage in the early 1980s prior to restoration.

Photo: Mervin Russell Stokes collection

One Stage Manager in the late 70s, Tony McEvoy, used to defy all health and safety regulations by jumping from the fly gallery to the stage while hauling on a fly rope and acting as its counterweight. This was not at all out of keeping with his character. Tony McEvoy was a larger than life figure, who loved theatre and performed on occasion himself - his last performance was in 'Kiss Me Kate'. Before he died, he approached Mervin and said he was going to leave, but the timing would be up to Mervin. Mervin asked him what he meant. He explained he had cancer and was soon to die. It would be either in twelve months with treatment, or six without. He wanted to die in the theatre itself, if at all possible. Mervin said if that was his wish, they would do all they could to accommodate it. Tony thanked him, and said he would like to take the six-month option.

Tony McEvoy, a former Stage Manager of The Gaiety Theatre

Photo: Island Photographics

He came to the theatre every day. Mervin and the assistant Stage Manager used to carry him into the auditorium where he would supervise, extremely critically, their attempts to stage manage. As his illness progressed, it became impossible for him to fulfil his desire to die there, and he finally died in a nursing home. Mervin knew he was planning a special send-off, but he had no idea that Tony's forward planning was so comprehensive. The first hint that it might be came when the undertakers called to ask if they might have access to Tony's room. When they explained they had instructions from Tony himself, Mervin let them in, but they were under orders not to explain what they were there for. Clearly, Tony had decided he would not allow any individual to know of the plans he had made and, for all those concerned, his funeral would come together bit by bit. Mervin had received a note telling him that the cortege would pause outside the theatre on its way to the church, and it would be appreciated if the flags could be lowered as it did so. This was done and, after the cortege left, Mervin went on to the church where the organist had been instructed to play songs from the shows. After the service, the Manx Youth Band was discovered on the path between the church and the hearse, which by now had been decorated with flowers and photographs of the many stars he admired - this had been the haul the undertakers had removed from his office. As the hearse set off, the Band struck up a selection of jazz favourites all the way to the crematorium, a full New Orleans send off. At the crematorium, Clinton Ford, a well-known singer who lived on the Island, sang 'The Sunshine of Your Smile'. After the coffin had passed through the curtains, the priest opened his instructions - which were to invite everyone back to the Sefton Hotel for a wake. As a fitting finale, the whole thing was reported in *The Stage*.

The pulleys above the grid were the original wooden blocks containing cast iron pulley wheels, but these had worn so much that the pulleys were prone to sticking and jamming without notice. The collected detritus of seven decades was everywhere - on either side of the fly gallery, the paint floor, and the area behind the paint floor where scenery used to be stored, known as the scene dock.

These Boffin-like piles of rubbish were continued to Augean proportions below the stage. It was simply packed with old props, bits of scenery, general waste, building materials, papers and all manner of other material, stacked to a height of a good four feet. Any orchestra playing for a show had to find its way through a tunnel of rubbish to the door under the stage which led into the orchestra pit, and even that needed a line of white paint to make it visible. There was little evidence of the understage machinery, only the remains of the grave trap and parts of the demon trap could be seen. For anyone performing there was no luxurious accommodation. The dressing rooms were in an appalling state. On the first floor some parts of the ceiling had fallen in exposing lath and green mould. Putting make-up on would have been a matter of approximation only since the lighting was totally inadequate; removing it even less appealing as there were no shower facilities at all. The rooms were decorated in peeling, sombre shades, and the furnishings consisted of dirty, second-hand carpets and old sofas. The roof at the rear of the building leaked badly and was one of the first repairs carried out by the Government once it took on the ownership of the site. Safety, such a popular feature when The Gaiety was built, had not been totally ignored. On either side of the Proscenium, there were still the original iron pass doors, which were replaced with less conductive materials on the advice of the Fire Services once the Government took over. The hand-operated safety curtain was plain white, a mild steel frame covered on both sides with asbestos and stuffed with rock wool. It may have had advertisements on it earlier, but had been painted plain white to act as a screen for films during T.T. week. The whole thing was fairly swiftly removed and replaced with the modern, motorised, steel curtain that is still in use. A selection of tatty drapes made up the stage curtains.

The originally gorgeous and luscious act drop was in a state of disrepair amounting to decrepitude. It was absolutely filthy with stains running its entire length and discoloured all over. There was a tear at the centre from its collision with a protuberance somewhere in the grid (possibly Tony McEvoy, or one of the least rigid fly bars) and various other holes that were sewn together with twine. The tacks that held it to its frame had rusted in the damp, and caused the canvas near their heads to rot, so it clung to the frame only by the most fragile tenacity. The winding gear for the act drop, though still operational, was reaching the end of its life. Its condition was hardly helped on the night Mervin wound the mechanism the wrong way, hauling the counterweights up instead of the act drop. The burden became too much, and he let the handle slip, sending the weights crashing down to the floor knocking them out of their guides. As a result, the drop, deprived of some of its weights, sank slowly to the floor while Mervin repeatedly tried and failed to lift it out of sight. For a while, it looked as though the evening would be spent with the drop rising and falling gently into and out of the action like a swooning maiden aunt being briefly revived with *sal volatile*. Eventually, another member of the stage staff realised what was wrong and came round to correct it, holding the handle in place throughout the show. Meanwhile, a terrified Mervin had disappeared to perform some other function such as tearing tickets or counting ice-creams. The system was repaired the next day by which time Mervin had confessed his fault to Bob Wilkinson who was extremely understanding and said: "Oh well, never mind. Accidents happen in the best of families".

The details were no less depressing than the generalities. The signage was the sort used on building sites to indicate a 'Hard Hat Area', which was perhaps apt - a slab of plaster fell from the roof in the early 70s. There was no attention given to architectural detail. Windows were replaced with bathroom glass and handles were found in a standard hardware store. The lighting board, where the technician watches the show and changes the lighting, was in the stage left box. There were large speakers at the side of the proscenium beside

the statues. The stage lighting consisted of four batons - ordinary bulbs rather than ones that can be focussed - hanging above the stage, and a set of footlights. Projecting from the front of the dress circle was a wide shelf, held up by iron straps, on which were three lanterns. These could be coloured by placing gels in front of the light, but as they got hot they would create a heat haze which made the performance for those sitting in the centre block of the dress circle seem as if perpetually in a dream sequence.

A dressing room before restoration.

Photo: Island Photographics

The whole building smelled like a church crypt - a damp, unholy church crypt. The heating system, when turned on at the beginning of summer (essentially to air it) and occasionally in the winter, would cause the seats to steam. It seemed to be, and probably was, falling apart. People would watch shows wrapped in coats or blankets and carrying hot water bottles. Another first can be claimed in that The Gaiety was probably the only theatre that would heat the tea urns before the performance in order to fill patrons' hot-water bottles. Up in the gallery and amphitheatre, raincoats were a sensible clothing option and there are those who claim umbrellas were a handy accessory for some. This is not authorial invention, although there is some doubt whether umbrellas were ever unfurled. It is a testament to the good fortune that prevented the theatre collapsing and the determination of audiences to keep it viable. As a place of entertainment, it had all the inconvenience and discomfort of an outdoor theatre without the concomitant sense of properly taking Nature on and beating her. It is a proud achievement of the British to believe that sitting in the damp, getting cold and being unable to see or hear the performance properly is the optimal method to enjoy high art. No wonder they conquered the world. Any nation that willingly sits outside for four hours to watch Shakespeare in the northern latitudes has a constitution more than able to take on the indigenous peoples of the veldt and plain.

There is something to be grateful for in this level of decay and neglect. Had the theatre been a continual success, making money and being regarded as a valued asset throughout its life, there can be little question it would have been

The boxes at stage left in the mid-seventies. The curtained-off area hides the lighting board and technician. The speaker system is all-too-visible. The No Smoking sign is out of keeping and the boxes have had all of their drapes removed.

Photo: Mervin Russell Stokes collection

fundamentally altered. Whole sections would have been removed and redesigned, new seats, perhaps even new functions given to areas within the building. Under only slightly different circumstances, it could easily have become a two-screen cinema or a bingo hall. Even if its principal function had remained the same, there would have been substantial building work undertaken to modernise it, and it would then have been lost almost certainly. What decoration was done to The Gaiety was superficial rather than wholesale. The box offices were retained rather than removed and replaced with tinted Perspex ones. The lights were largely untouched, not substituted. The decoration, where it was touched at all, was only painted over, and the plasterwork, including its gold leaf and paintwork, left entirely alone.

The kind of damage that can be done by the more drastic sort of shortsighted intervention is evident in most towns and cities, but there is a striking example of it immediately next to The Gaiety itself. The Villa Marina Arcade was completed in 1931, and was a magnificent example of Art Deco work. It had sharp, angular lines, but softened by slight changes in the tone of the decoration, which was pale with a jet-like black surround, and beautifully symmetrical. It was filled with precise detail, such as the decoration on the lights matching the ventilation grilles and the iron door surrounds. It used the latest in contemporary materials for a glossy finish, and even the toilets were exceptional. The design was sparse but not unforgiving, clean without being antiseptic. Everything chimed with everything else, and combined to create an airy, elegant space. Time and lack of care had their effect, of course, and gradually it fell into the kind of quiet decay which overtook The Gaiety. But the Arcade suffered at the hands of those who felt they had to try and add to it, with the result it now has light-fittings of smoked-glass bowls installed along its length; benches; large, round, blue flower-tubs; hanging baskets, and handrails painted red to protect from rust in the middle of the staircases. It has lost all the style, cohesion and clarity that marked it in the first place. Now that the Manx Government has taken over the ownership of The Villa Marina, a proper restoration of the Arcade may be considered, but a lot of rebuilding will be required. Thankfully, that was not the case with the theatre. Stripping back layers of ugly additions and gradually restoring the original is not necessarily easier or cheaper than a complete rebuild - and it is unquestionably slower - but there remains a far truer indication underneath of what the original was really like. Beauty-board may not be pretty, but

at least it doesn't completely destroy what it covers.

It would be nice to report that once Mervin started working and getting to know the theatre, he saw it for what it was and, in an architectural epiphany decided it needed to be brought back to a stuccoed life from its Anaglypta tomb. It would be nice, but it would also be completely inaccurate. He had no idea of its value for years and nor did anyone else. No-one seemed to know it was a Matcham and no-one would have cared had they known - he simply was not a significant figure to anyone but the most specialised groups at the time. It took Mervin some fifteen years working there before he recognised its value as a building and worth to the Island. Although the prospect of a restoration *per se* was fairly appealing, it had little to do with anything other than a natural discomfort of being in so run down a building and a desire to see it in a better state. As for the notion of a fully researched academic restoration, it was simply never considered. At least, it was not considered until Mervin became the General Manager and happened across Dr. David Wilmore.

Nevertheless, the smallest germ of an idea, or perhaps his natural affection for Victoriana, must have been at work in the back of his mind before then. In the early eighties there had been a plan to remove the box offices and replace them with more spacious, efficient, modern ones. Mervin argued successfully against this. However, there was a determination from the management to improve the foyer nonetheless and it was decided some carpeting would be a useful addition. This was probably true, but would require masonry nails to be hammered into the tiles. Mervin adopted a tactic he has employed since with great success, which is to get a problem solved to his satisfaction without telling his employer until it has been done. On this occasion, he persuaded the carpet-fitters to use strong, double-sided tape rather than the nails. To go to this effort for the foyer floor is evidence of some concern about the fabric of the building and its worth, especially as Mervin was at that time in no position to move forward the idea of preserving it. His saving of the act drop is easier to understand. It came about because the safety curtain was to be replaced, but the way the various bars were hanging meant the drop was in the way. So it was suggested it be broken up and removed. This was not unreasonable given the state of the drop and the importance of a safety curtain, although it might have been argued that a theatre as damp as The Gaiety was unlikely to burn at anything higher than a weak smoulder. However, Tony McEvoy and Mervin decided it was not right to remove the drop altogether, but had to get it out of the way so the safety curtain (or 'iron', as it known) could be hung correctly. They persuaded those from the suppliers of the new safety curtain, Telestage of Bury St. Edmunds, that they all looked very hungry, and could find an excellent meal at good value at The Sefton Hotel next door. Telestage thought this a thoroughly acceptable idea and went for their dinner. With them out of the way, Tony and Mervin managed to move the drop far enough back on the grid to leave space for the iron. The drop was saved. The value of its saving was demonstrated many months later. An entirely fallacious rumour was spread by the Management Committee's Dr John Bethel who, with tongue firmly in cheek, suggested the drop had been sold to the United States. At the conclusion of a performance where there was a full house, as the audience was rising to leave, the drop was slowly flown in. The result was electric. After a moment's silence, the audience erupted with cheers and applause.

By the late 70s more influential people than Mervin were taking some notice of the decaying nature of The Gaiety. The Manx Government had recognised further and more substantial work would be needed to keep the building operating. They had carried out some essential repairs, re-roofing the building and effectively making it safe, but there had been no attempt at restoring any of the architectural detail that made the theatre such a pleasure to visit.

With the millennium of the Manx Parliament approaching (in 1979), Victor Glasstone was appointed to produce a report on the value of a restoration. Mannin Entertainments had ended their lease of the building, partly because if they had continued it, it would have forced them to accept a crippling obligation to maintain it. It would have been completely beyond them to effect the repairs that were required, so The Gaiety became the responsibility of the Department of Tourism (known as the Tourist Board at the time). They carried out purely superficial maintenance at first, but it was soon clear that much more work was needed and they called in the advice of an expert.

Victor Glasstone was the man they chose, and with good reason. He was an architect, theatre consultant and historian who had been concerned exclusively with theatre for nearly thirty years. He had written extensively on theatre architecture for both specialist and national publications and contributed to the theatrical encyclopaedias *The Oxford Companion to the Theatre* and the *Encyclopaedia Dello Spettacolo*, and also to *Frank Matcham: Theatre Architect*. His books include *Victorian and Edwardian Theatres*, and *The London Coliseum*. He was a committee member for the Society for Theatre Research, the Theatres Advisory Council and the Housing the Arts committee of the Arts Council of Great Britain. His credentials could hardly be bettered.

Victor Glasstone's report was presented in April 1978. In many ways it was a brave attempt at something largely untried, but he was constrained by a tight budget and by what had already been done. He started with a bold assertion: 'My very strong recommendation is that everything should be done to put The Gaiety back, as closely as is possible, to its original scheme of decoration. Fortunately, this should not be difficult, or too exorbitantly expensive.' This was an extraordinary, almost visionary, statement to have made, and may have rather disappointed those locals who were hoping for a brand new, radically designed playhouse. His instincts and knowledge recognised just how unique The Gaiety's survival was and he saw the value of keeping it. He was aware of the value of the act drop, and saw the large speakers beside the stage as ugly impositions. He recognised that the existing light-fittings in the bars and promenades were, by and large, unacceptable, calling the chandeliers 'modernistic horrors'. But then he suggested painting the exits lime green and placing an off-gold, vinyl, flock wall paper on most of the walls. 'Chocolate pattern on pale mushroom ground' is how he describes it, and he continues: 'Stunningly hideous and vulgar, but just right . . .'. He recommended painting the wall below the dado at dress circle level green. He suggested the hotch-potch of seats was perfectly adequate. Yet he referred to an article about the opening night, and even included it in his report, that indicated what the décor was like. He had started by saying everything should be done to preserve it as closely as possible to what it was, and then recommended that it be painted and decorated like a contemporary restaurant. He believed the 1930s chandelier in the foyer was perfectly in keeping with the building as a whole, despite being unhappy with the shades on those in the auditorium.

Other aspects of Glasstone's report seem surprising today in view of his determination to restore it to original condition. One was the suggestion that a wall should be built at the place where the gallery and amphitheatre join. He felt the area should be put to some other use, although he had no suggestions as to what, possibly a cinema or a rehearsal room. He rightly pointed out it was never used and at that period never likely to be, but it seems strange now for a man with historical accuracy in mind to suggest erecting a partition

The auditorium corridor showing 1970s contract carpet, plain, Anaglypta walls and modernised doors.

Photo: Mervin Russell Stokes collection

wall clad in an acoustically absorbent material. Second, there was no mention made of the stage itself, its flying equipment or the backstage area. Third, and even more startling, is the fact that he simply never mentioned the understage machinery, the stained glass or the sun-burner. These crucial elements to the building's function and decoration appear to have been completely overlooked. It was not until Dr David Wilmore became part of the restoration team under Mervin that the whole area of the understage was revealed.

Whether these oversights were through lack of time, desire to keep the cost down or omitted from the final report because of some instruction in his brief is unknown. However it seems likely he was told to consider the building solely from the audience's point of view, and had to spend money where it would produce the maximum effect. After all, people were having to watch plays wrapped in warm clothing and with waterproofs in case of a shower. It is easy now to be surprised that a man of Glasstone's qualifications did not refer to these aspects of the building, given the position they hold in its history, but ideas and tastes about restoration were deficient in the 70s. It should be remembered, too, that theatre restoration was at the time a very new business, and Tynwald's decision to preserve and maintain the theatre was a rare act in itself. To then call in someone of Glasstone's position with a view to having it restored amounts almost to heroism. Glasstone deserves his place in the story of The Gaiety, because he established the possibility of a full restoration, and started the process that others were later to follow. On some points he was a model of dogmatic determination that Mervin would follow with rigour. About the boxes, for example, he was explicit and correct. The curtains must be replaced exactly as they were (he underlines the word 'exactly'), and without any kind of fitted pelmet: 'This has spoiled many a recent restoration.' But he was also pragmatic and did not suggest, for example, that the lighting board be removed from its place in one of the boxes. Instead he suggested there should be a better curtain to cover it up more effectively. Equally, he seems to have had no objection to a neon sign being placed on the front of the theatre; his only concern was that it should be moved down a few feet.

The report was accepted, and much of what he put forward was implemented in phases as money became available, while general repair and cleaning work was undertaken as well. The plan to build a wall across the Gallery area was discarded, possibly because of the cost. The painting of the exits lime green was never carried out, probably because it was considered of no great importance what colour they were painted. The exit corridors, which Glasstone said needed to be brightened up, were covered in Portafleck, a substance that is about as romantic as it sounds, which is a thick paint that develops globules of a different colour to become textured and multicoloured when dry. It is extremely clever and very useful, but hardly in keeping. On the ceilings in the emergency corridors at the front of house was artex, another thick and almost immovable substance that caused great problems when the full restoration began. The mahogany doors had their garish paint stripped and the plasterwork on the ceiling was cleaned. That is not to say it was properly cleansed and restored. It was sponged down, and would need substantially more work later. The wallpaper that Glasstone had recommended was hung, which although not correct was an improvement, and made the auditorium less like a vast hangar with ornamental plasterwork. New carpets were laid and the boxes had curtains and valences returned. Around the corridors at dress circle level, the Anaglypta was repainted in an uninspired brown, and a similar scheme was adopted in the coffee bar. A new carpet was laid on the grand staircase, in the corridors and the coffee bar. Unfortunately it was in a standard design of patterned red, which was not an entirely happy marriage of colour. With Mannin Entertainments gone, the four offices in the dress circle bar area were removed and the room returned to roughly its original proportions and purpose. A long bar was installed, and the same red carpet laid on the floor, with pink moiré vinyl paper on the walls.

All this was disappointing in view of the report's initial statement of intent. However, while the final result differed painfully from the original design, there was no question of the Government's commitment to saving the building, and Victor Glasstone would have been the first to admit that there was a long way to go to a complete restoration. But The Gaiety was usable, relatively comfortable and clean. It also had the endorsement of a recognised and respected expert in his field as evidence of the Government's good intentions. Yet, this investment in the building could have been disastrous. Having spent that time and money on making it a workable theatre, the Government could have decided enough was more than enough and left it at that. The idea that this might be only the beginning of the reclamation of The Gaiety was never considered by anyone on the Island - except by Mervin, whose dogged enthusiasm and curiosity was leading him to the Manx Museum with a few queries about who designed the theatre. Once the name Matcham was rooted from the Museum files, he began to realise the potential significance of The Gaiety. He researched the life and work of the man, discovered what the theatre had originally looked like and found scraps of information to piece together a complete picture of the building and its history together in his head. Over a number of years he became, almost imperceptibly, the authority on The Gaiety. And somewhere in the back of his mind the notion of a more complete restoration began very quietly to take shape. It would have to remain quiet for a while.

Mervin had been chastened by an experience of restoration some years before. When more than forty pantechnicons of rubbish were being removed from the understage area, he had noticed there were some paintings in rather nice frames being thrown away. He asked the then Manager if he could have them. The pictures were taken from the lorry, and he took them home. Once there, he began to restore the dozen pictures, just in case there was a Rembrandt hiding beneath the grime. In that respect he was disappointed, but there were pictures of genuine quality in all the frames, all of them filthy and all in need of considerable work. So he set about restoring them in his spare time. This was not an altogether altruistic action, since there was a chance of resale value or recompense for the work he was doing. However, he had been the one to save them from ending up in a landfill site and so felt a certain proprietorial right to them. Once all twelve were thoroughly presentable, he offered them to Government in the hope that they would hang in the theatre, as they were all of the Island and of the correct period. It was perhaps naive to expect a generous cheque and hearty thanks for managing to bring old and neglected beauty back to life, but even someone experienced in such matters would have been surprised at less than £10 per picture. The argument from the Government was that the pictures were Government property and he should not be charging for them at all. The fact that the Government were going to throw them away without a second glance and he had rescued them was irrelevant, as was the fact he had restored them, which in itself was work worth far more than they were offering. £100 was all that was forthcoming. Even the request for his expenses was refused. Government got their pictures, but it is unclear where they are hanging now. With this experience behind him, it would have been reckless to ask for the funding of a complete restoration of the building, or to start it on his own, just after the expense of the work already done. So he adopted a much more delicate approach.

Once he became General Manager, he started on the long and frequently lonely campaign to tell the Island all about its theatre. He took a slide show to Women's Institutes and Rotary Clubs. He started to use the space in the local papers and a regular slot on the local radio to promote the building as well as shows. He started offering tours around the building. He made himself the face and voice of The Gaiety, contacting other Matcham theatres to compare notes, discovering more and more about the architect and his creations and finding inspiration and comfort from those who had attempted restorations already. This was not just to reassure himself about the importance of the building. It was also to gain an understanding that with sufficient background work in place, launching a campaign to completely restore The Gaiety would be far easier. He would need public assistance, but not in terms of tax. The Gaiety was in the hands of Government already, but there are problems associated with public money. First, obtaining it is no easy matter, because everyone has a good cause and there are innumerable calls upon it from all sections of society. Second, in the case of The Gaiety, it would mean Government control that would entail a fair amount of delay while each suggestion was considered by the appropriate committees. Mervin realised there were some things the Department of Tourism was responsible for and would continue to pay for. He also knew there were things the Department might, quite reasonably, be less inclined to pay for, and which he could more easily achieve without having to go cap in hand to them.

This meant there were two avenues to pursue: the private sector for commercial sponsorship, and the public themselves. The public's involvement was not just in the hope of raising funds but also for a more nebulous support. Mervin believed that The Gaiety was not just a place for plays, but a national treasure of genuine significance. Just as much as historical monuments, it deserved more attention and respect from the Island's people. His belief had been to some extent given a boost by Sir John Betjeman, the Poet Laureate, who had described the theatre as the finest outside London. This insight was respected, and a great boon to those who were to work so hard to keep The Gaiety alive, but was not in itself sufficient to guarantee a restoration. The performers and audience had accepted it and made clear their desire to keep it, but had no notion of its importance in terms of theatre archaeology, quite apart from its inherent but hidden beauty. Mervin set about telling everyone all about it. With their understanding and approval, any plans put forward to the Department

Sir Laurence and Lady New with, standing behind left to right: Mervin Stokes; Harry Galbraith; Michael Wood ADC; Jack Cretney, then president of the Douglas Choral Union; Jillie Wood.
Photo: Sir Laurence New collection

Dr David Wilmore.   Photo: Mervin Russell Stokes collection

could be bulwarked with the knowledge there was a significant number of the populace who liked the idea. Moreover, any restoration would be the result of the public's direct involvement, rather than their being simply onlookers or tax-payers.

Anyone who has ever thrown a penny in a collecting-tin for the restoration at The Gaiety has made a personal contribution to the work carried out there, a fact which has made the whole project a matter of considerable pride on the Island. It has also been the cause of considerable irritation to those who did not much like the way Mervin operated, or who felt the work was not worth the effort.

Even for someone as enthusiastic and resilient as Mervin, however, the job of remaking a Government-owned theatre as it was built, with suitable modernisation to keep it functioning as the Island's only playhouse, was draining and demanding. It should be remembered that, to begin with at least, he was working full-time as the General Manager, responsible for every aspect of running the theatre. This ranged from counting the ice-cream money to negotiating contracts with touring companies; or from advertising forthcoming attractions to being present at the show to greet the audience. This was sometimes a rather baffling experience. There was one evening when a man asked if he could have a reduced price for his ticket, claiming it was a legitimate request because he had a wooden leg. He explained that since his whole body could not be present at the show, he should not have to pay full price. Very well, said Mervin, I will happily give you a reduced-price ticket. He got up, measured the man's full height, then measured his leg and one or two other dimensions, and then stepped back into the box office. After a few seconds furious calculating, he said the missing part of the leg equated to twelve per cent of his bodyweight, and the ticket would be reduced by that amount. The man agreed, and Mervin accepted the money. As he turned to go, he was stopped by Mervin saying: "Hold on sir; the usherettes will help you into the auditorium." The man was nonplussed. "No, thank you, I can walk on my own." "Ah, sir, you don't understand. Your leg has not paid the admission price, and I must therefore ask you to leave it with me in the box office to be collected after the performance." The man was not much amused by this, and complained vociferously of his treatment before storming from the theatre. The money was placed in the Guide Dogs for the Blind collection box.

Mervin was doing the work of a General Manager, a House Manager, a Marketing Manager, box office staff member, salesman, and more

besides, while at the same time promoting the value and significance of the building as a kind of sideline. He was also dealing with the bureaucratic obligations of any other civil servant. As the General Manager, he was also answerable to Government, who not only owned the building but also subsidised it. This meant he had to ensure the returns were sufficient and the audience numbers high enough to justify their continuing to do so. Given all this, if he was going to achieve what became his life's work, he would need some help.

He found two of his greatest allies in Dr David Wilmore and Sir Laurence New. Sir Laurence was appointed Lieutenant Governor shortly after Mervin became General Manager and he and his wife, Lady New, were avid theatre-goers. Indeed, Sir Laurence had first performed on The Gaiety stage as an Island schoolboy some forty years earlier. They struck up a close friendship, and on more than a few occasions could all three be found knee-deep in rubbish examining a new find under the stage or above the grid. Sir Laurence was Patron of the Friends of the Gaiety - later to become President - and provided moral support and advice, as well as being influential in an organisation that was vital for The Gaiety's continued survival, providing staff free of charge, and later substantial fund-raising for the restoration. David Wilmore became effectively Mervin's right-hand man in the theory and practice of rebuilding the theatre.

David Wilmore was born in 1957 in Lancashire. He studied Geology at the University of Newcastle-upon-Tyne, which proved useful only when digging through the accumulated layers of rubbish beneath The Gaiety's stage. He completed a Post Graduate Certificate of Education in Drama at Newcastle, largely in an attempt to stay on another year so as to be near his future wife, Catherine. While studying, he performed in Gilbert and Sullivan and became President of a society that had found itself without a theatre. This potential disaster led to a meeting that would have profound implications for the rest of his professional life. In his attempts to find a venue to perform, he went to The Tyne Theatre and asked if he could hire it for a week. He could, but it would cost £500 (In the Isle of Man in 2000, twenty-eight years later, it costs £625 for amateurs to hire The Gaiety for the same period). Although the price may have been a little steep for a University operatic society, it was the best bet, and it led to his meeting Jack Dixon, the Chairman of The Tyne Theatre and Opera Company, and it got David into the theatre. Once inside, he was shown the derelict machinery under the stage and effectively fell in love with Victorian stage workings and the theatres that housed them. Despite being involved with his PGCE, he started researching the traps, sloats, bridges and cuts, and came to the conclusion that teaching was not for him. While trying to decide what was his ideal career, he was offered a job on an oil-rig; but before he took up the post, he received a call from Jack Dixon. David's interest in the understage machinery had been evident, as such infatuations inevitably are. Jack Dixon wondered if he would care to spend his summer holidays supervising the installation of the refurbished and new machinery. What was to have been a summer job lasted three years and led to a shift in his academic direction and the carving out of an entire career. He spent three years at The Tyne Theatre, and decided to study for a Ph.D. at Hull University, there being no Drama Department at Newcastle. As a result, he has a Doctorate in Victorian Theatre Technology and is probably the only person with such a qualification. This exclusivity can be admirable in the workplace, but in the mid-80s there were few posts advertised requiring his particular skills and so he created a company to perform musicals with students and local performers. Looking to produce something creative and new, he approached Alan Hull of local folk/rock band Lindisfarne to write a musical based on their work for performance in March 1986. However, on Christmas Day 1985 the stage and the whole area surrounding it - fly gallery, understage and backstage - of the Tyne Theatre was completely razed by fire. All the work installing the new machinery, all the years of effort, were burned to the ground. Only the safety curtain saved the auditorium.

This crushing event could have done more than just dampen the spirits of anyone else, it could have been a cause for legitimate despair. Not for David; indeed it indirectly led to his current career. Perhaps he simply wasn't going to let circumstances deprive him of his work. Perhaps the effort of restoring the machinery in the first place seemed like ideal practice for this disaster. In short, he set about restoring the whole thing for the second time. In less than a year, The Tyne Theatre was brought back to life, and it would have been a sub-editor of rare strength who avoided mentioning Phoenixes and flames when reporting on the extraordinary speed with which it was recreated. The theatre was reopened in November 1986. It was at this point David set up his own company, Theatresearch, and started work as a freelance Theatre Consultant, presumably on the basis that the reason more vacancies weren't advertised for the role was because theatres didn't recognise it was needed. It was not long before it became clear how

many did need him. His first commission was for The Playhouse Theatre at Charing Cross in London. From there, he went on to become Stage Director of the Tyne Theatre Repertory Company, and when that was wound up he moved on to work for the Gateshead Garden Festival for a year until 1990. He and Catherine married, and he moved on to become Technical Director of Harrogate International Centre. His work as a consultant on theatre restoration includes: Her Majesty's Theatre in London where he was the machinery consultant for Phantom of the Opera; The Royal Hall, Harrogate; The Everyman Theatre in Cheltenham (originally The New Theatre and Opera House); and the Newcastle Theatre Royal. He has advised on aspects of Victorian theatre for film-makers including Ken Russell and Mike Leigh, who used his expertise in the Oscar-winning 'Topsy-Turvy' about the relationship between Gilbert and Sullivan.

He is a National Lottery assessor for the Arts Council of Great Britain, but sadly, this does not mean he has been able to bring in thousands of pounds of British Government money to help with The Gaiety. The Island's status as an internally self-governing Crown Dependency means it is not entitled to any. This creates a slightly bizarre arrangement with regard to lottery tickets on the Isle of Man. There used to be a Manx lottery, but once the glittering prizes of the United Kingdom's one became apparent, more and more money was sent to friends and relatives across - a colloquial for 'in Britain' for the Manx - and it was discontinued. This had a serious and none too pleasant effect on local charities who were deprived of much-needed income because they had no access to the funds the British lottery generated. So a complex legal agreement was drawn up allowing the United Kingdom's tickets to be sold on the Isle of Man with a percentage of the takings going to the Manx Government which then distributes the funds as it sees fit through a special committee. The amount the Manx Government gets from the deal is significantly less than the amount that goes to the U.K. Treasury, but none of the Island's concerns are able to apply for any funding from anyone but their own Government. The projected return is expected to bring in much the same as was raised when the Manx version was at its height, but the amount to be given to good causes is not absolutely guaranteed.

One of the more unusual commissions David has had - and one thankfully undertaken with plenty of assistance - was to dismantle Dunfermline Opera House brick by brick for relocation in Sarasota, Florida, an act sufficiently bizarre to

The lowest of the low: The Gaiety Theatre in the mid 1960s with the iron canopy clad in hideous square-cut boards helping the theatre to resemble the seediest of seaside venues.

Photo: Mervin Russell Stokes collection

suggest that all urban myths have at least an element of truth in them. He is currently working on the latest edition of *Curtains!!!*, a gazetteer of historic theatres in the British Isles. He is the editor of a biographical study of Frank Matcham, the biographer of Edwin Sachs and has written a book on nineteenth-century British theatrical patents.

The friendship and professional partnership with David Wilmore was pivotal in The Gaiety's restoration. It was also the first happy accident in Mervin's life that could be said to point his way towards the realisation of that idea. David met Mervin by falling through a stage in Newcastle. He damaged his back and was laid up for some time. By nature a restless and ever-active man, this was tantamount to a variation on the Chinese water torture. He had known of The Gaiety's understage machinery, and even seen a photo of what was visible, taken by a friend. His wife-to-be thought some kind of restorative therapy would help and suggested that he pay a visit to the Island's theatre. He went to stay with a friend, Coll MacHarrie who, as it turned out, knew Mervin. It was perhaps inevitable that, with any connections at all to the Island, David should meet Mervin. Fate, if you like; Island life if you don't. Coll suggested Mervin showed David around. As soon as he saw the theatre, David was impressed. Far more importantly, however, each recognised in the other a shared belief not just in the possibility, but the necessity, of complete and detailed reinstatement of the theatre's original features.

It is uncomfortable to dramatise such moments, and they only have their future resonance in hindsight, but this meeting was absolutely crucial to the restoration. The connection with the Island and the accident in Newcastle led to a friendship and professional understanding that would allow Mervin to crystallise his fragmented ideas about bringing The Gaiety back to life. With David's support, he had the academic, theoretical and practical backing of the best qualified and most practised person in the country to help him advance the job. For David, it was a chance to work on the best theatre of its kind in the country with someone not just sympathetic but brimful of enthusiasm with detailed knowledge of and insight into the fabric of the building. They began working to make it possible. This required planning and considerable patience. The Island still needed to be made more aware that there was something worth saving, and most importantly, the Government had to be kept informed of developments, and had to approve of them. A slow accumulation of evidence, professionally compiled, was presented to Government as layers of history were uncovered. From the outset, it was to be a slow, careful and accurate restoration, while having to keep constantly in mind the need for the theatre to remain fully functioning and up-to-date as well. There was one immediate hook on which to hang the whole process - the 90th birthday of the theatre itself. That would do to start with, and would prove an invaluable means of initially galvanising public support for the fund-raising activities that were to come. It also clearly indicated the closing date for the work - the centenary, on 16 July, 2000.

RESTORATION

Much as it had been between 1900 and 1970, The Gaiety was left largely to its own devices between 1978 and 1990. There had been no significant work undertaken. Mervin took the idea of the restoration to Laurence New, officially in his capacity as Patron of the Friends of The Gaiety. Unofficially, Mervin needed the approval of a man he trusted and who could be relied upon to offer impartial and knowledgeable advice. He approved. The next step was to put it to the Friends.

The Friends of The Gaiety were established in 1978 with the basic intention, as one founder member had it, of putting bums on seats. They believed in the value of live theatre and recognised some encouragement would be needed to fill a building that was falling apart in front of their very eyes. By the time of their formation, the Government had taken possession of the theatre and was preparing to introduce the recommendations of Victor Glasstone. The problem was getting people to come to see the shows. The Friends started by organising coaches from different parts of the Island to make it easier for the audience to reach the theatre. This was a brave and intelligent step that made a palpable difference. They also organised, thanks to the help of Steve de Haven, a salesman at Manx Radio, half-price radio advertisements for shows put on by local amateur groups, an arrangement that still stands. This gave the Theatre, and the Friends, a radio presence. As their membership grew, they developed into a group that would work hard to provide entertainment for themselves, and not just at The Gaiety. This meant trips to other theatres in the United Kingdom and similar outings, all of which helped foster a sense of community among the members. They put on shows, such as a version of 'The Good Old Days' with John Inman that filled the theatre with people dressed in Victorian style. This alone raised £7,000. They started working for free in the theatre itself, providing box office and other staff. They were tireless and ceaseless in their generous dedication to the building and the performances, becoming profoundly involved and important in the restoration and its funding. Along with the amateur societies, the Friends of The Gaiety were the public expression of the Island's determination to keep the building and theatre alive.

The Friends, or 'Fogies', had another role as well. They were a well-established, credible and respected society, recognised as working for the benefit of the theatre and therefore the Island as a whole. Mervin wanted his restoration to be entirely legitimate, seen as such and granted a kind of warrant that the Fogies' approval would represent. Moreover, just as he needed the support of Laurence New, he had to be sure the Friends agreed with his aims to provide him with a solid administrative backing through the long haul ahead. They would also provide a buffer zone between any powerful people who might not approve of what Mervin was doing, but who would have less chance of scuppering the committee of the Friends. If the theatre Manager had asked to raise and spend £100,000 on an aspect of refurbishment, it could have been laughed out of the Department, and rightly. After all, Mervin had no qualifications for attempting such a thing, and they had already commissioned the Glasstone report and acted on its consequent alterations. If a committee of a well-established organisation with a Lieutenant Governor at its head asks for it, it has a far greater chance of being welcomed. As far as Mervin was concerned, without their approval, there could quite possibly have been no restoration. To his great relief, the Friends agreed and established a sub-committee headed by Charles Sentance on 22 May, 1990. The aims were to restore the fabric of The Gaiety to as near as possible to Frank Matcham's original design in order to re-present it to the Island on its centenary. Mervin was never given absolute *carte blanche*; the sub-committee was to report back to the Friends for their approval on each development. In general, however, and not surprisingly, they have said yes to each proposal, if occasionally after some debate. Their dedication to the theatre has been reflected in their adoption of the restoration as a cause meriting their wholehearted support. They have been devoted fund-raisers, maintaining their presence at the theatre with their own shows (receipts to the restoration fund), run stalls and held coffee mornings, assisted with all aspects of running the theatre, all with an extraordinary generosity and brio. The Isle of Man is typically a generous giver to charity and the Manx are quietly proud of this. The spirit of this is exemplified in the Fogies, who have provided literally hundreds of unsung heroes to the cause.

Charles Sentance.   Photo: Island Photographics

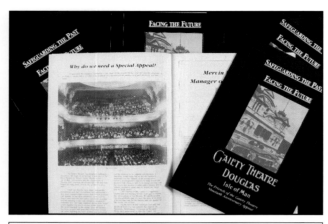

'Safeguarding the Past - Facing the Future'. The document that was used to launch the restoration appeal.

Photo: Island Photographics

From the start, it was decided to go about the restoration in a series of projects. This is unusual. Normally, a large pot of money is made available, the theatre is closed for ages and all the work is done in one go. This was neither possible nor desirable at The Gaiety. If a theatre is closed for any length of time the audience is lost and it takes more than the grand re-opening to get them back again. People need to develop the habit of looking to see what's on and deciding to go on a regular basis. Once those habits are broken, once no-one is talking about the latest production, the theatre as a venue becomes defunct in the imagination of the people who make it a viable concern. The Gaiety was the only theatre on the Island so it was essential to keep it running. More importantly, it was clear to Mervin and David that The Gaiety was perhaps the last theatre in Britain that could be put back as Matcham intended. This would require them to take longer over the job in order to avoid the financial or temporal necessity to cut corners. Once again, the fact that the Island was being largely ignored by the tourists, and the arts by the Government, meant The Gaiety was uniquely able to have such a detailed and extensive restoration undertaken. Another advantage of the Gaiety's situation was the fact that the theatre closed for two months as a matter of course after the pantomime. This was partly because of a lack of demand and partly to prevent the audience becoming frozen to their seats. This eight-week shutdown, unthinkable in almost any other theatre, allowed two months for major works to be undertaken with no greater disruption than was usual. It was also easier for the builders who would not have to down tools every evening and set the theatre up for a performance. On the other hand, it does mean the major building works of the restoration have been completed in a total period of twenty months, a remarkable achievement in itself and testament to the hard work of the Friends and the Government.

There was also the matter of keeping the theatre going as a live place of entertainment despite all this activity. It was open and running shows, both local and imported, for the other ten months of the year. The shows varied from one-night-stands to six-week seasons, incorporating repertory theatre, dance, comedy, musicals and concerts in an ever-shifting attempt to keep the audience coming. There are perennial favourites, such as Ken Dodd, as well as attempts at capturing the younger market. When Boyzone appeared at The Gaiety, Mervin failed to recognise them as the star turn and was convinced, when he saw them standing outside the stage door, they were a group of dangerous youths up to no good and ordered them to get away from his theatre. It took a quiet explanation to convince him that they were the evening's main attraction.

Roy Castle faced a different dilemma when he was presenting a summer season. He and his family had been out exploring the Island, and went to Niarbyl Bay. Roy's son, Daniel, fell from the cliffs and had to be taken to hospital with serious injuries. At the theatre when the news came through, the staff were waiting to hear that the evening's show would be cancelled. But Roy arrived on time and the show went ahead with the audience unaware of the off-stage drama. At the end of his show, Roy asked for requests. Someone called out 'Danny Boy!' There was a pause. For a moment, Roy turned his back on the audience. Then he gave a signal to the orchestra and sang the song. The footlights were the cut-off point. Everyone on the stage side knew exactly what was going on and was gripped with sympathetic tension. Everyone on the other side was having a night's entertainment from a hugely popular star. By the following day, though, the story had got out and the theatre was packed with fans and well-wishers choked with goodwill to see the man who sang 'Danny Boy' for his audience when his son was so ill.

The Gaiety also required such a comprehensive overhaul because it had never been the subject of any serious redevelopment and as a result there was practically nothing known about the fabric of the building. With other works of this sort there will be a history, or a guide at least, that makes it easier to determine what the finished article should look like. This does not, however, necessarily mean it is refurbished correctly. The other thing that a ten-year period allows is a great deal of fund-raising which in turn means a great number of people are involved, affected and informed. It was essential the community throughout the Isle of Man was all three.

The whole project was officially started with a gift of £3,000 from the Friends of The Gaiety to the Restoration Fund. Mervin went to the Isle of Man Bank with a view to obtaining sponsorship to produce a fund-raising restoration document entitled 'Safeguarding The Past - Facing The Future.' The bank was enthusiastic, and the document was made available to the public on 16 July, 1990. In the theatre that night there was a performance of 'Seaside Romp' that starred Molly Sugden and Jack Douglas. Molly became most famous for her work on television's 'Are You Being Served?' and lives on the Island. That connection was more than enough to prompt co-operation from the cast in the new restoration venture. They joined in the celebration, re-enacting the speeches and poems of the opening night. To round the evening off, there was a silent collection, in which paper currency is the only variety allowed. Following on from that, the Theatre Chaplain the Reverend Alec Smith wrote a Service of Thanksgiving to bless the restoration. Alec has been a loyal supporter of the whole project, and is a generous man with a fine sense of proportion and humour. He was a Chaplain to the Forces for many years, and was Director of religious broadcasting for the British armed forces in Germany. His

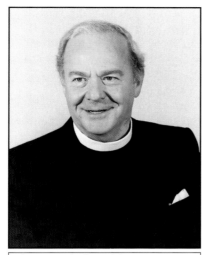

The Reverend Alec Smith
Photo: Morrison Photos

dedication is matched by the sympathetic creativity he brings to his vocation. The service he wrote for The Gaiety became the benchmark for others of this type, and has been adopted as such by the Actors' Church Union. Lessons were read by Molly Sugden and Jack Douglas, with other readings by Marion Shimmin and Ethel Brookes. Harry Galbraith and Linda Watterson were the soloists accompanied by John Riley. All this was covered in the local press, which gave the appeal exactly the kind of kick-start it needed. The Friends of The Gaiety set about publicising the restoration and generating money for it with a regular series of lunches on the stage of The Gaiety on Fridays, with Mervin and Charles Sentance as hosts. These lunches proved to be the most valuable source of business sponsorship, or at least the starting point for what would become business sponsorship. Senior members of the Island's business community would be telephoned by Charles or Mervin and simply asked to come. The Isle of Man is a small place and one of the great advantages of this is the accessibility it affords - after all, not many places list the Chief Minister's home number in the phone book.

The businessmen and women contacted out of the blue seemed to appreciate the personal approach, rather than receiving a formatted invitation to a corporate function and this made them all the more relaxed about accepting. There were other good reasons for the hospitality working. It was unusual for a start, and it involved a meal out, both likely to whet a curious appetite. It gave an opportunity to describe and show local businessmen and women what went on under the stage, and metaphorically under their very noses. This was a revelation and a matter of genuine astonishment to many who discovered, as Mervin described the history of the place and the workings of the traps, there was a treasure buried in their back garden and Mervin had a spade and a map. It also did no harm to offer a couple of glasses of wine to the guests before asking them to get their chequebooks out. By the end of December 1990, £33,595 had been raised.

The first project, funded by a bequest from the Martin family, was to save the act drop, which proved sufficiently testing to demonstrate some of the complications to come. Mervin approached the National Trust and English Heritage to find out whom they would recommend to carry out such a delicate and specialised task. From the short-list, the Fine Art International Consultancy in Bristol was chosen, a company that has been at the heart of the restoration work ever since. Their pedigree spoke for itself since they had worked in stately homes and churches all over the United Kingdom as well as on Capitol Hill in Washington; but it was their sympathy with the nature of the project that made them ideal. Restoring the act drop nearly became entirely unnecessary after Mervin and David, of all people, nearly destroyed it. To carry out the work, the drop had to be removed from its flying-bar at the front of the stage, walked (that is, moving one end forward a few feet while the other remains stationary, then repeating the process with the other end) halfway to the back, rotated through 180 degrees, then re-flown and the cleaning done from the paint-frame floor. When Mervin and David were releasing it from its fly-bar onto the floor, the side struts of the drop were so weak that they nearly buckled. The canvas ballooned out like a wind-caught sail; a few seconds more of the strain and the drop would have been gone forever. If the struts had given in under the pressure, or the tacks not held the canvas in place, the whole

The Service of Thanksgiving for 90 years of The Gaiety Theatre and to launch the restoration on the 23 July, 1990 at St Thomas' Church.
Photo: Island Photographics

Sticking point: moving the Act Drop.

Photo: Mervin Russell Stokes collection

thing would have been ruined. Mervin and David, with what was great presence of mind, managed to haul it back into its original position on the fly-bar and decided another method would probably be safer. It would, however, take more time.

They fixed the drop by three ties along a bar. It was moved back one side at a time, one bar at a time, with them both clambering up and down ladders to secure it or untie it, to the centre of the stage. Once there, two of the three ties were released and the centre one left alone. The intention was to rotate it, so the painted side faced upstage and be attended to on the paint frame floor. But as they turned it, they realised it was three inches wider than was available. This was not a design feature of the drop or a miscalculation. It was because a bridge between the left and right sides of the fly-floor gallery had been built at the front of the stage, making it impossible to turn the drop round. This bridge was not in the original theatre, and has since had to be removed to allow the house curtains to rise correctly, but it was very much present at the time. Faced with the choice of cancelling the first project of the restoration or dropping the act drop onto the floor again, they chose a much more straightforward means of solving the problem. They cut a chunk out of the bridge. While this was going on, the doorbell was ringing as the arriving company for that week's show were turning up with their articulated lorry of equipment hoping to do their 'get-in' (an expression which means exactly what it says, as does the one used at the end of a run, the 'get-out'). Mervin and David were standing with a 90 year old painting the size of a house, the only one of its kind in Great Britain, at 90 degrees to its correct alignment with a professional touring theatre company waiting to come in and put their set up, check the lights and sound, see the dressing rooms and generally prepare. The two on stage must have felt like house-burglars with swag bags when the bell went. But having come close to destroying the drop already, the two were loath to hurry the process along too much. They managed to free the stuck corner, continue working slowly back and haul the drop up to the frame floor, just in time to avoid serious complications.

Once in position, the backing canvas was removed. On the painted side of the canvas itself, the copper-headed nails that held it to the frame had oxidised and rotted the canvas in the immediate area. It is impossible to estimate just how little time there would have been before its own weight dragged it free from its nails and onto the ground. Its delicacy meant it had to be repaired *in situ* and the frame rebuilt around it.

The frame was repaired in the same wood as the original, the canvas edges strengthened, and the whole thing effectively re-affixed to the frame in sections. Only once this was done could the picture be cleaned. Even with all that preparation the business of cleaning it was far from straightforward. In order to avoid glare when lit by the footlights the drop had been painted in stage paint. This is a powdered water-paint mixed with size - a sticky, globby, gel that serves as a fixative. However, as it was water based, if the surface was rubbed the paint smudged immediately. To clean it required an intermediary layer between the surface and the restorer's brush. It was achieved using mulberry tissue paper, infused with a liquid that caused the dirt to soften on the paint surface and stick to the paper, leaving the clean paint of the original drop underneath.

Once cleaned - a painstaking, inch-by-inch task - the canvas was repaired, its holes and tears filled, and the additions overpainted to match the original. Its triumphant re-presentation to the Manx public later that summer was as neat and satisfactory a conclusion to the first project as could have been imagined.

The next section to be restored was the amphitheatre. It had been redesigned, and the differentiation between it and the gallery removed, and the whole thing called the upper circle. The rake had been greatly exaggerated during the 1930s when The Gaiety was a cinema, and the tiering altered to accommodate tip-up seats. These seats were a hotchpotch of various designs from other theatres and cinemas around the Island. The plan was to reinstate the front half of the Upper Circle as Matcham had designed, with a barrier between it and the gallery. First, the seating throughout the whole area was removed, and the tiering in the front section excavated to find the original levels of the seats, and the treads and risers of the stairs. These were easy to find under the alterations, and would be reinstated, thus returning to the theatre the magnificent sightlines so painstakingly designed by the architect. While the newer seats were being removed, a stanchion from the 1900 bench seating was found. This was used as a template for the seats that were to be placed in the restored amphitheatre. Similarly, a scrap of material formed the basis of the new seat covers. This system of discovery and implementation would be seen in many parts of the completed restoration.

Also found under the seats was a network of pipes leading to radiators, a part of an expanded heating system that had been growing sporadically over the past ninety years. This was removed (as it

later would be throughout the building), and the seats reinstated at their proper level. This was about two feet lower than it had been when the tip-up seats were in place. As a result, the brass safety rail that ran around the front of the amphitheatre had to be reinstated as well, or people sitting a couple of rows back would have had a horizontal rail interrupting their view of the performance, which was hardly in keeping with Matcham's principals on sightlines. It was something of a relief to discover the part of this rail that had been changed had only been lifted, not destroyed and replaced with a contemporary one. The 1930s work merely involved cutting the rail where it joined the amphitheatre from the slips and lifting it up on wooden stanchions. While this alteration was being reversed, the barrier between the two seating areas was reintroduced, its design based on

a photograph taken in 1900 of the theatre's interior. By the end of 1991, the amphitheatre had been completely renewed.

The comfort of those in the expensive seats was not forgotten. 200 seats were removed from the stalls, and the whole area re-spaced. This gave enough room for members of the public to move in and out of the rows without the discomfort and embarrassment of forcing everyone else to get to their feet. Also, at the rear of the stalls, space was created for twelve wheelchairs with seats beside them to allow carers or partners to sit beside their charges. This facility came courtesy of the Public Lottery Trust.

In the same year the rose window was restored. At the launch of the restoration appeal, Mervin secretly thought it would never be possible to raise the money needed for the work, however much he

Peeling away 90 years of nicotine and grime as the act drop begins its transformation.

Photo: International Fine Art Consultancy

The amphitheatre showing Matcham's original steps and the 1930s alterations.

Photo: Island Photographics

The amphitheatre in 1991 restored to Matcham's original specification.
Photo: Mervin Russell Stokes collection

next few months, he pieced together on this home-made light-table the patterns and shapes of the window from the broken bits of glass in the buckets. There had been three sections to each pane of the window, and eventually he managed to put two thirds of the largest segment in place, giving him the patterns and the colours. For the missing parts, he and David used their combined knowledge and imagination. There was evidence of stained glass work elsewhere in the building, such as above the box offices and the windows on the facade. Matcham was known to use certain styles from his stock books. So it was believed that if they could find an appropriate design in another theatre built at around the same time, there would be enough information to finish the remake of the one in The Gaiety. The Richmond Theatre in Surrey was built in the same year and in the dress circle bar was just the window they were looking for. With this as their guide, a design was drawn up that was effectively two-thirds Gaiety Theatre and one third Richmond Theatre, but all Frank Matcham and 1900.

Firms were invited to tender for the business of making the glass to size and fitting it. The Victorian Stained Glass Company of London was chosen, and had to incorporate certain modifications to comply with modern health and safety regulations. The area of unsupported glass had to be smaller than in 1900, so larger pieces were cut and leaded. The lighting for the window would have to be changed, too. Originally, it had been a ring of bulbs around the crown of the window. This was deemed a hazard, in part because of the possibility of danger to the audience and in part because it was a possible threat to the safety of whoever would be changing bulbs, who could slip and find themselves a part of the furniture below. Instead of a ring of lights, there were four theatre lanterns hung at equal points on the perimeter of the window with the light diffused over the whole of it, rather than simply focussed on its crown. A sheet of milk Perspex was built above the original window - that is, on the side between the window and the roof - protecting it from anything that could fall from above and further helping to diffuse the light.

At the same time, it was decided to restore the sun-burner since the effect of the restoration of either would be enhanced by the restoring of the

knew the green hardboard filling the framework was out of keeping with the rest of the ceiling decoration. Nevertheless, he decided to find out what was there originally. In the reports on the theatre's opening night, there was a description of how attractive it was, and how well it lit the auditorium. Armed with this, he spoke to David, who happened to be on the Island at the time. It was an August bank holiday and the two of them believed a couple of hours up in the roof space above the window would be all that was required to see if there were any clues to what might have been there. Two days later they came down. What they had found was to some extent expected - rubbish, newspapers, light bulbs and old programmes. But they also found, scattered on the floor, six bucket-loads of broken stained-glass shards. This was reverently taken down and transported to Mervin's home, where it was washed and polished and taken indoors. David went back to Harrogate, full of protestations to his wife that his bank holiday hadn't been all ice-creams and sandcastles. Meanwhile Mervin got an old patio door, put it on bricks in his dining room and placed three fluorescent lights beneath it. For the other. For the first time in around fifty years, the whole of the burner was lowered. The 1930s Odeon-style luminaire was discarded. Mervin contacted Sugg Lighting, a London-based organisation and specialists in the field of Victorian lighting and gas appliances. For such a company familiar with many devices like the sun-burner, The Gaiety was a straightforward job. But Mervin faced one of the perennial problems facing any restoration, but one particularly difficult when dealing with a building that still has to serve a purpose and function. Should he restore the burner as it was, with its gas jets and capacity to draw hot air out of the auditorium? If he did not, would that be to invalidate the restoration itself? Safety obligations came to the rescue. If he could manage to get the same effect without the concomitant concern about very hot gas jets and very old roof timbers, he would be true to the aesthetic and satisfy common sense. There was also the fact that a burner would go on bringing dirty air up to a ceiling that had just been cleaned, which is hardly good housekeeping. Equally, the aesthetic value of the lights under the rose window would be maintained, but the practical purpose of the burner itself was no longer a consideration. Audiences in the 1990s were a good deal cleaner than they were in 1900 and there was no smoking in the theatre so the need for something to draw hot, fuggy air out of the building was largely negated. In the end, the functionality was not a consideration, but the appearance mattered in the grand scheme. Facsimiles of the burners were made and fitted into the original frame. At end of the gas jets where flames would have emerged, small halogen bulbs were installed which, when slightly dimmed, create a very reasonable gas effect from the floor and stalls.

While restoring the sun-burner, its gas-feed pipes were unearthed. Typically, rather than just remark on its appearance, Mervin and David decided to trace the pipes back. The pipes travelled through the proscenium, into the substage area, through the orchestra pit wall, under the Stalls floor and into the box office on the right as you enter the foyer. Here it disappeared behind the Beauty-board. Once this was removed, the control panel was revealed, untouched since its placing there in 1900. This route is the most labyrinthine possible to get from the burner to the control panel and, although there is no evidence to support the theory, it seems likely there were controls for the supply situated, for example, at the side of the stage for the Stage Manager to dim the burner. Finding this piece of the building's internal workings was satisfying in

itself, but it had far greater significance for theatrical and engineering historians. At the time, although such a supply to the burner was known, it was not clear who had designed and patented it. On The Gaiety's panel, it stated not only the name and home town of the manufacturer, Tollerton of Leeds, but also gave a clear patent number for the system. Tollerton was also responsible for other stage works such as the gas feeds into the stage area. Just as nowadays there are flaps or dips on a stage floor with electric sockets under or in them, so the gas engineers in 1900 placed gas power sockets under the Gaiety stage, and each of the gas covers was stamped with Tollerton's name.

The episode of the rose window and the sun-burner epitomises the entire project. The detective work, the months of perseverance and the incidental discoveries are littered throughout this second building of The Gaiety. Similarly, the hunger for the work to be right allied to the need to keep the theatre functioning in a modern environment has been a recurrent theme. It has to be as modern as possible in terms of its safety and performance capabilities, but look and feel one hundred years old. It must be accurate without compromising modern standards and modern without compromising the accuracy. The commercial sponsorship was essential and demonstrated how the new finance sector was saving the building created by the tourist trade. Corporate involvement was needed because major projects required substantial sums to be available immediately, and raising the money through the public would take too long. This meant the public's continued generosity went into the general fund to be used for other works or ones with no specific sponsor. Also, in the window and burner project as with every other part of the restoration, Mervin and David were involved from conception to completion, learning more as work progressed, insisting upon the quality of the result and achieving magnificence. The value of having the time to research in detail aspects of the building only revealed through the minutest inspection perfectly demonstrated in this project.

1992 saw the ceiling paintings of the four seasons and the surrounding plasterwork cleaned. This required a kind of Michaelangelo scaffolding arrangement to be erected above the stalls at a height that would allow people to work on the ceiling. First, the ceiling itself had to be conserved, because it was clear a substantial section of the plasterwork was in danger of collapse. It was also revealed that the large puttis (there are eight) round the light fittings had moved away from the bed of the ceiling by about an inch. Just to make it

The sun-burner restored and being hoisted in to position by Robert Jones (left) and Mervin.

Photo: Island Photographics

The control for the sun-burner discovered behind panelling in the box office.

Photo: Island Photographics

Restoring the ceiling using a false floor erected above the auditorium.

Photo: Island Photographics

Taping the ceiling cracks . . .

Photo: Island Photographics

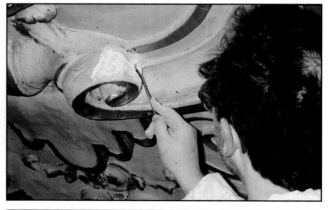

. . .and then filling them.

Photo: Island Photographics

discussed. A complete redecoration, while it would have been the safest means of reinstating a ceiling, was dismissed as completely out of keeping with the restoration. In the end, each crack was individually treated with a specially formulated filler that would contract and expand as appropriate. This work took weeks, each crack requiring the skilled attention of one of the restorers armed with a tiny spatula to force the filler home. Then the cracks were painted over and the ceiling given a thorough wash.

During this whole process the delicacy of the ceiling's original colours was being gradually revealed. After decades of smoke and grime being pulled up to the roof, the colour had become essentially a plain and rather dull, nicotinish brown. Under this drab covering, there was cream, caramel and *vieux rose*, all highlighted with 23²/3-carat gold leaf. This last is still in perfect condition on The Gaiety's ceiling and would cost £750,000 to replace. Once cleaned, the entire paint surface was covered with a specialist protective layer which means that when the theatre is cleaned in the future, the actual paint surface will remain protected and not fade as a result. There was a similar line of thought behind placing a milk Perspex sheet over the rose window.

Rather as cathedrals have tiny signatures of craftsmen carved into little niches, the plasterwork was covered in graffiti. This was left alone during the restoration and demonstrates, or seems to, that Kilroy was alive and well (and here) in or around 1900. There was great care taken not to remove any of this during the restoration work. Among the comments is: "If this theatre wasn't here, I could see the Conister Rock - Locke", a statement which is irrefutable, and about as revealing as irrefutable statements always are. It has the ring of proverb about it: true, but self-evident and pointless. Very odd. The Gaiety's second manager, Fred Barwell, who worked there from before the first War and was still a regular almost up to his death 1990, used to say when he arrived at the theatre: "My name's up there. I wrote it down before I went off to fight in 1914, just in case I never came back." Mervin used to take this with a pinch of salt, a small grandiloquence from a man who had some claim to the fabric of the building; but it was there, as Mervin was able to testify when he went up the scaffolding.

The *trompe l'oeil* murals on either side of the orchestra pit were conserved and restored, as were the two frescoes in the dress circle. There had been some concern these last were not original. As the cleaning began,

a little more complicated, the method of preventing a collapse of the whole ceiling almost brought it about. It was made secure with several hundred stainless steel tie-rods. These held the ceiling and pulled back into position the section that was due to fall down. However, the result was to make the whole ceiling crack like a well-struck egg. This left everyone with a serious concern about what should be done next. Each crack was individually taped while the possibilities were

Fred Barwell, the Gaiety's second Manager and later a Director of The Palace and Derby Castle Company.
Photo: Doreen Barwell collection

Fred Barwell's signature on the ceiling dated 1914 - just prior to his departure to serve in the First World War.
Photo: Mervin Russell Stokes collection

it became apparent that what had been visible was an overlay, which is why it looked out of place; the real Binns ones were discovered underneath and restored. It was during this stage of the operation that there was a growing conviction that the general colour scheme was originally of a turquoise and sea-green hue, rather than royal blue as had been believed before. Colour had always been a problem. There were reliable early photographs of the theatre, inside and out, but they were sepia. The descriptions in the press were a starting point, but no more than that - describing colour is a notoriously nebulous matter. Without physical evidence there was not much to indicate what the whole theatre looked like. There were theories about the colours of the sea, but no proof to back it. As each layer of the theatre's decoration was cleaned and polished, buffed and repaired, tones, tints and hues were springing into life again.

Even in the last weeks before the centenary, new evidence was being found to show that the colour of the barrier between the amphitheatre and gallery was in a caramel tinted rose colour. Shades of green were found in the dresses of the goddesses painted on the frescoes of the dress circle ceiling. Then there was the tiling in the pit area, and the curtains on the act drop, surely painted to give the impression they were the same as the theatre's real ones. The colour was beginning to reappear almost of its own accord.

The modernisation of the stage was also continuing. 1989 had seen the removal of the hemp lines and their replacement with a double-purchase counterweight system. The grid was strengthened as well, and another gallery built to make loading the counterweights possible. 1992 was to see another nine sets of counterweights put

in place. All the equipment came second-hand from The ABC Theatre in Blackpool, which supplied similar materials for another Matcham house, The Opera House at Wakefield, and was installed by A. S. Green and Co. of Liverpool.

It was also in 1992 that the original artwork of the 'Nibs' cartoon of Frank Matcham came to be in The Gaiety. The cartoon had appeared in 1911 in *Vanity Fair* when Matcham was profiled in the magazine's 'Men of the Day' series. This was the last year Matcham did any significant work.

Rediscovering Binns' frescos in the dress circle.
Photo: International Fine Art Consultancy

The original artwork of the Nibs cartoon of Frank Matcham that appeared in 'Vanity Fair' which is on permanent loan to the Gaiety Theatre.

Photo: The Gaiety Theatre

Perhaps being *Vanity Fair*'s 'Man of the Year' made further achievement unnecessary; perhaps being cartooned by a man whose real name was - magnificently - Drummond Niblick, was the perfect end to his career. In 1991, Mervin decided a print of the cartoon should belong to the theatre. He went to London and scoured all the print shops, but the one of Matcham was not as popular as the stereotypes of judges or golfers, and he was advised to try the National Portrait Gallery, where a copy was in their archives. Mervin asked for a copy, and battled the unwillingness of the staff who felt their copy was not really of high enough quality for reproduction as it had a crease down the middle. Mervin would not be dissuaded, and the copy arrived to be hung in the foyer. Some months later, there was a phone call from a man in Sheerness in Kent saying: "I understand you have a Matcham theatre. Would you be interested in the original artwork of the Nibs portrait of Frank Matcham?" Mervin said yes in as calm a voice as he could muster. However, there were other theatres in competition, and he was asked if he would bid for it. Mervin said he wanted no part of an auction but wanted to know the price. He was told. After a brief pause to catch his breath, he approached the Government who were sympathetic, but didn't see it as a priority. There was a similar story at the Manx Museum and National Trust. As a last resort, he approached a private individual who generously bought the picture and gave it on permanent loan until the price could be refunded. The individual and the price are still a secret, although the price, while substantial, was considered by Christie's to be about right, given the associations of the theatre and the subject of the picture.

For every lucky break or generous donor, there were setbacks. The safety curtain motor burst a seal, sending oil dribbling down the act drop. Fortunately, the restorers working on the ceiling paintings were on hand to deal with it. With equal good fortune, Mervin had insured the drop for just such a contingency. The motor has since been moved.

The exterior of the building received most of its substantial work over the next year, 1993. The canopy was removed for two reasons. The first was simply because it was in a desperate state. After all those years with the sea only feet away, most of the ironwork had rotted and rusted. The process of removing it was as carefully monitored as the rose window. It was taken down piece by piece, and anything seen as a later addition was discarded. All the original ironwork above the level of the columns was sent to the Cast Iron Workshop in Wakefield. The original columns had managed to remain in relatively good condition and were left in the pavement as a starting point for the rebuilding work. As each piece was removed, it was drawn and photographed. Once the canopy was out of the way, access to the facade of the building from street level was possible, which was the second reason for removing the canopy. Once the scaffolding was in place, all unnecessary signage could be taken down and thrown away. The Day-Glo was no more. All the electrical cables were removed, as were those of the recently installed computer system. The facade was then surveyed for missing architectural details. There was a good deal that needed replacing or remaking, including stone spheres that formed the finials sitting as a relief above the *oeil de boeuf* windows. To have a stone sphere carved was extremely expensive, and an alternative had to be found. In the end, a football was the answer. A latex mould of half a ball was made, and then cast in concrete. The process was repeated, the two halves cemented together, put in place and when painted were indistinguishable from the originals. Restoring other details such as garlands used a similar casting technique because there were examples extant on the building. For each damaged or disappeared section of laurel leaf, there was a whole one available to take a mould from.

All the work on the façade was paid for by the Manx Government. This is quite significant. The restoration campaign was of sufficient solidity to merit Government involvement and they continue to assist substantially in the restoration programme to this day. They are also responsible for providing the capital funds for such major projects as the stage relaying, the lights and the sound system. Government also provides a significant annual subsidy to cover the maintenance of the building and the cost of running it, including wages and insurance.

Having completed the work of rebuilding the outside, and given it all due care and inventive attention, there was one question unanswered about it, and an important one at that. What colour should it be? The Gaiety was not painted at its opening, but scrapings through the layers of exterior paint indicated the first scheme was cream masonry work relieved by leaf green iron and wood work. This was true for the whole of the outside, except for the doors. These were mahogany throughout, unless visiting the Pit or the Gallery, where *faux* mahogany was in place. The lower orders did not merit the real thing, but the overall impression needed to be consistent. For the restoration, the real thing would be used

throughout. Having removed the ugly additions to the signage of the building, it was necessary to replace it with something more suitable. Mervin was convinced the gold leaf so generously applied to the ceiling was to be found lavished on the letters spelling out Gaiety Theatre and Opera House on the wall facing the promenade. Nobody else agreed with him; so he laid a bet with a member of the Government Department that was involved with the work. The Department was so sure that no-one would place gold leaf lettering on the outside of a building beside the sea that it agreed to the bet's condition - if it was gold, they would replace it. Mervin has never disclosed what his forfeit would be if he were wrong, but it was immaterial. After scraping through the various layers of paint, the glint in Mervin's eye was matched by the gold of the letters, a gold that is now back in place and still glinting. The work on the front of the building was a transformation. As a blue and white theatre with orange signs, it looked rather shabby despite the brightness of the colours. The change effected by the work was more than just a lick of paint and a clean up. It was finding the right paint, attending to the detail and following the sense of the whole. It was an achievement of understanding the design and respecting its context. Given the proper attention, The Gaiety regained its elegant and cheerful frontage and became a pleasure to look at.

The stained glass windows in the facade werereplaced. The patterns for the fenestration and the design within were evident in the photos from 1901, and the colours chosen to match those of the existing windows. Once this was completed, the canopy could be re-erected.

The filigree ironwork on the top of the canopy had disappeared, so the photo of 1901 was examined minutely. A scale drawing was made, then scaled up to the actual size on block board. This was then cut out with a jig-saw and carved to a clean finish. This wooden carving was used to create a mould from which a new casting of the original design was made. Much the same system

was used for the stained glass used all over the canopy, using a photograph from 1947. Again, the Victorian Stained Glass Company was responsible for all the glazing work on the canopy.

The statue of Progress had her arm replaced in pearwood by local sculptor Simon Buttimore, with the flame in gold leaf. The bronze flambeau atop the building was rediscovered. It was a popular feature when The Gaiety was built. There are still some in existence at various gentlemen's clubs and at Harrogate's Royal Hall. As a feature, it was presumably intended to show a brotherhood with the aspirations of classical Hellenic civilisation and a disregard for gas bills. The one in Douglas was cleaned and painted and, at the time of writing, negotiations are continuing with the local gas supplier for its reconnection.

Back inside the theatre the work continued. The fresco above the proscenium was cleaned and restored, again using the International Fine Art Consultancy. A significant development was the building of the Matcham Suite, a hospitality room. The importance of the room is not so much in the architecture as the purpose. It allowed sponsors of shows to have a private reception, to be made to feel separate and special. Private functions could be held there, and fund-raising events. Originally it was the gallery and amphitheatre bar, which had been a temperance bar when the theatre opened. It had been divided to form on the one side a corridor between the left and right of the gallery and, on the other, a prop room. When cleared of its contents, half the original bar was discovered, with its ornate mirrors intact. It must have felt like cleaning a picture of a dull landscape to find half a Renoir behind it. Or, given the money-raising potential of the Matcham Suite, like finding a pocketful of notes in an old pair of trousers.

Mervin had known the space was there and realised the value of a reception area. Throughout the restoration work, he was responsible for coaxing, chivvying, encouraging and occasionally bullying the money for the

A football transformed! Improvising the construction of stone spheres for the facade.

Photo: Mervin Russell Stokes collection

A bet won! Re-gilding the lettering on the facade in gold leaf.

Photo: Mervin Russell Stokes collection

Creating the mould and templates for the new canopy.

Photo: The Cast Iron Workshop, Wakefield

The amphitheatre and gallery bar transformed into the Matcham Suite.
Below: The foyer, before and after.

Photo: Island Photographics

which had previously been a poster store.

Elsewhere in the building, the grand foyer and staircase were redecorated and repapered, thanks to Douglas Round Table, who made the theatre their charity of the year, and raised over £16,000. As part of their work, they created a 500 Club, and brought The Gaiety to the attention of at least that number of people.

The last major work undertaken in 1993 was the replacement of the entire central heating system. Originally, there had been just the four radiators and a coke boiler. But over the years more had been added and pipes laid throughout, like a 3-D sketch illustrating the meaning of 'higgledy-piggledy'. As a result, there were radiators from every decade and in every design, making it a haven for the collectors of such ephemera, but not at all in keeping with the designs for The Gaiety. All the pipes were stripped out and a duct created under the stalls floor to enclose the new ones. Attached to those pipes was a complete set of Victorian radiators. The original four were restored and placed where they were in 1900 and a set of 25 that looked much like them put in position. It was considered too costly to remake the entire set and they were not part of the original design, so it seemed unnecessary to go to the expense. Replacing the heating was a major job, and required all the time available. As the curtain came down on the pantomime, the work started. It finished just in time for the reopening in late February. Stewart Clague Services were the company responsible. For some of the audience, the noise of building works as a curtain came down must have been eerily reminiscent of the night a few years previously when The Palace Coliseum Theatre was demolished. Then, the wreckers moved in while the audience was filing out.

As the radiators were removed for restoration, they revealed their secret cache of memorabilia. There were bus, tram and train timetables, ticket stubs, flyers and a pair of false teeth. Some unfortunate had taken his or her teeth out for whatever reason only to see them slip irretrievably behind the thick radiator grille; set in an iron and dusty prison, perpetually smiling at the world.

This was a substantial amount of work to have completed in just three years or so, and should

projects from the Island's companies. And not just the restoration work; he generated income for the shows as well, finding sponsors to cover the costs of productions. He went and spoke to them, he took them to lunch and dinner, he haggled and persuaded, wined and dined them at home to make it possible. He would arrange special one-off performances to generate funds and was still working to raise awareness of the theatre locally and anywhere else he could.

It was discovered that the bar had been decorated like the staircases in two-tone pink with brown linoleum on the floor. This was pleasant enough in the staircases but not ideal for top-flight financiers and their wives. So it was decided to remake it with Matcham designs and use appropriate wallpaper and carpets. The bar was re-created as a buffet area, with period fixtures and fittings added to furnish the room in the correct manner. Here again, a mixture of common sense and appropriate invention kept the space useful and serving a necessary function in keeping with the new requirements of the theatre. It was not an accurate remake of the original but it used the original to create something functional and in keeping. Funds from the Friends went on creating a modern kitchen in a room next to the suite, have cost a fortune. Indeed it did, but nothing like as much as it could have done. Much of the work was done for free. David Wilmore, although technically employed as a consultant, always worked for the absolute minimum. But thousands upon thousands of man-hours were donated for nothing, and the obligation to keep the costs down - but not cut corners - meant every penny was carefully scrutinised. The Friends of The Gaiety Restoration Sub-committee was a vital force in maintaining strict cost-control throughout, and the hours of work exerted by the volunteers were fundamental in making the work possible. Generally, the Friends of the Gaiety have contributed some £50,000 each year to the restoration. Sponsorships of seat plaques or boxes raise substantial amounts and there have been major donations for specific projects, such as the house curtain, the rose window and the canopy. They have worked in tandem with many of the charitable trusts of the Island, such as the Gough Ritchie Trust, the Public Lottery Trust and others, and have used the subscription fees raised by members to meet administrative costs.

They have also made personal contributions to the understanding of the restoration itself. Charles Sentance has stood in for Mervin when the latter was unavailable and Helen Callister, David Butterworth and Mike Davies have carried on the theatre tours after Mervin started them. They have increased the theatre's appeal by changing its use. It can be used for a school prize-giving or a conference. It can be included as part of a corporate package for the non-golfing members of a visiting business. The Friends are responsible for the use and running of the Matcham Suite and, such is the devotion they have for the building itself, one member wanted her wake to be held there (sadly, practical problems prevented it). Nowhere else on the Island offers such a setting, quite apart from its capacity to seat nearly a thousand people. The sponsorship is also, paradoxically, a vital part of the sense of community. Corporate sponsorship is about a presence in an area associated with whatever is being sponsored. Exposure as a supporter of a popular cause brings reflected popularity. For the companies who placed large sums of money into the trustworthy hands of the Friends, there were tangible benefits such as good seats at the opening night, a reception for themselves and their clients, their name on programmes and posters. But the intangible benefit was as important. It showed them to be behind a project that was supported by the whole Island. For companies coming to the Island from outside, establishing a presence as part of an insular world was relevant and useful. Their work might not be with the Island itself but their staff and their home were. Commitment to both could be demonstrated by a commitment to The Gaiety. It also carried the advantage of being classless; everyone on the Island could, and did, go to the theatre. The total number of people going to The Gaiety each year during the restoration to see a show averaged over 50,000. The population of the Isle of Man is approximately 75,000.

There were also benefits for those who gave to the restoration fund in terms of its status. It was well run, efficient and properly administered. It was also cautious. The Friends had no collateral, and no loans were going to be forthcoming. This caution made them all the more trustworthy, as did the visibility of their work. All the money was spent on restoring the building, and the results of any donation or sponsorship were almost immediately evident, and the results themselves were in creating a magical world that was apparent from the moment the building was entered. Long before the curtain rose on a show, the sponsor or benefactor could see and sense the contribution was having an effect. The charity was also independent of Government even though the building was not, which made it more appealing to benefactors. Despite this, the relationship with central Government was one of the triumphs of the work. There was a friendly understanding built up over the years with those senior officials of Departments who were involved. This was made even easier by the profound enthusiasm for the project the Friends and Mervin demonstrated. They found that if you had enough interest in it, people came with them. The Government has been one of the closest companions and, of those involved, Gerry McGarvey, Dick Holtham, Eric Cleator and the late Denis Corkill have been long associates in The Gaiety's continuing maintenance and restoration.

1994, and the external work saw the canopy completed with the reinstatement of the four large canopy lamps and the two hanging lanterns. These were all reproduced by William Sugg and Company using the photograph taken in 1901. The designs and proportions were worked out, and then Sugg was instructed to manufacture them. When the larger lanterns arrived, Mervin was initially rather scared - they looked about the size of a phone box. Once in place, however, their scale became relative to the rest of the building and they worked perfectly. They are substantial, certainly, but the Victorians were never scared of building big; indeed, they revelled in it. This

The newly-installed lanterns on the completed canopy.
Photo: Island
Photographics

confidence is not always rewarded with great or lasting beauty, but was typical of their attitude to their environment. The Gaiety is a successful example. It is big, but not overbearing, and suits its place perfectly. As evidence of the Government's increasing awareness of the scale and value of the project, the lanterns were switched on by the newly-appointed Minister for Tourism, Tony Brown, M.H.K. The fact that his Minister had only recently taken up office rather threw Mervin, and he could not remember his name in the speeches. He could hardly invent one, and so hoped honesty would prove a serviceable option: "I'm terribly sorry, I've forgotten your name," he admitted, not a little shamefacedly. "It's Brown, and you've just lost your job!" was the reply from the Minister, who was, thankfully, smiling as he said it.

Inside, work in the foyer was completed by replacing the red, hotel carpet with a copy of the Matcham original. This was determined by using a sample of an original from The Buxton Opera House, a Matcham theatre in much the same colours as The Gaiety. Buxton had had their original remade and part of this was brought to the Island, and tested against the rest of the design. It looked perfect and, as it was believed to be from a stock design, was installed.

The original stencilling on the grand staircase and the quarter landings, just before entering the corridor running across the back of the circle was destroyed. This was no sudden impatience with the obligations of the restoration. The stencils had been overpainted so much and the plaster was in such poor condition, that all the *trompe l'oeil* effect was lost. The fact they were stencils and therefore mechanical rather than the handiwork of an artist meant removal made aesthetic and financial sense, as well as taking much less time. But this was not to avoid replacing them. Before being taken down, they were photographed. Then the design was traced onto paper, and pricked out. The ceilings were made good, and jeweller's rouge - a powder paint in this circumstance, normally a fine powder used to clean jewels - was splashed at the paper which had been stuck in place where the original had been. This left an outline through the pinpricks for the International Fine Art Consultancy to repaint, following the photos, and made it possible to recreate the full three-dimensional appearance of the designs.

The next project was the dress circle wallpaper. The design was known from photographs. Mervin had bought these early pictures of the theatre from the local auction house many years before. He had offered them to the theatre, but was told there was

no money to frame them and he was encouraged to keep them by all means but not to trouble the management with them. They had provided useful guidance for several aspects of the theatre's restoration, but lacked any indication of colour. Finding the right colours for the wallpaper in the dress circle was essential. To find them took time, once again illustrating the value of the ten years put aside for the work. Despite searching behind radiators and under floorboards, there seemed to be no trace of the original. Then one day at the entrance to the gallery, a set of baize doors had to be removed. The builders had not yet performed this, and were being reminded of the need to do so on a regular basis. Eventually, a man arrived to do the work. Mervin noticed something lurking behind the door frame as it was being removed, and asked the man to stop working while a kettle was found. The man, having been the subject of opprobrium for not doing the job before, was incensed at being told to stop and promptly stormed off. But Mervin knew what he had discovered, and steamed it off the wall. With this tiny sample, he was able to recreate the right colour for the dress circle. It was a turquoise, as he was beginning to feel certain it should be, and not royal blue as had been thought. Rolls of the newly found design were recreated by Alexander Beauchamp of Cumbria.

As for the rest of the house paper, Mervin was one day idly picking at the existing wall coverings, knowing that somewhere underneath there must surely be evidence of the original. There are not many people who would be able to do this with the combination of cherubic innocence and complete self-belief that Mervin possesses. He has not always been regarded as a specialist whose opinion was of consequence and is not universally seen that way even now. His reputation as a slightly eccentric obsessive is frankly not helped by habits such as randomly picking at wallpaper, claiming "The truth is in there". But he was right, again. Under layers of additions, there it was, intact. An area was stripped and a section removed and sent down to Beauchamp's. The original paper had been covered with a series of borders placed to make it look as though it was panelled. This panelling effect was a later addition (probably in the 20s) to modernise the appearance at minimal

Re-making the stencils on the grand staircase.
Photo: Island Photographics

Re-creation of the auditorium wallpaper.
Photo: Island Photographics

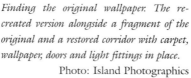

Finding the original wallpaper. The re-created version alongside a fragment of the original and a restored corridor with carpet, wallpaper, doors and light fittings in place.
Photo: Island Photographics

expense, and it was no hard decision not to recreate it. The colours of the original paper in the foyer, the dress circle, coffee promenade and the corridors around the auditorium were essentially green, rose, and turquoise. However, technology and health regulations posed difficulties in remaking it. The first was that the colours had to be approximated. The paper had suffered from the gas fumes of the Theatre's original emergency lighting system. The effect of wallpaper paste on top of it, quite apart from the wear and tear of a century, had compounded the problem. The second difficulty was that the original ink had an arsenic base that could not now be used. So that, too, had to be approximated. The other colours - the turquoise and the rose pink - matched other parts of the interior where the original had been discovered, and the whole internal scheme was developing as the coherent and complementary whole it had been when Matcham designed it.

COMPLETING THE CIRCLE

The destruction of so much of the nineteenth century's understage machinery and the skills associated with it is a genuine loss in terms of Britain's industrial archaeology. If a water-wheel or windmill is discovered lying unkempt and dilapidated, there are bodies who dedicate themselves as a matter of course to its preservation, display and educational use. The artefacts are automatically cherished and the knowledge gained informs future generations of the way of life in a previous age. The workings of theatre machinery, however, have been ignored and with this neglect has come a huge loss of information about a part of everyday leisure and craftsmanship.

The development of new techniques and technology also dissolved a tacit religious iconography running through any stage presentation of a hundred years ago. If the stage can be seen to represent Mother Earth, the flies were the Heavens, whence came angels and fairies. Beneath was the underworld, where demons and devils lived, to spring up and startle the unwary through traps. This notion of the order of things was implicit in practically all plays as a symbol of the moral positioning of Man in God's universe. To lose all connection with the physical representation of a previous generation's beliefs is to lose more than just a technical understanding, but to break a cultural connection that still has complex resonances in contemporary thought. How people imagined the world and presented it to themselves is an essential part of understanding how current attempts at the same thing developed. The how is intimately connected with the why. This is one reason why The Gaiety's restoration is important socially as well as aesthetically. On a purely practical level, the lack of existing information about technical elements of stagecraft in Victorian theatre made one part of The Gaiety's restoration particularly difficult - the Corsican trap presented an almost impossible conundrum.

The other understage material was relatively easy to procure. In a sense, the invisible part of the project was not quite a restoration. There was very little actually left under the stage itself. All the appropriate cuts on the stage itself were in place, so there was no question of what should have been underneath. But the physical remains had gone, apart from the grave trap, which was still in place. As a result, the rest of the restored material has either come from other theatres or been rebuilt. In this regard especially, the fact that David Wilmore was a part of the team was absolutely essential. For years, he had been collecting unwanted bits of machinery and making sure it was kept in storage. His work with organisations such as the National Trust meant he had contacts and access, quite apart from his experience, in precisely this area. If theatres were being rebuilt or demolished he knew about it, could find out if there was anything of value in it, and save it. The first part of The Gaiety's understage to be restored was through just such knowledge.

The Lyceum in Sheffield was being renovated, and they had some demon traps they did not wish to keep. David made sure they were not destroyed, and brought them to The Gaiety. The traps are not simply the square section on the stage. They include the six feet or so of the wooden framework, the square on which the actor stood, the ropes, paddles and all the other moving, working, sliding, grooved and prepared parts that allow an actor to be propelled almost instantly from the depths of the underworld into the full glare of the stage. The traps were brought to the Island some eighteen months before the official restoration got underway, in 1988, and was followed in 1990 by the major acquisition of the machinery in The Lyceum in Edinburgh. Again, the building was being renovated, and since a newer theatre had different technical requirements - and the area under the stage could be used for something else - the stage machinery was going to be thrown away. There was no consideration of its usefulness, value or interest; it simply amounted to a lot of heavy and inconvenient wood. Again, David knew about the plans and liaised with the people responsible. Their concern was simply to be rid of the stuff, and he was told he could take what he wanted. What he wanted were both the bridges, all the attendant workings, four sloats and various other pieces. He was also keen to obtain as much of the timber used as structural support as possible to help with any rebuilding that might be needed. He went to The Lyceum to establish the best means of loading the material and saw there was a large open space that would make it relatively simple to load two, twenty-eight-feet long, ten feet high wooden bridges and the rest. However, when he returned some months later to collect his spoils, a building site had sprung up, as had a 100-foot high new building. Any loading of bridges was completely impossible, and it looked as though The Lyceum's

The stage machinery arrives.

Photo: Island Photographics

David and Mervin oversee the installation of one of the bridges from the Lyceum, Edinburgh.

Photo: Island Photographics

machinery was destined to be scrapped. However, as is often the case with large new buildings, there was a large crane and, after a brief negotiation, David persuaded the crane driver to hoist the bridges up and over the new building and onto the waiting truck. The bridges were then taken to The Tyne Theatre and Opera House in Newcastle, where their years of wear were repaired and their height reduced to fit The Gaiety. Once shipped across, they slotted perfectly into their new home. The ease of the last part of the operation is because the Victorian wooden stage was built to fairly universal specifications. The width of a trap was almost always twenty-four inches and any theatre of the time would be equipped with gaps in the stage to accommodate such a width. This standardisation gives the work at The Gaiety a validity it might otherwise be felt to lack because what is there now, despite coming from different places or being a modern replacement, is of a proportion and size entirely consistent with what was there originally. Moreover, there has been no attempt to stain the various woods used, which means the machinery tells its own variegated story about the restoration. The fact it is all in place under a stage also gives it a context in which it makes sense.

David had worked with the National Trust in various theatres in Britain where there had been stage machinery. In some of his restoration work, David had ensured that surplus machinery was put into storage and, as a result he was able to draw on these reserves for The Gaiety. For example, the drum and shafts originally came from The Theatre

Royal in Bristol. The Trustees gave it to the National Trust who in turn passed it on to David.

With many of the recovered pieces, repairs had to be done, usually in Newcastle. Parts of one would be added to sections of another to re-create what is now under The Gaiety's stage. This was in many ways what would have happened in the past. Wooden structures are not only man-made but eminently alterable, and carpenters throughout the ages would have adapted what they had to meet the changing requirements of the producers. More recently, film makers have required the atmosphere of the theatre's underside to be created. Before it came to the Island some of the machinery at The Gaiety appeared in a film, when it was used as a set for 'The Fool' with Derek Jacobi.

The carpet cut has not been replaced, although the shape to accommodate it is cut out on the stage. However, all the service pipes and cables run under that part of the floor, and again common sense determined its value did not merit such a comprehensive relaying of wires and pipes. The other cuts, which take flats and are essentially just thin slices out of the boards at the side of the stage, are all in place. Thanks to decades of garnering and storing, studying and collecting and the constant work to raise the necessary funds by the Friends of The Gaiety, David had replaced and re-created The Gaiety's understage.

Not all of it fell as neatly into place as the bridges, however. The Corsican trap is a problem because there is no instruction manual. The evidence for the other machinery is fairly clear if you know where to

Under The Gaiety Stage - a lost world re-created.

Photo: Island Photographics

look and how to read it. But the Corsican trap was an extremely enigmatic piece, the design for which was never, apparently, written down. It is an example of the kind of alteration to a stage mentioned above, one which was an adaptation of existing materials. The trap had to be in a particular place on the stage for the effect to work. Most stages were able to remove a section when required, and The Gaiety's is built to the normal dimensions of its time, so incorporating it would not have in itself been a problem. Over twenty years, David pieced together what little evidence there is to make The Gaiety's reconstruction the first full-scale working example for almost 80 years. Charles Kean introduced the Corsican trap when he produced the play 'The Corsican Brothers' in the middle of the nineteenth century. Where he got the idea was as uncertain as how he made it work. The play was extraordinarily popular, and many companies toured it, so it is possible the machinery was portable, requiring the theatre to remove a section of the stage to allow the trap to be inserted. Some theatres had their own, though, such as The Citizens Theatre in Glasgow, The Theatre Royal in Bath, The Tyne Theatre and Opera House in Newcastle, all of which contain tantalising hints as to how it operated. It is unclear whether The Gaiety did or not. The Gaiety has the traditional dimensions required to allow a portable one to be inserted, including its rake. This is a slight slope on a stage that means the rear of it is higher than the front, making it easier for the audience to see everything. On The Gaiety stage, the rake is one in twenty-four, the standard angle. On the other hand, it is possible the theatre was built on the assumption the play would be performed there and incorporating it into the design.

David works on the basis of the architectural and documentary research he and his company do, and the architectural and documentary evidence for how the Corsican trap works was maddeningly small. The architectural evidence is drawn from minute hints within theatres, such as the scouring marks on the wall of The Citizens Theatre in Glasgow, which indicated how one element of the system functioned. It has been a rule of thumb for David that if something on a recovered fragment of machinery appears senseless, keep it in any reproduction anyway. There will be a reason for it but it may take some time before that reason becomes clear. This tenacious belief in the fundamental soundness of Victorian engineering was sternly tested but eventually demonstrated with the Corsican trap. Much of the written evidence comes from a work known as the Eyre Manuscript. Eyre was the Manager of The Theatre Royal in Ipswich from the middle of the nineteenth century,

and he kept a record of the changes and alterations there. Among his jottings is a tiny reference to the Corsican trap and how it was made. This, along with David's years of research and practical understanding of understage mechanisms, meant he knew the trap needed at least three people to work it, and would be counterweighted to make it operate smoothly. However, he needed to know a lot more to make it work again. Joiners, carpenters, enthusiasts and experts have all helped in the attempt to bring this machine back to life and resolve a personal quest for David. The problem was that there are two sections of the stage that have to move at the same time, at the same speed, but over different distances. One was the two-foot wide area of the visible stage, the other was a square sled underneath, on which the actor stood, that was built onto an inclined plane in a manner which kept him perpendicular to the stage. The opening in the upper section had to remain immediately above him while both he and it were travelling across the stage for the illusion to work. This seemed to require a single winding point and a gearing mechanism to control both upper and lower sections. It was known the upper section was made of 'scruto', that is, planks of pitch pine, joined by jute strips underneath, so what is seen on the stage is just the wood. The jute allows the necessary flexibility for the effect to work. This whole section of the stage had to be winched from one side to the other, thus moving the opening built into it across as it travelled. There had to be enough of the scruto to fill the gap behind it with usable stage as well. As an example of just one problem involved with the Corsican trap, where and how was it possible to store the yards and yards of scruto? If it was attached to the winding wheel, that wheel's diameter would increase with each rotation and affect the speed at which this upper part moved. This is where the scouring marks in Glasgow had their impact. David noticed the marks were on the timber joists under the stage where the workings for the Corsican trap would have been positioned. The marks were evidence of a huge, single wheel, which meant one rotation would have been enough to carry the scruto from one side to another without affecting the overall diameter of the wheel. With another wheel on the other side of the stage, it could be repositioned for the next performance.

This was a significant breakthrough, but was not enough to solve all the Corsican's mysteries. Models had been built, but they never satisfactorily dealt with the problem of moving the actor up the inclined plane beneath the stage at exactly the same speed. Fixing the sled on which the actor stood to the underside of the aperture using telescoping

Mr Martin Harvey in 'The Corsican Brothers', from an early London production.

Photo: Theatresearch

The Corsican trap in long shot, stage right, using the sled guides and sled platform in its lowest position during its reconstruction.

Photo: Island Photographics

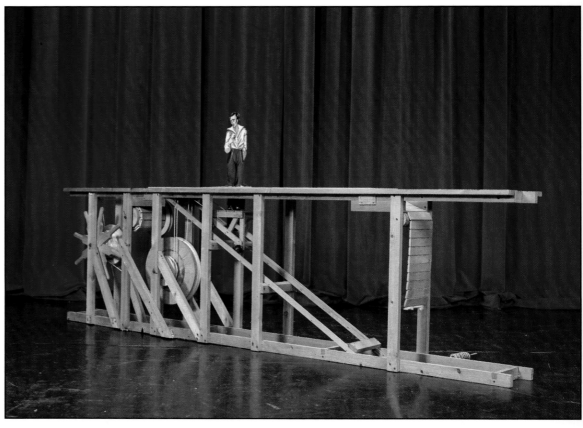

support struts was a possibility, but there was no architectural or archaeological evidence that this was done. One element David discovered that works better than most was to place the actor's sled in grooves, rather than put it on wheels as most models have suggested. This added to its stability, however much it made the three people that are working the trap strain a little harder. The other elements that models failed to demonstrate fully were friction and extension. It was these that allowed David to successfully create a full-scale, functioning trap for The Gaiety.

When it was being built in the theatre, some months prior to the centenary celebrations, David was working in the belief that the gearing system of driving the two wheels would be the one that worked. This was what all his research told him, and what all other texts suggested. He calculated the distance in travel between the scruto and the sled, and then worked out the different ratios required between the driving shafts of each wheel. He was then able to calculate the different sizes of the shafts to drive the sled and the scruto at the same speed to make sure the hole in the upper section stayed immediately above the actor's sled underneath. Having by this method calculated the two circumferences of the drive shafts to move the two sections, a process that seems about as

straightforward as logarithmic tables and a quadrant for determining longitude, he pulled on the line to make the whole thing move smoothly across the stage. What should have happened was a victory for close scrutiny of original evidence, a triumph of patient reasoning and craftsmanship and something of an historical event. What actually happened was the sled travelled far quicker than the scruto with the result that, had an actor been standing on the sled, his torso would have reached the other side of the stage some time before his head managed to. Such a disastrous experiment called for careful checking of the complicated maths involved. After all, it was quite a complex series of sums, and a single mistake might have been the cause for the inaccurate ratio. Despite extremely careful re-examination, it seemed all the calculations were correct. This might have perturbed someone of lesser mettle than Mervin and David, but David had survived the destruction by fire of three years' work in Newcastle and had to reconstruct the whole thing in a year, and Mervin had spent a ten year slog remaking The Gaiety, so the immediate dismissal of twenty years' research was no more than a bagatelle. Clearly, there was another factor, which had not been allowed for in the models and theories up to now. It is not an easy matter to realise all your thinking up to this time has been flawed, and it takes a particular kind of strength to accept it and carry on looking for the truth. In one of those tiny moments of insight that can make the heart sing, David realised the problem was not more complicated gearing mechanisms or ratios of distance, the problem was the fact that the jute stretched.

When the scruto is put under tension, as it is when hauled upon to be moved across the stage, the fabric expands and the whole length of scruto becomes longer. This compensates for the difference in the length of travel between the scruto and the understage sled. When the mechanism was tried without the gearing system, without the differing shaft widths, without algebraic computation, it worked. The two parts of the Corsican trap travelled in easy fellowship across the stage with only one rope being needed to operate the whole movement. This obviated any fears there were over the difficulty of driving two separate movements using a natural fibre rope. David had been concerned that the stretching of the hemp lines would make a difference to the delicate calculations and had toyed with the idea of using wire rope instead. This would not have been anachronistic, since it was invented in the 1830s, but there was no evidence it had been used with the Corsican trap and his instinct was always to follow the evidence. His instinct had been right. After the trap has been used, the jute contracts to its original size, and is ready for the next performance. It was that simple, and once again David's belief that reconstruction should precisely mirror the original was vindicated. The right materials under the right conditions would function correctly. The Gaiety's Corsican trap was successfully given trials on Thursday and Friday, the 17 and 18 of February 2000, with weights up to fifteen stone on the actor's sled, and it was shown the whole system could be operated by two people. For the first time in three generations, there is a working example of the Corsican trap, and it is another paradigm of The Gaiety's reconstruction as a whole. Painstaking, well-informed, principled and inspired, it functions as an example of the way things used to be done and has genuine educational value. It is equally something future theatre companies may want to use in productions and it has no detrimental effect on the theatre's ability to present plays, musicals or concerts of any sort. It is part of an understage area brimming with revived vitality, important and valuable in itself. It has its own story and is part of a much larger tale as well.

One event of 1994 was to add a further dimension to the entire process and practice of the restoration. Séamus Shea became The Gaiety's Stage Manager. An ally, friend and colleague of Mervin's as well as a highly qualified professional, he was to add a contemporary edge to the refitting, and be a vital part of a major lecture tour promoting The Gaiety. He went to the Central School of Speech and Drama, where he studied technical theatre and stage management and qualified in 1987. He became the touring Assistant Stage Manager for Field Day Theatre Company, where he worked with Brian Friel, Stephen Rea and Séamus Heaney, on a play that transferred to the Royal National Theatre. He returned to Ireland, after a brief spell with a touring company in Western Australia, and he became Stage Director of The National Theatre of Ireland, which comprises The Abbey and The Peacock Theatres. He was there for two years, notably working on 'Hedda Gabler' directed by Deborah Warner, which transferred to London's West End where it won an Olivier Award.

Séamus' interest and knowledge of the restoration grew beyond simply being consulted on those matters that affected him. As his involvement grew, he also co-hosted the fund-raising lunches on The Gaiety's stage with Mervin and Charles Sentance. When he was promoted to Production Manager as a result of staff increases in late 1997, he was able to offer even more. It was in that year he and Mervin came up with the idea of the 'Rags to Riches' tour. This was to be a chance to promote The Gaiety's centenary, attract people to the Island, spread the word about the restoration, and do any amount of good to the attendance figures for the year 2000. It all came about because of an invitation to speak at the Association of British Theatre Technicians (ABTT). The ABTT was holding a seminar on Frank Matcham, rather an unusual activity for a group principally involved in the most modern technology. It is just possible it had something to do with David Wilmore since the event was taking place in Harrogate. If so, David did not inform Mervin or Séamus that the other lecturers, apart from himself, would include John Earl, then Director of The Theatre's Trust. And there was one other speaker of special significance. Brian Matcham, Frank's great-nephew, whose professional life was spent in the BBC, was presenting a lecture there. It was a slightly nervous Mervin and Séamus who presented their talk, but it was well-received and generated considerable interest.

It was later that year, at Wakefield, the idea of a lecture tour of their own emerged. Mervin, Séamus and Jackie Corkhill from the Department of Tourism were investigating a new sound system that they were considering for The Gaiety. They were offered the chance to see the pantomime that evening, and were given a glossy journal describing

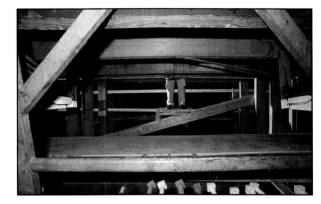

The Corsican trap from below and above during trials at The Gaiety in February 2000, with Production Manager Séamus Shea.
Photo: Island Photographics

Séamus Shea.   Photo: Island Photographics

A Gaiety Theatre presentation held at the Manx Museum, January 1999. Left to right: Séamus Shea; Nicholas Owen, Robert Fleming (Isle of Man) Ltd; Mervin Russell Stokes; Greg Horton, Robert Fleming (Isle of Man) Ltd; The Lieutenant Governor, Sir Timothy Daunt; Lady Daunt; Brian Matcham, great nephew of Frank Matcham.

Photos: Island Photographics

were presented at theatres all over the United Kingdom, as well as places such as the Theatre Museum in Covent Garden, the Theatres Trust of Great Britain, English Heritage and the Manx American Association, in America. This last was possible thanks to private sponsorship from Manx Telecom and the Manx Heritage Foundation. The rest of the tour was supported by Government, the Friends of The Gaiety and once again by Mervin finding sponsors.

From the early settlers and colonists such as Myles Standish, there is quite a powerful connection between the Manx and the Americans. Former Vice President Dan Quayle is descended from a Manx family, although that is perhaps a less persuasive argument for the Island's contribution to American life. Cleveland is seen by some as a parish of the Island, as it was founded by the Manx. As the Irish emigrated when conditions in their home country became untenable, so the Manx, and there are branches of the Manx American Association throughout the US. It's slightly unnerving how often a Manx connection appears. When planning the trip, Mervin told a friend of a friend which towns he would be visiting. "Oh! I've a friend who lives there. She could put you up I'm sure, and would you mind taking her this gift when you go ..." Taking the story of The Gaiety to America was by no means empty PR, however pleasurable it may have been; there are people who came to the Island as a direct result of the trip. One person who would have loved to visit came to a lecture in Washington. She had performed on The Gaiety's stage in 1920, and had never imagined she would see it again. At the end of the presentation, she came up to Mervin and Séamus in tears at the beauty of the restored building and the memories it evoked.

One evening lecture was particularly significant, and was held at the Manx Museum, just a few minutes walk from the theatre. Invited guests included the Lieutenant Governor and some of the Island's politicians. Séamus discovered that even people who had been associated with the building all their life were discovering aspects of it they had never seen nor suspected before, a fact that he found revealing and touching. Brian Matcham was also there. He had paid his first visit to the theatre that morning. Mervin led him in to see the auditorium at gallery level. He stood completely silent. As the silence extended, Mervin began to panic, fearing he had simply got it all horribly wrong and his guest was speechless in horror. Then Brian said: "I cannot believe that anybody would take so much trouble and lavish so much love over one of my great-uncle's buildings. Thank you." Later that day he said: "If the Old Man walked in

The Wakefield Opera House's centenary. Looking through the journal while in a bar before the show, they were discussing how to celebrate The Gaiety's one hundred years. There was no doubt they wanted to do it on a large scale. The Wakefield Opera House had put on a gala night; they wanted to do something altogether more adventurous - a season of plays? A book? Later that night (at another bar), after they had completed their duties at the pantomime, the idea was discussed further. Jackie had by this stage left the two alone and gone to her bed. Mervin and Séamus discussed centenary plans, working out how to present an extended celebration of a remarkable theatre. There would be a book. There would be a season of shows. There would be a reproduction of the musical that opened the building, 'The Telephone Girl'. The difficulty lay in telling the interested people in the United Kingdom about the theatre. How were they going to tell the target audience, and anyone else interested, about this extraordinary building and its rejuvenation? The best answer they came up with was simple in description, if a little labour intensive. They would have to tell them personally. So it was decided to produce a proper lecture, write to all the theatres that might be interested and organise a tour. The response from the initial letter was sufficiently promising to spur them into actually doing it. Over the next three years, their lectures today, it would be exactly as it was on the last day he saw it." Brian was a friend to Mervin, Séamus and David, and the restoration, until his sudden death in 1999. He pointed out, though, that Frank Matcham would have been surprised to see his work restored. As a man perpetually innovating and taking advantage of new technology he would probably have preferred, if given the chance, to rebuild the whole place. This made Mervin feel rather queasy, but delighted Séamus. The point is indicative of an aspect of their professional relationship. Mervin will determine where some new system for lights or sound must go, and what effect it may have on the fabric of the building. Séamus determines what that equipment should be. Both know The Gaiety has to maintain its role as the only theatre on the Island and introduce new technology regularly to keep it up to date with the expectations of touring companies and local amateur dramatic societies. The Gaiety's history is filled with neglect, and both know they have to ensure it is not ignored any longer. As a result, the pretty Victorian playhouse boasts some of the most advanced equipment in the world. This means Séamus' contribution to The Gaiety's survival is crucial. He is sympathetic to the building and Mervin's requirements concerning its fabric, whilst determined as Production Manager to ensure the best is available for his staff and the performances. At the same time, Mervin, who professes to be uncomfortable with anything built after 1903, knows he can trust Séamus' judgement on the installation of new equipment and be secure in the knowledge that the visual and architectural niceties will not be compromised.

1995 saw the gallery slips and the stalls papered. The result was that anyone sitting in the theatre would have a view of it more or less as it was in 1900. There were still major works to undertake, but halfway through the restoration project, The Gaiety's essential nature had been re-established for the audience. This was never going to be enough, though. There was a great deal more to do in rapidly decreasing time to bring the whole project to anything approaching its end.

The emergency lighting system was as chaotic as the heating had been. There was a great variety of different styles that apart from anything else could have been dangerous, and it was all removed. New emergency lighting was placed at floor level in the auditorium, a move applauded by the Fire Service. New lights were placed at the entrance to the stalls. These were reproduction lamps by Sugg Lighting Company of London and even this detail paid its respects to the spirit of 1900. Where it could be proved there had been a gas bracket for the original

emergency lighting, a reproduction gas tap was included on the new light fitting. At the same time, the plethora of differing signs, most of which were inappropriate as well as inconsistent in design, were removed and replaced with gold leaf on mahogany.

At the end of the year, attention turned to the frieze at the rear of the dress circle. The photographs suggested a plaster frieze running at the base of the barrel-vault. After closer examination of the original photograph from 1900, a canvas frieze seemed more likely. This was proved when removing the lighting box which had been taken to the rear of the circle in 1982. It was a hideous structure that protruded into the rear three rows of the circle, and there was no great unhappiness when it was removed and the space for the lighting controller made more sympathetic. During the demolition, under three strands of lead-covered electrical wiring, there was a fragment of canvas, painted with a design that matched the photographs. With the colours and the design of the frieze captured, Howell and Robinson, a local firm, were able to recreate and rehang it.

1996 was a relatively quiet year for the restoration. The old coffee kiosk in the promenade area behind the dress circle was removed and replaced with a kiosk that was designed from pictures of other Matcham bars and built to the correct scale for the room. It was given large mirrors that had the effect of appearing to double the width of a rather narrow promenade. The area was recarpeted in the Matcham carpet, and it was wallpapered as well, linking the foyer and the corridors together literally and in design terms.

Running concurrently with the work itself was the continuous effort to generate the money needed to do it. The Friends of The Gaiety Restoration Sub-committee was administering funds brought in from any number of different initiatives. There were special events and fund-raisers, from coffee-mornings to shows from the likes of Rick Wakeman, the Island-resident composer and pianist with the group Yes and a solo

The recreation of the frieze at the rear of the dress circle. At the top, an enlargement of the photograph from 1900; Middle: The fragment discovered below the lead-covered electrical wiring.

Bottom: The recreated frieze in position. Below: a 'before and after' of the promenade kiosk, reconstructed in Frank Matcham's style based on pictures from other Matcham bars.

Photos: Island Photographics

artist. There was a seat-plaque scheme where the name of the donor would be attached to the required seat in return for a donation. Performers were regularly asked to comment on the beauty of the theatre in a closing speech and to ask the audience to give generously towards the restoration on their way out.

The 'Manx Last Night of the Proms', a shameless copy from the United Kingdom institution, was started in 1985 and generates a substantial sum for the restoration fund each year. It is an example of an idea being taken up by the public and becoming almost self-perpetuating. It also allows business-minded friends a chance to use their entrepreneurial skills. A consortium of businesses headed by Clive Dixon of Moore Stephens, buys a substantial number of tickets, adds on a reception and a meal, and then sells the tickets to colleagues who know they will be treated to a fine night out of food and wine and throwing streamers during the chorus of 'Land of Hope and Glory'. The profits made on these tickets then go back to the Friends of The Gaiety. This one idea alone has brought in some £4,000 a year.

Mervin is not one to pass up an opportunity. The Isle of Man has in recent years been promoting itself as a film location. 'Waking Ned', for example, was made entirely on the Isle of Man and gave a small but growing industry a considerable fillip with its success. It hardly rivals the finance sector as a business - as yet, anyway - but it is unquestionably glamorous and wealthy, and means there will be people around the world who know of the Island for itself rather than as a typing error for the Isle of Wight (which has happened). The Gaiety has of course great potential as a location for period films, and when 'The Harpist' was made in 1996, The Friends of The Gaiety provided the audience in return for a donation to the cause. Film makers can create problems too, when they take over a location and turn it into the landscape for their production. Mervin was incensed when the one remaining vestige of The Pavilion (a sign painted on a wall on the stage left rear of the building) was painted over, and made his displeasure known to the director. It was reinstated very smartly and a donation to the restoration fund was gratefully received.

Early in 1996, the Minister for Tourism was at a concert at The Gaiety. On the side of the stage were stacks of large, ugly speakers that served as the sound system for the theatre. Mr Brown was so little impressed by the sound quality of the evening's entertainment, that he insisted Mervin and Séamus find a new system. This was something the two had campaigned for over quite a long period, but they lacked Ministerial authority. They did manage to ensure the remit for the expenditure included a requirement that whatever they purchased had to be invisible. The decision was taken to find the best sound reinforcement system (SRS) for the job. The difference between a proper sound system and an old touring set of speakers is immeasurable. The Gaiety had a second-hand touring system where parts of the speakers were broken, there was no proper balance to the sound, and it looked completely out of place. Despite all of which, it was better than its predecessor, about which the less said the better. The distinction between an SRS and a public address system is that the latter just shouts at you, while SRS brings the sound to you. It distributes whatever sound is on stage all the way around the theatre in little speakers that can be hidden away in walls and ceilings. The wiring is also invisible. To some extent, if you can tell you're hearing it, it's not working properly. The impression should simply be that you can hear what is happening on stage. There is no need for huge speakers that have to fill the theatre with noise, because each speaker only has to send the sound a few feet. It also includes a delay system. When you watch a play, you hear things as you are watching. Because sound travels much slower than light, you see the words being said slightly before you hear them. The body's innate understanding of this means that if you are any distance from the stage and hear a sound at the same time as you see it made, it is rather unnerving. So each speaker in the SRS has a delay fitted into it, which is set by the operator, to allow an appropriate time-lapse between the sound being picked up by the microphones on stage and being played through the speaker. The people at the front will hear the words or music just before the people at the back - exactly as they would without any amplification. It's a delicately balanced method of bringing the sound closer. The system is also very clever. If a particular

performer has preferences in terms of the sound he or she likes, this can be programmed in to make it easy to accommodate when the artist returns. Or the pre-set required can be sent by the performer's agent and fed in to the system in advance. It would even be possible to cater for an audience sitting on just one side of the auditorium, should such an event ever occur. The point is that the system is flexible and uses computing technology in an area that had previously relied upon brute force. The decision to go with a computerised sound control known as Media Matrix was a brave move, and one that typifies Mervin and Séamus' working practice. This was the first time such a system had been installed in a theatre on a permanent basis. There had been plenty of experimental versions and some placed in theatres for a brief period, but never as the full-time sound system. So The Gaiety Theatre, at some 96 years of age, was breaking new ground. A revolutionary new model had been installed which made no compromises in terms of quality and had no detrimental implications for the architectural integrity of the building.

A similar story was the case with the stage lighting system. The one in place when Mervin arrived lasted until the very early 70s, along with a huge Furse lighting board that was situated above the left-hand side of the stage. This was replaced with a set of proper theatrical lanterns, complete with a new dimmer-board. This was placed in the box on the right hand side of the auditorium. Lighting boards are the control panels that are operated to raise and dim the lights upon the stage and in the auditorium. It is by no means unusual to place them in boxes previously used by the audience, but it is a curious thing to do nonetheless. It usually means a box is curtained off, damaging the visual balance of the auditorium, and occasionally the operator can be seen at his or her task or peering inquisitively at the audience, neither of which assists the willing suspension of disbelief required for an ideal night at the theatre. At The Gaiety in the early 80s, Duggie Chapman decided to move the lighting board. His solution was radical, if not much more pleasing. He constructed a massive lighting box that ran the full length of the back of the circle, cut into three rows of seats, obscured the barrel-vault ceiling, and was double glazed, which meant no-one in it could hear anything. At least it rebalanced the auditorium. In the early 90s, Mervin decided to pull down the box, although keeping the lighting board where it was, but on a bench. This removed the separation between audience and technical staff, and the lack of soundproofing put an end to some of the more ribald (or slanderous) conversations between the staff, who are all able to communicate through microphones on headsets. Mervin reinstated the waist-high wooden barrier, and took out the last row of seats, which had been added in the 30s. For the centenary, the lighting board and lights were to be moved again. To reveal the front of the amphitheatre, the lighting bar was removed altogether. A new position in the gallery ceiling was created for a bar that can be retracted to suit the theatre's requirements. When there is a show on, it is lowered; when the theatre is dark or there is a tour of it under way, the lights are raised and hidden. As a result, stronger lanterns were required, since they were further from the stage. New follow-spots were added, also of a stronger beam, and the lighting and sound positions were removed to the gallery as well. This created a self-contained operational area for lights, sound and follow-spots and allowed the area at the back of the dress circle to become a promenade area again. The dimmer switches themselves, which are the electrical equipment that determine the intensity of the lights, were installed in 1995 and were in good order. Once again, a change has been introduced that allows new technology to be a part of a functioning theatre and is better for the operators and audience, but also sympathetic to the design requirements of a 100-year-old building.

For all its technological innovation, The Gaiety has its proper share of the paranormal. No theatre worth its salt is without a ghost and The Gaiety can boast at least three. There have been many people who have believed they were 'not alone' when in the gallery slips, and occasionally the follow-spot operators, perched at the point where the gallery meets the amphitheatre, have sensed someone watching them. The three ghosts who have been witnessed - rather than an unnerving sensation of 'something' being in the same part of the theatre - are a lady dressed in black, an unseen pair of hands and a man. Mervin has had two encounters with the lady. Once, after a show, in a hot but empty auditorium, he was in one of the boxes and noticed her sitting all alone in the stalls as if enjoying the performance. He turned away and when he looked back saw she was no longer there. He looked into the space she should have been but there was no sign of her. At that moment, he became extremely cold, and the hairs on the back of his neck shot to attention.

She appeared once again during a theatre tour, and was clearly visible behind the group who were being shown the progress of the restoration and given a brief history lesson. Tours were another means Mervin used to bring a greater understanding of the theatre to the population, and

it allowed people to donate to the cause once he had demonstrated what a fine and noble undertaking he was attempting. The woman was dressed entirely in black with a hat, and once again when Mervin looked away she disappeared completely. This may have been because she disagreed with him on some aspect of the tour but she has not been seen since to explain. The unseen hands have also made their presence felt twice. On one occasion, in the midst of a serious crisis, a troubled Mervin was walking upstairs to his office, and a hand gripped him by the shoulder hard enough to stop him in his tracks. He could feel the pressure of the thumb and fingers, but felt in no way threatened; in fact he felt considerably reassured. So much so that he said 'Thank you'; and the pressure was released immediately. The other occasion was again during a theatre tour. Mervin had arrived late and was racing upstairs to turn on the house lights. In his haste, he found he was lost and was stumbling blindly around in the dark when a pair of hands took his waist and pushed him forward against a light switch. He pressed it, and it was precisely the one he had been looking for.

The other ghostly appearance was witnessed by a Friend of The Gaiety, who was rather startled by a man walking out of the wall in a passageway between the street and the auditorium at stalls level on the audience's right. The man walked across the passageway and through the opposite wall. This is not a huge number of sightings in thirty years, but it is noticeable that the ghosts have only shown themselves when the theatre is busy.

One thing a theatre as venerable as The Gaiety requires is a fire alarm system. Before the late 90s, it was hard-wired detectors with lengths of cable fitted indiscriminately between them. This was an improvement on a method employed beforehand that required a pre-recorded message to be sent to the telephone operator if a fire was detected. On one occasion (a false alarm, thankfully) the alarm went off triggering the telephone call. Unfortunately, the recorded message malfunctioned, and all the operator heard was: "Fire at The G . . .". The operator had the presence of mind to work out what this strangulated message meant and called the brigade out, but the near-failure led to the newer, better but ugly installation. By 1997, an upgrading of the system was genuinely required, which was as well, because Mervin could hardly stand the one in place. The one chosen was the same as that installed at Windsor Castle after the disastrous fire there. A radio-controlled system was put in place with heat and smoke sensitive detectors (known as 'heads') placed in areas of the theatre where it would have been impossible before.

This was made possible because the heads were battery powered, and sent any signal by radio telecommunication. They were literally wire-less. Places that were previously inaccessible could now be protected and, where there had only been a couple of detectors, it was possible to place a cluster of up to eight heads. Again, this was the first permanent installation of this kind in a theatre and the policy of including the newest and best while retaining the aesthetic of the original was maintained.

Mervin's work with Séamus in these technical areas demonstrates how the effective use of contemporary technology can be matched with a nineteenth-century aesthetic to everyone's benefit. The theatre is better lit, has a better sound system and is safer because of the kind of innovative technology Séamus sees as necessary in a contemporary theatre. But that same innovation makes it all the more acceptable in a nineteenth-century one. Marrying the two allows the historical value of the decoration to be fully exposed while maintaining a workable space for demanding theatrical companies who have every right to expect certain standards of stage management. It also allows the audience an entirely satisfying evening at a theatre where they are surrounded by the pomp and luxury of the gilt and plaster-work, but can also see and hear the show properly, while the building itself is better protected than it has ever been from the threat of fire that destroyed so many other theatres of its day. With all these technical improvements, it was funds from central Government that covered the cost, as it was with the stage itself.

The performers were to benefit from the restoration as well. The stage had not been reboarded since it was first laid, and it was in a poor state by 1997. It had seized up completely in places, after years of being painted and hammered and trod and danced on. Age had had an impact, too; water reached it, warping the boards. In truth, it was not solely - or even principally - for the benefit of the performers that it needed to be redone. If the understage machinery were to be put back in working order, the stage had to able to accommodate the traps. This was not simply a matter of pulling up boards and getting pitch pine from a DIY store. Anderson Sawmills near Crewe were approached. They were sent precise instructions for the one-off project. The timber used was called Danta, a mahogany-like wood, and a renewable resource, capable of being grown and used in a sustainable fashion. The wood had to be of a certain density to satisfy fire services, and required precise milling to suit the complex

The removal of the old stage floor and the new one in place. Below: Jimmy Kelly of Charmer Builders, fixing the new tops to the bridge frames.

Photos: Island Photographics

requirements of the stage. It demands much more than tongue-and-groove because it has to do much more than stand still. Apart from being able to withstand the constantly shifting weights of the performers and the scenery, it has to be able to have substantial sections removed without losing strength, and has to shift in its place while remaining stable. It needs to be firm and extremely flexible. Séamus had to saw bits of the stage out to get the profile correct, which were then sent to David Wilmore. The timber had to be specially dried in a kiln then left for six weeks in the theatre to acclimatise. While this was being done, the old trap tops had to be ripped out, but they were carefully copied before they were destroyed. Almost the entire stage was reboarded with the new material, the areas unaffected by the traps being done first. 'Almost', because there is one area where there is a strip of original Gaiety stage still in place; the fire corridor on the right-hand side. This is because the corridor was added as a requirement of fire regulations brought in after the Summerland fire, a tragic and avoidable inferno at a family leisure centre. This corridor was built over the existing stage, and it is sentimentally reassuring that the old floorboards are still there.

The new flooring was installed by Charmer Builders, Limited, from Castletown, and in particular by Jimmy Kelly who was involved in many aspects of the work on the stage, and whose understanding and patience were invaluable. Charmers have worked on other prestigious restoration projects around the Island, including the renovations in Castle Rushen, Castletown. The new stage looked magnificent, and to maintain it, there is no painting or hammering into it allowed. It is covered normally with a black, dance floor to protect it, but it can be seen in all its roseate glory at concerts and recitals.

The technical staff at The Gaiety comprises Séamus and a team of four beneath him. Between them, they can adapt the theatre to accommodate full-scale ice extravaganzas to one-man shows and

The generating room, now cosmetically restored.

Photo: Island Photographics

The new double-purchase counterweight system.

Photo: Island Photographics

everything in between, and take a genuine pride in being able to deal with the historical obligations and the contemporary technical ones. Facilities backstage have been upgraded significantly, too. There is a crew room near where the generators are housed. One of the generators has been there since the thirties and one since the theatre opened; both have been cosmetically restored and look like magnificent, somnolent steam engines although neither is operational. There is a full internal relay system to the properly equipped dressing rooms, now complete with mirrors, heating and lavatories, as well as reasonable furniture. There are eight dressing rooms, a laundry room and two shower rooms, allowing some 60 or 70 people to be accommodated. The iron, or safety curtain, is electrically operated as is the house curtain, but this latter can be worked manually if required. The counterweight system is double-purchase, because the shape of the building restricts the vertical distance that the counterweights can travel. The double-purchase system means The Gaiety can still accommodate the scenic needs of the companies that visit the theatre. The paint floor has been restored, and the wing forks are still in use. This frequently causes a stir with touring companies, who are convinced they have seen everything a theatre has to offer. They forget, in its marriage of the unbelievably old and extraordinarily new, The Gaiety is unique.

1998 was nearly a disastrous year. Wet weather was among the causes of water seeping through into the left side of the auditorium. The damp removed all the paper from the amphitheatre level through the box corridor and down as far as the lower part of the stalls. There were, remarkably, benefits to be

One of the wing forks.

Photo: Island Photographics

had from this. During the investigations into the damage, it was discovered some of the roof cladding and roof supports were rotten, a finding that would otherwise have remained hidden and could have lead to substantially greater problems if untreated.

The Government paid for repairs to the cladding and supports and the insurance covered the other damage. It meant more work, though. Some of the stencilled frescoes in the Gallery Slips were delaminated as a result, and damage was also caused to the plaster dado just below the ceiling coving. This meant there was a chance to remove the frescoes and send them down to the International Fine Art Consultancy in Bristol for restoration. It also required Hales and Howe - fibrous plaster specialists - to come to the theatre and restore the coving.

When it came to the exit corridors, it was decided to go ahead with a restoration rather than simply making sure they were safe because there was reliable evidence from scrapings of what the original colours were. Two-tone pink, dark on the bottom, lighter above, with a black line separating them was the arrangement discovered beneath the Portafleck. At times, it felt as though keeping the top layer would have been an easier option. Removing the Portafleck from all the corridor walls took a huge amount of patience and effort from one man and his grinder. The ceilings, which had been an equally resilient Artex, had that removed by a similarly arduous process and were then painted a flat white. When the walls were scraped of all their paint, the back of an original Promenade arch of The Pavilion façade was discovered, in red Ruabon brick with its sandstone dressings. This has been left as a feature on one staircase leading to the gallery. The corridors from the back of the pit were found to be stencilled, a very unusual feature, with no explanation to account for it. The Briggs' Patent Panic Bolts on all the emergency exit doors were in different materials for the different classes. Brass was the metal of choice for the upper class, iron for the lower, and the difference is evident also in the handrails throughout the building. There are existing examples of this distinction at the Royal Hall in Harrogate, although at The Gaiety before the centenary they have yet to be reinstated.

More visibly, and very much more part of recreating the full splendour of the experience of theatre-going in 1900, the house curtains were reproduced as accurately as possible by Creasey's of London. The house curtains sit in front of everything else on stage and are the ones that are imagined rising when the expression 'curtain up' is used. In 1900, they cost £70 all in. In 2000, for the same specification, they cost £75,000. Among the features of The Gaiety's curtains is the fact they were tableau style. This was not in the slightest way unique to the building in 1900, but adds to the sense of occasion and is rarely seen in modern theatres. Curtains hung in the tableau style do not

Left: The original house curtain designs on opening night, 1900, enlarged from the original photograph.
Photo: Mervin Russell Stokes

Above: Discovering the original colour scheme in the fire escape corridors. Above right: The corridor restored with light fitting and stained glass also in place.
Photo: Island Photographics

Right: Original stencilling discovered under later paintwork in the stalls corridor.
Photo: Island Photographics

simply rise and fall, but are pulled apart from six to eight feet up, then sweep dramatically up. This leaves a curve - or swag - of curtain visible from the centre of the proscenium at its top down to the side, where a small section hangs down completing the elegant framing of the stage. The material was patterned mohair, while the valence and the swags of the boxes and the proscenium pelmet were the same colour, but crushed rather than patterned. The house curtains were decorated with ropes, tassels and fringes of a dark viridian green flecked with gold. These huge curtains weigh about 250 kilos each, and are too heavy to lift by hand, so their lifting mechanism is motorised. However, should the more modern style of straightforward rise and fall be required, it can be done manually. As with much of the work on The Gaiety, the correctness of the restoration depended on chance, detection, determination and skill. The material for the new curtains could be colour matched exactly because a patch of the original material was found snagged on a nail in the grid. That this was indeed the correct colour was confirmed by comparing the grid find with a piece of material still in position lining the back of the barrier at the rear of the pit. Creasey's have taken the colour and produced a copy that uses the same heavy mohair as the original. The new curtains were embroidered in a style similar to the

The original design for the box curtains, showing beaded glass shades.
Photo: Mervin Russell Stokes collection

lettering on those at The Royal Opera House in Covent Garden, but have the 'GTOH' (Gaiety Theatre and Opera House) monogram from Matcham's design found on the ceiling. Around this are placed the initials of the private companies that have sponsored the remake. The box curtains were replaced and hung as they should be, and the boxes themselves redecorated. Researching them, Mervin discovered the distinction between them and the other seats was even more pronounced, and their high status even more accentuated than simply being very private and expensive. They are papered in the same colour as the caramel of the ceiling with a small, sprigged flower design picked out in bronze colour on the paper. The boxes were lit by beaded glass shades suspended from four cupped petals of copper or bronze that hung down from the electric cable. The colour of the glass beads is unknown, although it is thought they paled in tone from viridian to white. Up to the centenary, these light-fittings had not been completed, but the existing lights were hung lower than previously on an electric cable covered in the same material as the box curtains as they would have been in 1900, with the existing crystal shades. As part of the work to complete the correct colouring for the auditorium, the padded, velvet tops to the tiers have been covered in crushed viridian mohair, as they were originally. Throughout, with the exception of the gallery and amphitheatre areas, the seats are of a standard cinema layout. This is partly an acceptable compromise, partly the cost and priority of reupholstering perfectly serviceable seats. They are not correct, but are better than if they had been replaced with entirely modern equivalents, and their royal blue covers will, in time, be replaced with the viridian mohair.

The same desire to have a continuity of colour was evident with the orchestra rail. A brass copy of the original was reintroduced to the auditorium, and the door to orchestra pit placed in the centre of the rail where it should be, as any Musical Director will tell you. The curtain that hangs from the rail was specially made along with its fringing, which was viridian with gold, mirroring the house curtains and the act drop. This thematic colouring continues in the light and draught excluders throughout the interior. These curtains are found wherever there is an entrance to the auditorium, and are to have their swagged pelmets reinstated.

The Manager of The Gaiety does not enjoy the luxury of a house on the premises, which is perhaps as well given how much of his life Mervin has already spent in the theatre. He might never have seen daylight in the last twenty years if he had no cause to leave. As it is, the offices used by Mervin are situated on the third floor at the front of the building in a room that used to be the poster room. That is not quite as small an area as it may sound, since it was the storehouse and paint-shop for the posters for all The Palace and Derby Castle Company attractions, which is a fair number of posters, and they were clearly kept in some luxury. It is by no means certain what the room was for when originally built since it only became the poster room later on, but it is possible that it was an office when the building was constructed. The room has a view over the sea from behind the statue of Progress.

Another room with a similar view was the dress circle bar, or retiring room for patrons in the fauteuils, Governor's and family Circles. It was above the foyer at first floor level. A handsome room of good proportion, it was square and had access to the balcony on the façade. Originally the room was laid out with a mahogany circular bar with a white Carrara marble top, and had corner banquettes. The original decoration above the panelling was a Chinese-style wallpaper in green with gold embossed chrysanthemums. This was very much in keeping with the continuing late-Victorian interest in all things Oriental, typified in the Gilbert and Sullivan's 'The Mikado'. The original paper still exists on the walls, but it was discovered too late to be recreated for the centenary. It is intended to have a copy made and the paper rehung on the walls in a few years' time. When the theatre lost, or simply failed to renew, its licence to serve alcohol, the bar area became the boardroom for the Directors of The Palace and Derby Castle Company. There is no clear reason for the decision to stop serving alcohol. As a result, the bar suffered the same fate as the rest of the theatre and became rather neglected and run-down. It was sub-divided into small offices until 1979, when the Government opened it up and returned it to its original use - having restored the licence. A straight bar was installed along one side. This was a great improvement, but the bar was very much a late 70s style and could hardly be said to represent a restoration. The centenary work brought it much closer to its original state. The bar could not be a round one because of modern health and safety requirements, so a half-round bar was fitted along one wall. This is a style Matcham had used elsewhere. The panelling was reinstated, as was the white Carrara marble. The wallpaper was of the same design as the foyer paper, and the carpet on the staircase has been carried through into the bar. When the ceiling was stripped, original stencil work was found under the layers of dirt and later painting, which will be reinstated along with the original design for the wallpaper. For the moment, the ceiling is painted in the caramel colour that forms such a part of the overall colour scheme.

There is only one original lavatory. This will be restored using original parts that have survived from the others in the building, and it is hoped the more modern ones will be refurbished in sympathy with the original designs when the time comes to upgrade them.

All the original parts of the box offices exist, but only the sections facing the foyer are in use. None of the original furniture inside remains, although the sun-burner control panel is still in the one on the right, and all the windows are original. Only one of the box offices is in regular use; the other contains the back-up computer system for the tickets and takings, but is designed to serve as a box office should demand require it. Even so, there is a vestige of The Gaiety's history in the regular box office. There is a wooden cash drawer - a block of wood with two smooth round hollows in it for money. All over it are the signatures of various members of the Barwell family - Fred, the second manager of the theatre; his brother who was killed at Dunkirk; and various other members of the family who have served the theatre over the years.

The Gaiety is also unique because of its reinstatement of those aspects of the original design that were class-based. The systematic series of distinctions between the lower and upper classes is part of the building's fabric. To restore the building with anything approaching a sympathetic understanding of its architecture required most of the visible aspects of this division to be re-created. So the fauteuils area has its wallpaper and perfect view of the exquisite ceiling, while the pit has its tiles and the plain underside of the Governor's and family circles. There have been, of course, additions to the house to accommodate the changes in audience expectations and blur these boundaries. The pit and fauteuils area is now simply the stalls, and there is carpeting throughout. All the seats in the theatre, except in the gallery and amphitheatre, are tip-up, comfortable and equally sized. There is no fifth row division between the Governor's circle and the Family circle - it's just the circle. All these tie in with the common sense aspects of a restoration in a working theatre, quite apart from having to be suitable for modern fire safety regulations. But the late twentieth century quite rightly deplores institutional class distinction, just as it does racism. For all the inconsistencies, this is the action of a civilised society attempting to further noble aspirations. It can lead, however, to a kind of outraged posturing at an imagined slight. Most people accept that seats nearer the Stage will cost more than those at the back. There is little complaint at boxes being more expensive. It is

generally understood that certain luxuries come at a price. This does mean that poorer people - or those who choose to pay less - sit farther away, but this is not based on a fundamental exclusion policy running through the heart of society. Within The Gaiety's fabric, such divides are visible and intentional.

The barrier between the pit and the fauteuils is a straightforward wall, a brutal division. It is much more obtrusive than the one between the gallery and the amphitheatre, where the division seems to chime in almost imperceptibly with the rest of the décor. Moreover, the one upstairs is not at the heart of the centrepiece of the building, and the decoration around it does not change with such abruptness as the one between pit and fauteuils. When Mervin decided to reinstate this latter barrier, there was powerful and vocal opposition on the basis it was reintroducing a class distinction and reducing those behind it to the status of second class citizens. To Mervin, this was a perfect example of MacAulay's 'periodical fits of morality' and just as ridiculous. There was no forcing people of any type to sit behind it and there was no loss of sight to those who did. There was not even a price divide at the barrier. This was deliberate on Mervin's part, who shifted the price change between front and rear stalls back three rows to accommodate the liberal community, demonstrating he was conscious of the problems he might face. However, the protests show the complexity of the issue for those who accept higher prices for better seats, but would see it as social exclusion if there were any formal distinction between the seats themselves. The irony is that everyone in The Gaiety can see and hear perfectly wherever they sit.

A change in price might be easier to excuse if there was an actual difference in the standard of comfort enjoyed by the patrons in different sections of the house. Mervin put the barrier back in place because the building demanded it, although he faced execration in some quarters for doing so. Those who were antagonistic did not raise any

The reinstated barrier between the fauteils and pit showing the dramatic changes in décor that separated the classes in 1900.

Photo: Island Photographics

The Bust of Frank Matcham by Amanda Barton.
Photo: Island Photographics

concerns about the view of the ceiling from the fauteuils being altogether better than from the pit; nor did they demand ornate gilt plasterwork be placed on the underside of the circle. Strangest of all, there was no comment from them when the barrier was reinstated between the gallery and amphitheatre. But then, those are the cheap seats, and hidden away from most people's gaze.

Having made the decision to reintroduce the barrier, Mervin had to hope it worked architecturally. Thankfully, it did. It ties the two sides of the theatre together and makes it more intimate, reducing any sensation of the space being like a large cinema. It has the additional advantage of accommodating a particularly small house, and giving the theatre the ambience of a studio, making audience and actors more comfortable if the numbers are low. However, the Fire Department was at first unsure of it for safety reasons. The idea of a barrier, after all, was to stop people moving from one place to another. Matcham's design in 1900 made it easier for different sections of the audience to reach different exits, and thus avoid the possibility of a panic rush to one door with the consequent crushing and slowing of movement. This was, however, inconsistent with late twentieth century thinking and could have presented an insurmountable difficulty. The brigade, though, were extremely helpful as they had been throughout the restoration work, and allowed it on condition that there were doors inserted in the barrier at the aisles, and that the seat that used to be situated in the fauteuils on the central aisle not be reinstated. In the Governor's circle and family circle the divide, which was always more notional than practical, has not been restored. This is partly because the circle area still had work to be done on it once the centenary was over, but also because it is less significant architecturally. It amounted solely to one seat at the point of each side aisle.

There are other aspects of these class distinctions that have yet to be reinstated. More could be done to emulate the experience of entering the theatre a hundred years ago. There used to be different floor coverings for different areas; now it is wall-to-wall carpet. There used to be benches; now most of the seats are the cushioned, tip-up variety. These changes are designed to make it more comfortable for a contemporary audience to watch a play. It is possible that the next generation will enjoy - even demand - a closer approximation to the original experience. The success of The Globe in London, designed to appear as it would have done in Shakespeare's day, shows there is such a demand. If people are prepared to stand exposed to the weather

in a re-creation of a pit with none of the conventional niceties of a contemporary venue, perhaps there will be a call for plain runners over bare boards in parts of The Gaiety. The veneer of equality in certain sections of the auditorium may be seen as unnecessary, even fundamentally flawed given the design of the building, and the work of the past decade completed through popular understanding rather than lone campaigning. Watching a play from the gallery or amphitheatre, restored to their original state is exciting enough, irrespective of the performance. As greater knowledge of what was entailed in late-Victorian entertainment becomes available to more people, the potential for this sort of virtual time-travel may increase, with the experience being part of the exercise of the imagination that theatre-going essentially is.

The Gaiety will continue to fulfil its role as the Island's theatre, even if other venues are created. It will still have to function as a modern, capable performance space and it is unlikely that it will be allowed to become a museum, even if its fabric and design can be protected by statute. For all its contemporary requirements, however, it is the embodiment of a way of life that is not so far gone, a living reminder of a facet of the past that gives it such a resonant presence. Thanks to the genius of its designer, it deserved to survive. Thanks to the dedication of a small group of enthusiasts and professionals, with the willing and generous assistance of its own community, it has. For all the little areas that have been changed, for all the necessary modernising, and for all that there are sections where the restoration has not yet reached, a decade's work has been completed. The Gaiety is the most perfect example of a theatre of its type in the British Isles, and has a value that spreads far beyond that. It bears comparison with any theatre in Europe, and probably the world. This is not just the grandiose pomp expected at a time of celebration; it is a bald fact, but it has by no means been fully understood on the Island. The restoration has been officially recognised as one of the finest undertaken and The Gaiety as the best example of what theatre-going in the Victorian age would have been like. The building has been called the prettiest theatre in the British Isles. Ten years of building, researching, discovering, financing, promoting, understanding, directing and managing, have been concluded, and all tied up with a celebratory bow on top for the centenary. There were special issue postage stamps, phone cards, the cover of the Island's telephone directory being a picture of the interior, and a specially commissioned bust of Frank Matcham for the foyer by Amanda Barton.

All that, however, is now past. It is also therefore irrelevant if the present state of the theatre is compromised in the future. The Isle of Man is in possession of a rare and precious building, one whose current exquisite state would be threatened and possibly destroyed by just one careless decision about the colour of paint to be used in redecorating. The fabric of the building has been reconstructed so carefully, so minutely, and so accurately, that its greatest danger is in its care beyond 2000. The Chief Minister of the Isle of Man Government at the time of the centenary, Donald Gelling, recognised the significance of the theatre within the Island's cultural and political world. The economy had allowed the financial assistance from Government over many years and, at the same time, the buoyancy of the finance sector made sponsorship possible. Equally, the work of the hundreds of Friends of The Gaiety and their constant fund-raising had shown how business, Government and the public could function together and bring about something 'really marvellous.' He was also clear about Mervin's role in making the restoration possible, saying it would be difficult to imagine anyone else bringing such enthusiasm to the task, and going to such lengths to make it right. Without this enthusiasm, it would never have been accomplished, a sentiment echoed by Eddie Lowey, who had been one of the people responsible for its purchase by Government and who was the political member with responsibility for it at the centenary. He said Mervin was the right man in the right job at the right time, and believed his work as Manager was a shining example of what could be achieved. Mr Gelling also recognised the significance of the building and the importance of maintaining it correctly. The Gaiety has come under the same ownership as its neighbour, The Villa Marina. In the future it is possible that a range of theatres will be seen as a necessary part of Island life. This would be something of a change in many ways for the Island.

The Manx traditions are in song and dance rather than theatre and the theatre was built for the tourists. But the population has changed and with it the expectations from Government. The danger is that commercial and convenient decisions will outweigh those made on the basis of the building's intrinsic worth. Donald Gelling believes the Government will ensure whoever is appointed to look after the building in the future will be able to offer it the same loving attention as Mervin, and is confident it will be maintained properly since so much work has been undertaken to restore it. But, as he admitted, finding someone else like Mervin to take it on is statistically unlikely, to say the least. This means the problem of proper care in the future remains.

Without some form of statutory guarantee to protect what has been done and maintain it, The Gaiety faces the danger of slipping into the disrepair that so nearly destroyed it before. It has been shown such a restriction need have no effect on its capacity to function as a place of entertainment, and its current elevation to the status of a building worthy of international attention shows it can be enhanced as a theatre, simply because more people will want to come and see it. The Gaiety Theatre and Opera House, Douglas, remains a sparkling, unique example of a spectacular talent. The future of The Gaiety looks better than it did thirty years ago, certainly; but its security and value depend upon its being cherished and valued for itself as an object of interest and beauty, not purely for its function. The Isle of Man has the chance now, in the centenary year of the theatre, to put a framework in place to guarantee its survival in the proper fashion. The danger is not one of impulsive destruction, but the gradual decline into indignity, a slow desensitising to the quality of the minutiae as well as the general. This creeping diminution can slide in through the back door unnoticed and requires the kind of tender attentiveness of a lover to see it off.

All the designs, therefore, all the architectural detail, all the patterns and colours must become the responsibility of the Island as a whole. The theatre itself was originally given to the Islanders and now it has been given to them again. Now it is time for them to accept the burdens and rewards of its preservation and promotion.

There have been many buildings of either beauty or significance that have slipped away from the Island, and become no more than nostalgic memories. The Palace Ballroom, Sir William Hillary's Fort Anne home and the general design of the whole of Douglas Promenade are just three examples within a two-mile stretch of Douglas alone. The Isle of Man is now a part of and party to a wider world, something that has not always been true in the past. Its separateness often meant isolation. Now it has the chance to present itself to a far wider market than before as a unique place constitutionally, historically and culturally. If The Gaiety is properly cared for, run efficiently and its restoration maintained, the Isle of Man will receive and deserve the world's envious admiration.

The restored auditorium.   Photo: Island Photographics

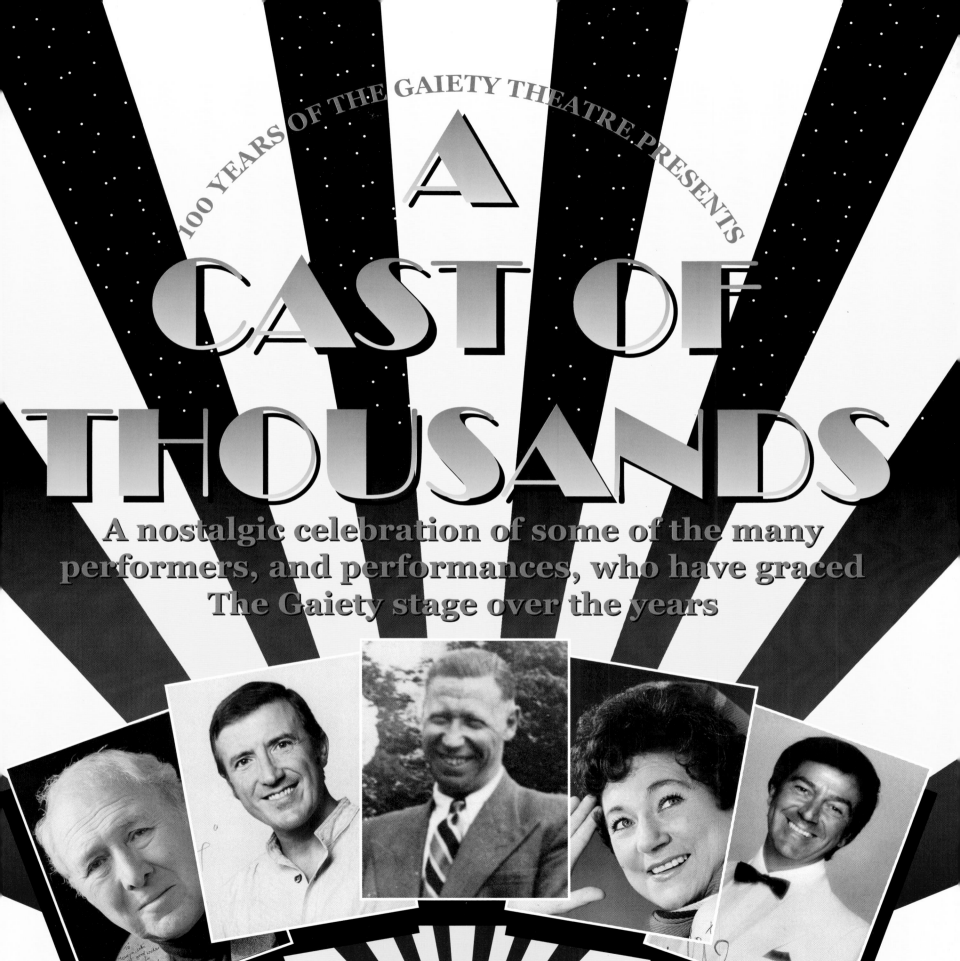

THE GOOD OLD DAYS

"Soldiers in Skirts" was an example of cross-dressers as a form of entertainment, filling theatres throughout the British Isles shortly after the Second World War. This photograph dates back to 1951, and features the cast which appeared at the Gaiety Theatre the same year.

Photo: Mervin Russell Stokes collection

Above: George Formby and his (then) wife, Beryl, pictured in the Villa Marina Gardens during a visit to the Island to perform at The Gaiety Theatre
Photo: Percy Morrison

Above: 'High Hazel', showing her considerable scale outside 'Avril's' Hair Salon in Douglas.

Photo: Mervin Russell Stokes collection

Left: The Manley Brothers, who performed at the Gaiety Theatre in 1947.

Right: Wally and Birdie's Punch and Judy show, featured at The Gaiety on September 13th, 1947.

Far right: Prolific stage performer of the forties and fifties, Doel Luscombe.

Photos: Percy Morrison

THE GOOD OLD DAYS

Stella Hartley, the energetic compere of her own variety shows 'Stella's Party Time' which she ran with her husband, Sid Myers. This would be a variety show, including accordionists, contortionists, singers and sketches. It was performed for some sixteen weeks, from May to September. It was family show of the end-of-the-pier variety, and it ran for over twenty consecutive years at The Gaiety Theatre, up to her final appearance in 1968.

Photo: Mervin Russell Stokes collection

ROBBY VINCENT
(ENOCH)

HARRY KORRIS
(MR. LOVEJOY)

CECIL FREDERICK
(RAMSBOTTOM)

HAPPIDROME

'Happidrome', a show developed and performed by Robby Vincent, Harry Korris and Cecil Frederick shortly after the Second World War.

Photo: Mervin Russell Stokes collection

1935

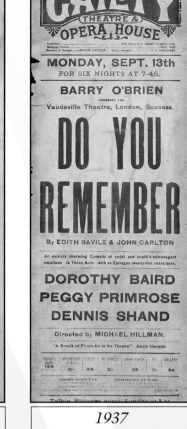

1937

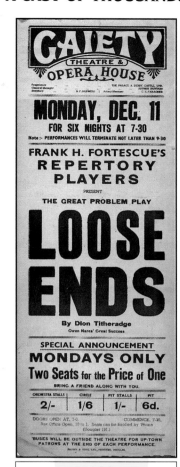

1939

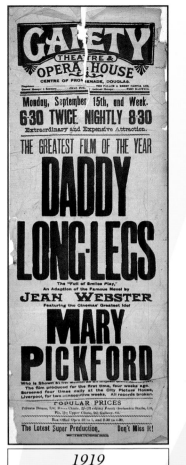

1919

1935

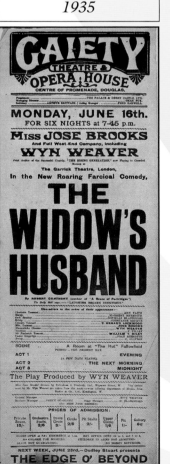

1924

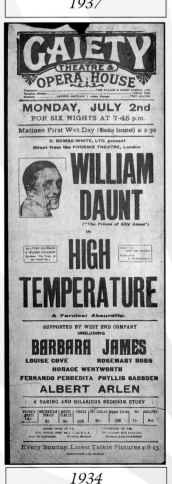

1934

1921

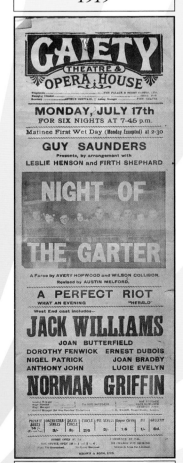

1933

1928

ALL THAT JAZZ?

Above: Acker Bilk and his band; above right: Chris Barber, and right: Kenny Ball
Photos: Mervin Russell Stokes collection

Clockwise from above: Stephan Grapelli; Cleo Laine and Johnny Dankworth; Humphrey Lyttleton; the Jaques Loussier Trio

Photos: Mervin Russell Stokes collection

MELODIES FOR YOU

Left: Classical violinist Leland Chen; above left: Country Music stars Sandy Kelly and George Hamilton IV; above: one of the nation's favourites - Anne Shelton

Photos: Mervin Russell Stokes collection

Clockwise from above left: the late, lamented Roy Castle; 'Hot Chocolate' lead singer and now solo success, Errol Brown; Dame Hilda Brackett and, alongside, accompanist Dr Evadne Hinge; presenter and classical music lover, Richard Baker.

Photos: Mervin Russell Stokes collection

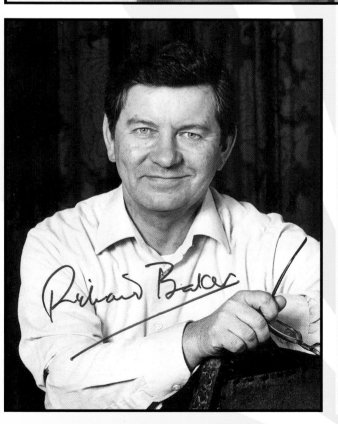

THE DRAMA CLUB

Above left: Ian Lavender; above, the distinguished star of stage and screen, the late Sir Anthony Quayle (who has Manx ancestry), who wrote " . . .with every hope for success in your venture", a reference to Mervin Stokes' plans for the restoration. Left: Film actor Simon Ward.
Photos: Mervin Russell Stokes collection

Clockwise from top left: The highly versatile comic actor, Victor Spinetti; Jack Watling; Gerald Harper; Shirley Anne-Field.
Photos: Mervin Russell Stokes collection

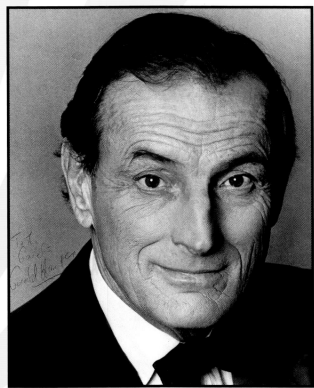

THE DRAMA CLUB

Clockwise from top left: Television regular Brian Murphy; Dame Peggy Mount, with a warm tribute to The Gaiety; Molly Sugden, a frequent visitor to the Island; distinguished actress Mona Bruce; John Bannen, renowned as "C. J." in the 'Reginald Perrin' series.
Photos: Mervin Russell Stokes collection

Above left: International star of stage and screen, Susan George; above: acclaimed actress Margaret Courteney; left: William Guest, as he appeared in 'Gaslight' at The Gaiety Theatre.

Photos: Mervin Russell Stokes collection

THAT'S ENTERTAINMENT

Left: The spectacular Danny La Rue; above: one of the Gaiety Theatre's biggest draws, Ken Dodd. A regular fixture over many years, Ken Dodd ensures a full house whenever he appears.

Photos: Mervin Russell Stokes collection

Clockwise from top left: Lounge singer and talented dancer, the late Dickie Henderson; magician Paul Daniels; the late Larry Grayson and Jack Douglas, pictured here in his "Alf Ippititimus" persona.
Photos: Mervin Russell Stokes collection

THAT'S ENTERTAINMENT

Clockwise from top left: Judith Ellis as Florrie Ford; supreme tenor Sir Harry Secombe; Dance master Wayne Sleep; television personality Jeremy Beadle; comedian Charlie Williams.

Photos: Mervin Russell Stokes collection

Clockwise from top left: Presenter Matthew Kelly; entertainer Lional Blair; comedian the late Bernie Winters who made a number of Island appearances with his brother Mike; the late Charlie Chester; presenter Nicholas Parsons; singer and television personality Des O'Connor.
Photos: Mervin Russell Stokes collection

FOLK HEROES

Clockwise from top left: Finbar Furey; The Houghton Weavers; comedic singer and guitarist Richard Digance; The Dubliners
Photos: Mervin Russell Stokes collection

1933

1924

1921

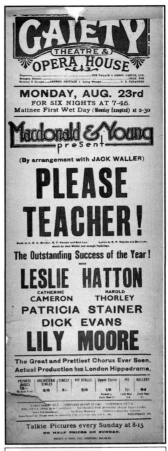

1937

1914

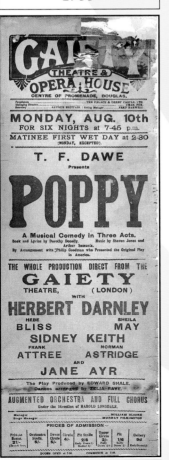

1925

1939

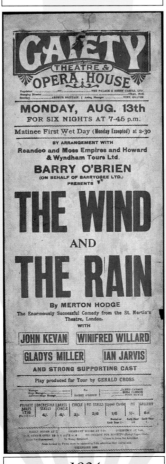

1934

1913

1902

LOCAL HEROES
The Douglas Choral Union

The Douglas Choral Union celebrated its own centenary in 1996, and continues to stage amateur dramatic productions on an annual basis. As one of Britain's oldest surviving amateur operatic socieites, the Douglas Choral Union has staged its productions at The Gaiety Theatre since 1900, when it performed 'The Gondoliers'

Winifred Adams (in white) with female "sailors" in 'Billee Taylor' (1898).
Photo: Douglas Choral Union

The male principals of 'The Mikado', in 1902.
Photo: Douglas Choral Union

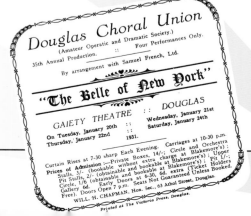

Douglas Choral Union
(Amateur Operatic and Dramatic Society.)
35th Annual Production.   ::   Four Performances Only.

By arrangement with Samuel French, Ltd.

"The Belle of New York"

GAIETY THEATRE   ::   DOUGLAS

On Tuesday, January 20th   ::   Wednesday, January 21st
Thursday, January 22nd   ::   Saturday, January 24th
1931.

Curtain Rises at 7-30 sharp Each Evening. Carriages at 10-30 p.m.
Prices of Admission :—Private Boxes, 14/-; Circle and Orchestra
Stalls, 3/- (bookable without extra charge at Blakemore's); Upper
Circle, 2/- (obtainable and bookable at Blakemore's) ; Pit 1/-;
Pit Stalls, 1/6 (obtainable and bookable at Blakemore's). (Ticket Holders
Gallery 6d. Early Doors at 6-30, 6d. extra Not Guaranteed Unless Booked.
Free). Doors Open 7 p.m. Seats Not Guaranteed Unless Booked.
WILL. H. CHAPMAN, Hon. Sec., 63 Athol Street, Douglas.
Printed at The Victoria Press, Douglas.

Right: Michael and Freda Uren from 'Fiddler on the Roof' (1973). Far right: Fred Bull as Mr Bumble in 'Oliver!' (1972)
Photo: Freda Uren

Eileen Pickard in 'A Greek Slave' (1927).

A scene from 'Bitter Sweet' (1953).
Photo: Jennifer Kewley

Frank Bull as Professor Henry Higgins in 'My Fair Lady' (1969).

THE
DOUGLAS CHORAL UNION
PRESENT

GiGi

AT THE
GAIETY THEATRE, DOUGLAS
5th-9th FEBRUARY, 1980

Above: A scene from 'Naughty Marietta' (1960). Back row, eft to right: Audrey Coole, Roy Nicholl, Wylie McDowall, Ethel Brookes, Frank Bull, Arthur Cowley. Front row: Avril Oates, Fred Bull, Betty Chapman, Allan Wilcocks, Pat Quigley, Henry Cregeen and Margaret Butterworth.
Photo: Ethel Brookes

Right: Christine Kinvig and Ernest Thorn, principals in 'Carmen' (1994).

LOCAL HEROES

The Manx Operatic Society

Formed over fifty years ago, The Manx Operatic Society have performed on The Gaiety stage annually. Their first Gaiety show was 'Vagabond King' in 1950.

'Show Boat' *(1952)*

'The Dubarry' *(1955)*

'Oklahoma!' *(1969)*

'Brigadoon' *(1961)*

'The Three Musketeers' *(1959)*

'Valley of Song' *(1965)*

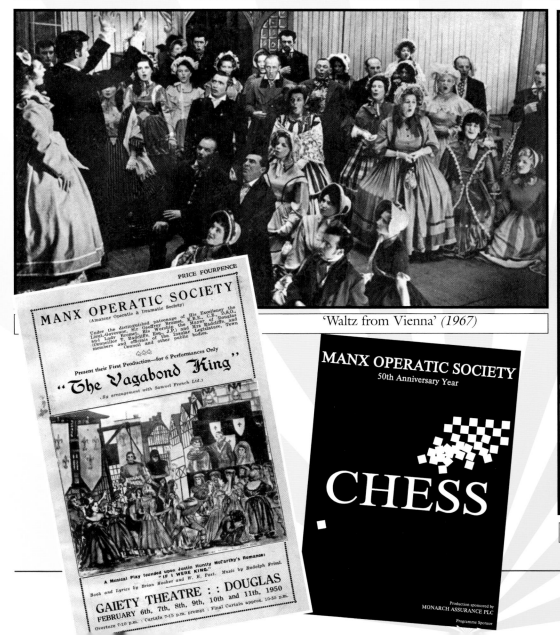

'Waltz from Vienna' *(1967)*

Lisa Danks takes the lead in 'Chess' (2000)

LOCAL HEROES
The Legion Players

In 1932, a group of fifteen young men, each of them veterans of the First World War, formed an acting troupe to help those who had returned from the War less fortunate than they. Thus, 'The Legion Players' were formed, and they have performed an average of three plays or musicals every two years ever since.

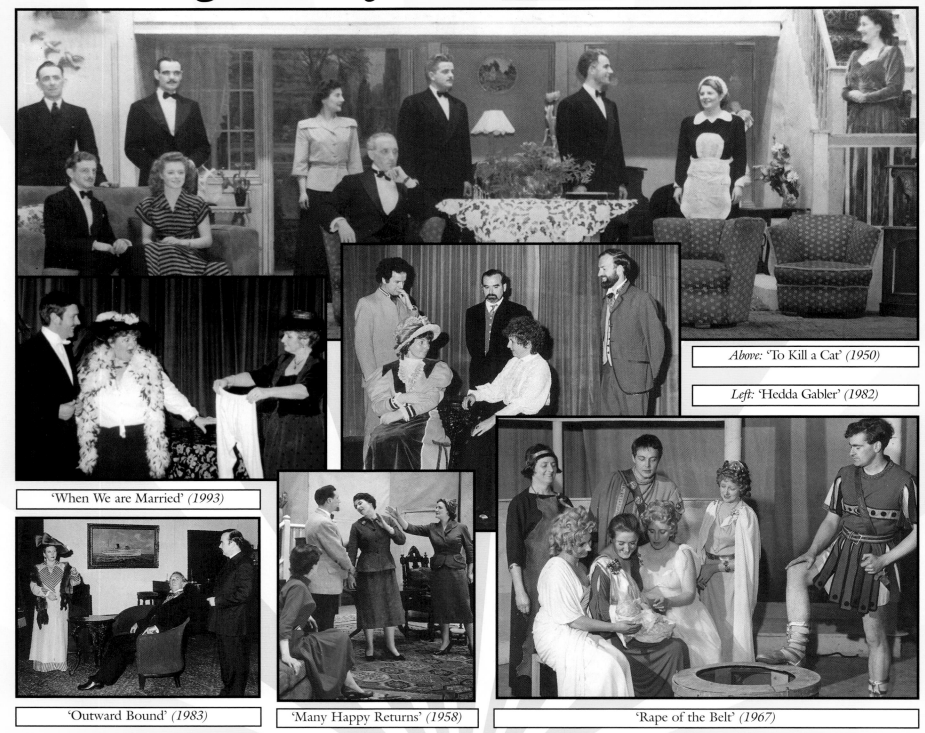

Above: 'To Kill a Cat' (1950)

Left: 'Hedda Gabler' (1982)

'When We are Married' (1993)

'Outward Bound' (1983)

'Many Happy Returns' (1958)

'Rape of the Belt' (1967)

LOCAL HEROES
Christine Wild Theatre School

Every two to three years, Christine Wild, a classically-trained dance instructor, produces spectacularly-staged musical shows which always delight both local residents and visitors. Comprised almost exclusively of children from aged five upwards, the Christine Wild Theatre School spends literally two years in rehearsal of brilliantly-choreographed routines which always result in energetic, colourful performances to full houses of appreciative audiences.

LOCAL HEROES
Albany Theatre Group

Regular performances from The Albany Theatre Group have been staged at The Gaiety Theatre in recent years. Formed in the 1980s, the Albany Theatre Group is one of the Island's newest-established ensembles.

The then Lieutenant Governor, Sir Laurence New, meets the cast after 'For the Children', a show in aid of The Save The Children Fund in 1990.

'Breath of Spring' (1986).

Rehearsals for 'A Tomb with a View' (June 1994).

Four 'evacuees': Brian Harrison, Jacques Evans, Charlotte Evans, Kimberley Manning in 'In which They Served' (November 1994).

LOCAL HEROES
The Manx Ballet Company

Young dancers backstage

'La Boutique Fantastique' *(December 1999)*

The Manx Ballet Company was formed in 1995 and, in November 1999, became a registered charity. Artistic director Ms Janette Alexander, a former pupil of former island resident and classically-trained dancer Ms Monica Mudie, revived local ballet with this company, after an absence from the local stage of almost thirty years. The Manx Ballet Company performs at The Gaiety Theatre every two years, drawing talent from schools based throughout the Isle of Man.

'Goldilocks' *(1993)*

After the first night of 'La Boutique Fantastique'.

LOCAL HEROES
The Service Players

The late Jon Pertwee, who found fame on radio and later on television, as 'Dr Who' and 'Worzel Gummidge' founded the Isle of Man Service Players in 1944. The Isle of Man was used to accommodate prisoners and, as such, soldiers, who began to perform at The Gaiety whilst stationed here. One of Jon Pertwee's legacies is the Service Players continued amateur dramatic success.

Jon Pertwee, founder of the Service Players in the Isle of Man.

Alf Devereau and Vera Craine in 'Fresh Fields' (1948).

'Here We Come Gathering' (1952).

'One Wild Oat' (November 1982).

'Rose Without a Thorn' (November 1977).

CENTENARY SPECIAL ISSUES

A set of six commemorative stamps have been issued by the Isle of Man Post Office Authority in celebration of the centenary of The Gaiety Theatre. The designs, pictured below, feature six aspects of the Theatre, namely Ballet, Musicals, Opera, Drama, Comedy and Pantomime, merged with images of The Gaiety itself. John Shimmin MHK, Chairman of the Isle of Man Post Office, said: "When deciding on which subjects to commemorate for our year's programme of nine stamp issues, it was never in doubt that The Gaiety Theatre's centenary would be top of our bill for 2000. Our stamp issue was inspired by the fact that The Gaiety is not a museum piece, but a living theatre, where a huge variety of productions is performed at both amateur and professional levels. We have tried to capture the very essence of what 'treading the boards' is all about with each of the six stamps."

For further information on the Theatre Stamp Issue,
contact the Isle of Man Post Office, P. O. Box 10M, Douglas, Isle of Man.

Manx Telecom have issued a series of six 'Phonecards' featuring different aspects of The Gaiety Theatre's unique design.
For further information on the Phonecard Issue, contact Manx Telecom, Victoria Street, Douglas, Isle of Man.

Designs for both the Stamp Issue and the Phonecard issue by The Agency Limited

The following twelve pages contain a reproduction in its entirety of an early London stage production of 'The Corsican Brothers' at the Royal Lyceum Theatre. The programme, beautifully designed, tells the tragic story for which the Corsican Trap was created - a hugely innovative creation designed to give the impression of, in this case, a ghostly apparition rsing from under the stage.

The rare and now fully recreated and fully operational Corsican Trap under the stage of The Gaiety Theatre will once again be used as the technological showpiece of The Corsican Brothers, as the play is performed especially during The Gaiety Theatre's centenary season.

The cast list is punctuated at its foot with the names of the Royal Lyceum's Stage Manager and Acting Manager; the latter being one Mr. Bram Stoker who, of course, journeyed into literary immortality with his creation, 'Dracula', a book dedicated to Hall Caine.

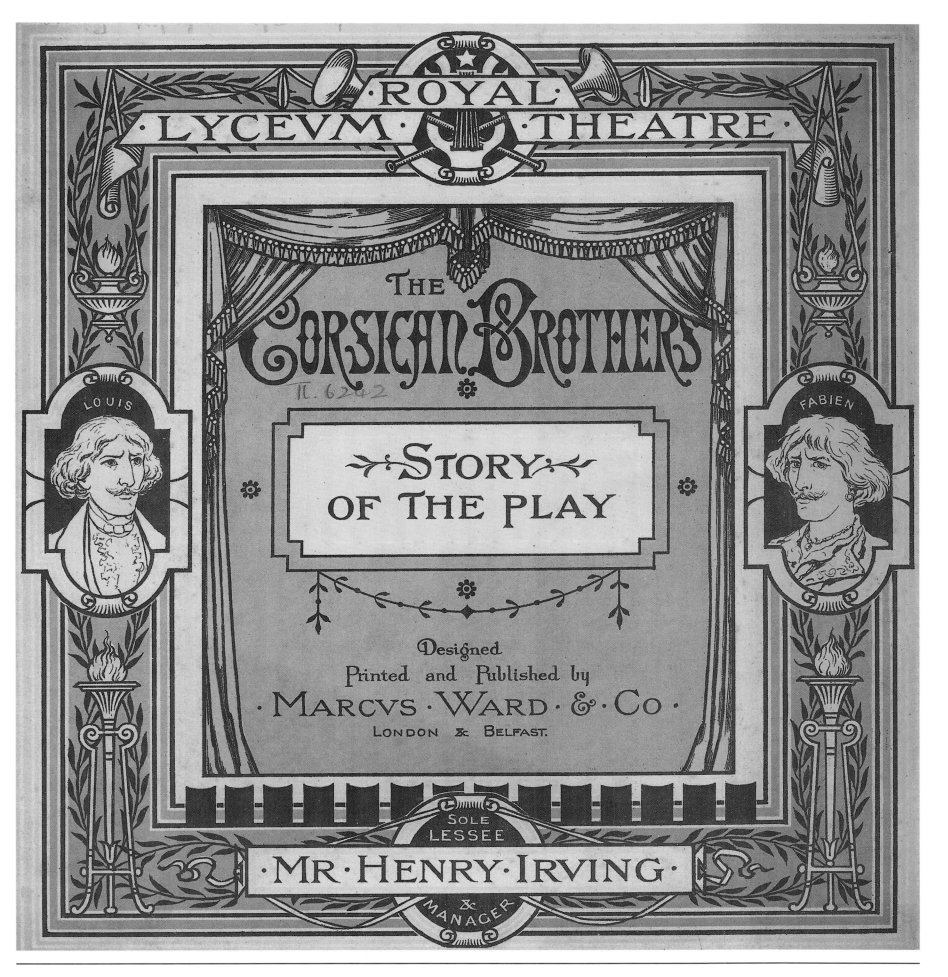

ROYAL LYCEVM THEATRE

LOUIS

FABIEN

THE CORSICAN BROTHERS

Story OF THE PLAY

Designed Printed and Published by

MARCVS WARD & Co

LONDON & BELFAST

SOLE LESSEE & MANAGER

MR HENRY IRVING

THE
CORSICAN · BROTHERS

A Legendary Drama

Founded upon DUMAS' Novel, "Les Frères Corses," and altered for the
English Stage by DION BOUCICAULT.

Scenery by HAWES CRAVEN, W. CUTHBERT, and H. CUTHBERT. Figure Paintings by C. CATERMOLE.
Overture and Incidental Music composed and arranged by HAMILTON CLARKE.
Costumes by KERSLAKE & CO., Mrs. REID, and Madame CARREE.
The Bal Masqué arranged by J. LAURIE. Machinist, Mr. MATHER. Appointments, Mr. ARNOTT.

DRAMATIS PERSONÆ.

M. Fabien dei Franchi ⎫ *Twin Brothers*		MR. IRVING.
M. Louis dei Franchi ⎭		
M. de Château Renaud		MR. W. TERRISS.
M. le Baron de Montgiron		MR. ELWOOD.
M. Meynard		MR. PINERO.
M. Martelli		MR. TYARS.
Colonna ⎫ ... ... *Corsican Peasants*		⎰ MR. JOHNSON.
Orlando ⎭		⎱ MR. MEADE.
Antonio Sanola ... *Judge of the District*		MR. TAPPING.
Griffo		MR. ARCHER.
Boissec ... ... *a Woodcutter*		MR. CARTER.
M. Verner ... MR. HUDSON.	Tomaso—*a Guide*	MR. HARWOOD.
M. Beauchamp MR. FERRAND.	*A Surgeon* ...	MR. LOUTHER.
Madame Emilie de Lesparre		MISS FOWLER.
Madame Savilia dei Franchi		MISS PAUNCEFORT.
Marie ... MISS HARWOOD.	Coralie	MISS M. THORNTON.
Celestine ... MISS BARNETT.	Estelle	MISS HOULISTON.
Rose ... MISS COLERIDGE.	Eugènie	MISS MORELEY.

CORSICANS, PIERROTS, FOLLYS, DEBARDEURS, &c.

PERIOD, 1840.

Stage Manager ... MR. H. J. LOVEDAY.   Acting Manager ... MR. BRAM STOKER.

· ACT · 1 ·
CORSICA · Hall and Terrace of the Chateau, of the Dei Franchi at Sullacaro.

· THE ARRIVAL ·

THE STORY OF THE PLAY

THE scene is the old hall of a Corsican château, the time evening; the setting sun floods with crimson the hills beyond. The speaker is Fabien dei Franchi. "There is," he explains to his guest, a Parisian, and friend of his brother Louis, "a strange mysterious sympathy between Louis and me; no matter what space divides us, we are still one in body, in feeling, in soul. Any powerful impression which the one experiences is instantly conveyed by some invisible agency to the senses of the other. For the last few days, despite of myself, my temperament has changed. I have become sad, uneasy, gloomy, with a depression of the heart I cannot conquer. I am convinced my brother is unhappy." The Parisian, unable to comprehend so strange a sympathy, inquires further as to its origin. Then, amid the gathering gloom of night, in the old hall of the Corsican château, he learns from the lips of Fabien the following story, "well attested in the annals of the Dei Franchi":—

"Three hundred years ago, the extraordinary attachment to each other of the two sons of the founder of the house of Dei Franchi was the theme of Corsica. Arrived at the age of manhood, they bound themselves by a solemn oath, that not even death should separate them; he who died first was to appear to the other. About two months after, one of the brothers, far away from home, was waylaid and murdered. At the very same moment, the other, writing a letter to him, was seized with a vague and terrible sense of danger. As he impressed his seal upon the molten wax, he heard a sigh. He turned, and saw his dead brother

· ACT · 2 ·
· PARIS · Interior of the Opera House ·
· MASQUERADE BALL & CARNIVAL ·

· THE WAGER ·

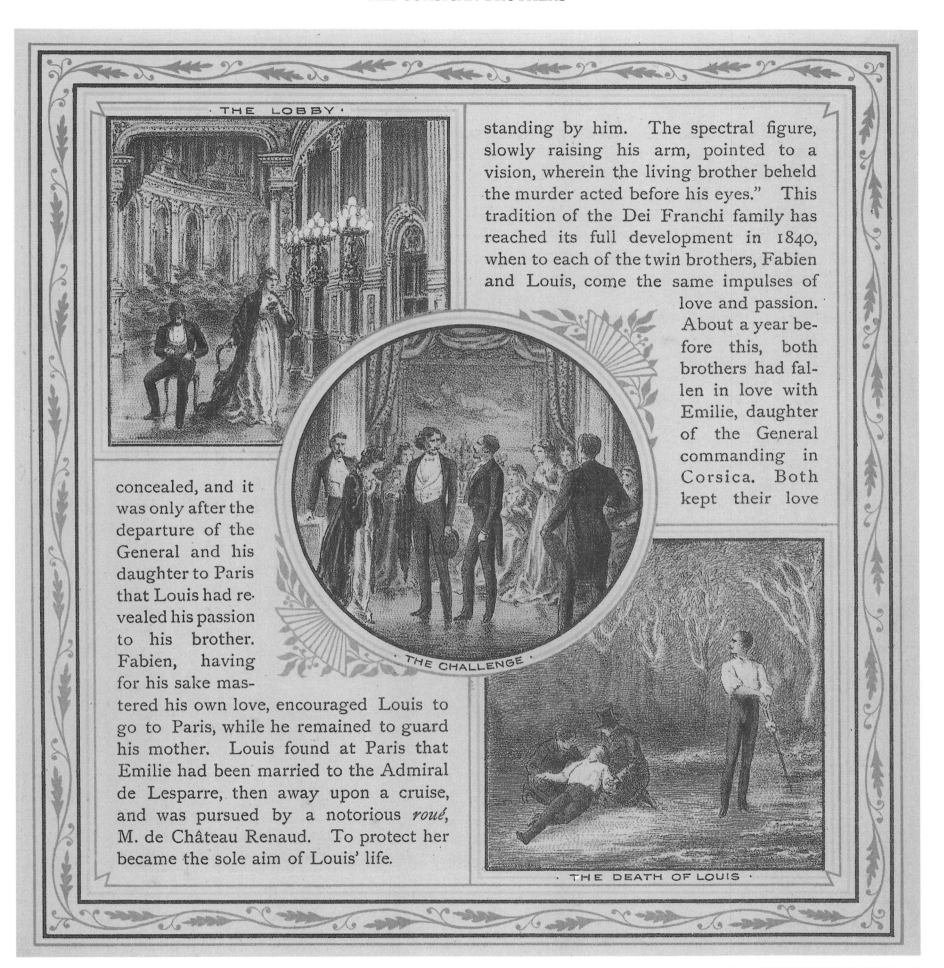

THE LOBBY.

THE CHALLENGE.

THE DEATH OF LOUIS.

standing by him. The spectral figure, slowly raising his arm, pointed to a vision, wherein the living brother beheld the murder acted before his eyes." This tradition of the Dei Franchi family has reached its full development in 1840, when to each of the twin brothers, Fabien and Louis, come the same impulses of love and passion. About a year before this, both brothers had fallen in love with Emilie, daughter of the General commanding in Corsica. Both kept their love concealed, and it was only after the departure of the General and his daughter to Paris that Louis had revealed his passion to his brother. Fabien, having for his sake mastered his own love, encouraged Louis to go to Paris, while he remained to guard his mother. Louis found at Paris that Emilie had been married to the Admiral de Lesparre, then away upon a cruise, and was pursued by a notorious *roué*, M. de Château Renaud. To protect her became the sole aim of Louis' life.

A great *bal masqué* is held at the Opera House, at which Emilie meets Château Renaud, in order to obtain the promised return of certain letters. He conceives the idea of compromising her reputation; requests her to await him in the lobby, and, returning to his friends, makes a bet that he will bring Madame de Lesparre to a supper at the Baron de Montgiron's rooms by four o'clock. Louis, overhearing the infamous wager, accepts the invitation he had before declined to the supper, in order to protect the woman he loves. In the lobby, Château Renaud promises to return the letters, and, by a base subterfuge, persuades Emilie to accompany him. On arriving, she finds herself in the midst of a gathering of rakish companions of the Baron. She places herself under the protection of Louis, who, declaring that "his blood to the last drop" is hers, leads her away, and accepts the challenge which Château Renaud forces upon him.

In the grey winter dawn they meet, and the less skilled Louis falls by the blade of the accomplished duellist. Before the dying eyes of Louis rises his old Corsican home, where his brother, in a vision, gazes with horror-struck face upon the scene then being enacted—and lo! at midnight, in the old château, the horror of three hundred years ago is once more repeated. Fabien, overcome by his mysterious anxiety, is in the very act of sealing a letter to his brother in Paris, when the apparition of the murdered Louis rises beside him, and mournfully points to a vision of the woful scene of his own death. Thus the living and the dead stand face to face.

Five days afterwards, Fabien, in pursuit of the murderer of his brother, sees the carriage of Château Renaud break down in the Forest of Fontainebleau. Drawn by the hand of fate, the assassin finds himself at the very spot where the blood of his slaughtered victim still stains the snow-clad forest glade. Château Renaud, unaware of the avenger close upon his track, feels his heart sink with foreboding as he recognises the frozen pool at which the duel had been fought, and the great tree under which Louis had fallen. Unnerved by the mysterious conjuncture of time and place, Château Renaud would fly from his fate, when suddenly the avenging Fabien stands before him to demand an account of the murder. Driven to bay, the duellist asks him to name hour, place, and weapons. Fabien answers him—"The hour? I have sworn it should be at the moment when I met you. The weapons? With the sword you slew my brother, with the sword you shall encounter me. The place? The spot where we now stand." From far away over the wintry landscape the distant stroke of a chapel clock tolls the same hour that tolled at Louis' death. Confidence in his own skill once more nerves the arm of Château Renaud. He attacks Fabien, who parries every thrust with a "wrist of iron." Baffled

· ACT · 3 ·
· FONTAINEBLEAU · Frozen Glade in the Forest ·
· THE DUEL ·

· RETRIBUTION ·

at every point, Château Renaud recoils. Fabien gives him breathing-time. Again they meet; the sword of Château Renaud breaks; his second, Montgiron interferes. "The duel is over; the chances are no longer equal." "Not so," says Fabien, as he breaks his own sword across his knee, "they are equal now." The duel is renewed, with the broken sword points used as poignards. The end is not far off. As the opponents stand face to face, Fabien springs at his adversary, and for a moment they stand locked together in the death-grip. Château Renaud seems to get the better of the struggle; but the Corsican with a sudden wrench frees himself, stabs his adversary to the heart, thus completing his Corsican vengeance, and stands over him for a moment, triumphant: then, as he turns away, his mournful cry goes up—" Louis, my brother, I can weep for you now."

A ghostly silence steals over the scene; from the laden branches fall spectral flakes of snow; the crimson hues of the winter sun shine dim through the forest stems. Fabien sits with his head bowed beside the spot where his brother had fallen, and where now his murderer lies. From beneath the snow rises the pale face of Louis; the dead and the living stand side by side; while in the solemn silence of the forest aisles, Fabien hears the voice he knows so well :—" Mourn not, my brother, we shall meet again."

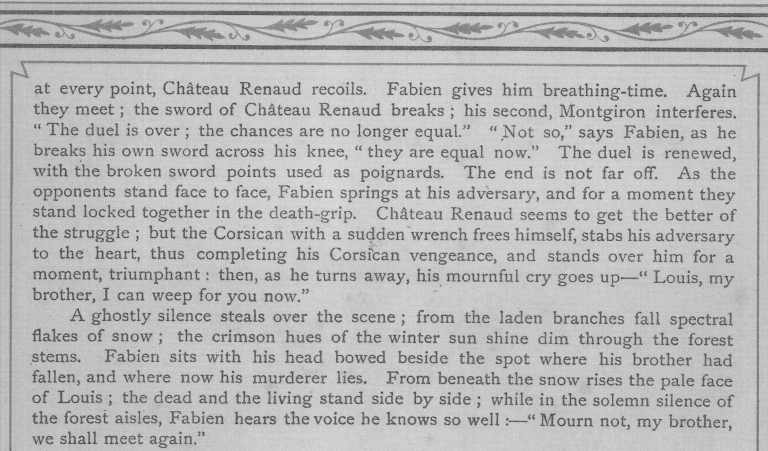

A CENTURY OF PERFORMANCE

1900

DATE	PRODUCTION
16th July	THE TELEPHONE GIRL
23rd July	THE LADY OF OSTEND
30th July	THE PRINCE OF BORNIO
13th August	THE LADY SLAVEY
20th August	MISS FORTESCUE AND HER
	SPECIALLY SELECTED LONDON COMPANY
20th, 22nd, 24th	MOTHS
August 21st	SHE STOOPS TO CONQUER
August 23rd	SCHOOL FOR SCANDAL
August 25th	PYGMALION AND GALATEA
27th August	THE DANDY FIFTH
3rd September	MR ARTHUR ROBERTS
	In CRUISE OF HMS IRRESPONSIBLE
10th September	THE MOODY MANNERS OPERA COMPANY
September 10th	FAUST
September 11th	LOHENGRIN
September 12th, 14th	CARMEN
September 13th	TANNHAUSER
September 15th	BOHEMIAN GIRL

1901

DATE	PRODUCTION
February 12th	A GRAND MISCELLANEOUS CONCERT
	which was postponed owing to the death of her Majesty Queen Victoria
	will consist in the first part of SACRED and in the second part
	of SECULAR MUSIC both vocal and instrumental
1st July	MISS MINNIE PALMER
8th July	TRIP TO CHICAGO
15th July	MR W S PENLEY IN
	CHARLEY'S AUNT
22nd July	THE LADY OF OSTEND
29th July	THE ENGLISH MILITARY COMIC
	OPERA THE DANDY FIFTH
5th August	THE MESSENGER BOY
12th August	MISS LILY HALL CAIN
	IN THE CHRISTIAN BY HALL CAIN
19th August	MR C P LEVILLY'S
	ORIGINAL LONDON COMPANY
	IN LA POUPÉE starring Miss Stella Gastelle
26th August	MISS FORTESCUE AND
	HER LONDON COMPANY
August 26th, 29th	MOTHS
August 27th, 30th	PERIL
August 28th	SHE STOOPS TO CONQUER
August 31st	THE LADY FROM TEXAS
2nd September	SANTOY
9th September	THE WRONG MR RIGHT

Monday 16th September	MISS EMMA HUTCHISON'S
	COMPANY: MRS DANES DEFENCE
23rd September	THE CASINO GIRL

1902

DATE	PRODUCTION
7th July	THE CASE OF THE REBELLIOUS SUSAN
14th July	MR WEEDON GROSMITH IN
	THE NIGHT OF THE PARTY
21st July	A TRIP TO CHICAGO
28th July	KITTY GRAY
4th August	SHERLOCK HOLMES
11th August	SANTOY
18th August	THE TOREADOR
25th August	THE MUMMY AND THE HUMMING BIRD
1st September	LA POUPÉE
8th September	A CHINESE HONEYMOON
15th September	MR EDWARD TERRY AND HIS COMPANY
15th September	HOLLY TREE INN
	followed by MY PRETTY MAID
16th, 19th September	SWEET LAVENDER
17th September	HOLLY TREE INN
	followed by LOVE IN IDLENESS
18th September	HOLLY TREE INN
	followed by THE PASSPORT
20th September	THE TELEPHONE
	followed by BARDELL -V- PICKWICK
	to conclude with THE CHURCHWARDEN
22nd September	FACING THE MUSIC
	preceded by Buxton's Comedy
	THE GOOD FOR NOTHING

1903

DATE	PRODUCTION
29th June	THE NEW BOY
	preceded each evening by a
	dramatic episode entitled THE
	SHADOW OF THE GUILLLOTINE
6th July	BROWN AT BRIGHTON
	preceded by a Duologue by
	Albert A Drinkwater entitled
	TWO IN A TRAP
13th July	MICE AND MEN
20th July	LA POUPEE
27th July	THE TORREDOR
3rd August	MR EDWARD TERRY
	AND HIS COMPANY
3rd, 4th August	THE TELEPHONE
	followed by YOU NEVER KNOW

1903 (continued)

DATE	PRODUCTION
5th August	MY PRETTY MAID
	followed by BARDEL -V- PICKWICK
6th August	SWEET LAVENDER
7th August	KERRY followed by LOVE IN IDLENESS
8th August	THE TELEPHONE followed by THE PASSPORT
10th August	THE CHINESE HONEYMOON
17th August	THE NEW CLOWN
	preceded each evening by the
	original play in one act
	JUDGED BY APPEARANCES
24th August	SAPHO
31st August,	
1st , 2nd, 5th September	THE LIARS
3rd, 4th September	MRS DANES DEFENCE
7th September	KITTY GRAY
14th September	MRS GORRINGE'S NECKLACE
	preceded each evening by
	MRS HILARY REGRETS
21st September	THE LITTLE FRENCH MILLINER
	Preceded by HIS LANDLADY

1904

DATE	PRODUCTION
Whit Saturday	
for six nights	OUR FLAT
30th May	CONFUSION
	preceded by OUR NEW BUTLER
6th June	JANE
	preceded each evening by THE ADMIRAL
13th , 14th, 15th June	OUR FLAT
16th, 17th, 18th June	OFF THE RANKS
	preceded by the Comedietta
	IN THE STRICTEST CONFIDENCE
20th June	THE BRIXTON BURGLARY
	preceded each evening by the
	Muscial Comedy A HAPPY PAIR
27th June	THE PRIVATE SECRETARY
	preceded each evening by
	THE LITTLE LAUNDRESS
4th, 5th and 6th July	OFF THE RANK
7th, 8th, 9th July	JANE
11th July	NIOBE
	preceded each evening by the Comedy Drama
	GOOD FOR NOTHING OR NAN
18th July	ARMORELLE
25th July	ARE YOU A MASON?
	preceded each evening by the
	Comedietta HUSHED UP
1st August	Mr Arthur Roberts in PACKING UP
	and a new Comedy in three acts COUSIN KATE
8th August	THE TORREDOR
15th August	THE CHINESE HONEYMOON

DATE	PRODUCTION
22nd August	THE GREAT DRAMATIC
	SENSATION - ZAZA
29th August	THE ORCHID
5th September	THE GIRL FROM KAY'S
12th September	Miss Louie Freear in BOY BOB
	preceded each evening by the
	Comedietta GOOD FOR NOTHING
19th September	THE NEW CLOWN
	preceded each evening by THE TEST
Monday 26th September	Fred Carno's celebrated company
	in HIS MAJESTY'S GUESTS

1905

DATE	PRODUCTION	% BOX OFFICE & TAKEN
Sunday July 30th	LINDEN TRAVERS	
	Illustrated lecture and songs - pianist and lantern operator;	
	Miss Lindan Travers and Miss Daisy Allow (Duettists);	
	H Rusworth, (accompanist); Mr Pat Jordan (Violinist)	
August 16th	LINDEN TRAVERS	
	Miss Francis and Miss Allow (Accompanist); Mr Clifford Kershaw (Cello)	
August 13th	LINDEN TRAVERS	
	Miss Emily Hall (Soprano)	
August 20th	LINDEN TRAVERS	
	Miss May Proctor (Contralto)	
August 27th	LINDEN TRAVERS	
	Mr Dodd (Baritone)	
September 3rd	LINDEN TRAVERS	
	Miss Bessie Clarke (Soprano); Sam Robinson (Violin)	

LINDEN TRAVERS was paid Ten pounds for each of these concerts, The Soloists one guinea and The Accompanists twelve shillings and six pence.

DATE	PRODUCTION	% BOX OFFICE & TAKEN
June 12th	THREE LITTLE MAIDS	62.5%
July 3rd	LEOPALDS	55%
July 10th	DAREDEVIL DOROTHY	52.5%
July 17th	WALLS OF JERICHO	52.5%
July 24th	SERGEANT	60%
July 31st	EDWARD TERRY	55%
August 7th	THE ORCHID	65%
August 14th	THE CINGALEE	65%
August 21st	THE ADMIRALS LADY	65%
August 28th	A CHINESE HONEYMOON	62.5%
September 4th	THE CATCH OF THE SEASON	66 2/3%
September 11th	BEAUTY AND THE BARGE	66.2/3%
September 18th	SATURDAY TO MONDAY	55%

1906

DATE	PRODUCTION	% BOX OFFICE & TAKEN
June 4th - July 9th	H RALLANDS STOCK CO.	50%
July 16fh	LA POUPEE	65%
July 23rd	AMORELLE	65%
July 30th	LEAH KLESCHNA	45% Monday to Wednesday,
		50% Thursday to Saturday
August 6th	BRIGADIER GERARD	65%
August 13th	CATCH OF THE SEASON	75%

DATE	PRODUCTION	% BOX OFFICE	£ TAKEN
August 20th	THE BLUE MOON	60%	
August 27th	THE PRODICAL SON	60%	
September 3rd	THE DAIRY MAIDS	62.5	
September 10th	FREEDOM OF SUSANNE	55%	
September 17th	WHAT THE BUTLER SAW	55%	

1907

DATE	PRODUCTION	% BOX OFFICE	£ TAKEN
March 31st	LADY OF OSTEND	52.5%	
June 3rd - July 8th	H RALLANDS STOCK CO.	50%	
July 15th	THE PRINCE OF PILSON	60%	£208
July 22nd	WHAT THE BUTLER SAW	55%	£475
July 29th	THE EARL AND THE GIRL	60%	£479
August 5th	SEYMOUR HICKS TRIPLE BILL	66.2/3%	£930
August 12th	THE BOUDMAN	52.5%	£933
August 19th	THE DAIRY MAIDS	62.5%	£1241
August 26th	THE PRODICAL SON	50%	£585
September 2nd	THE BLUE MOON	62.5%	£751
September 9th	TOM JONES	65%	£811
September 16th	MISS TOMMY	55%	£204

1908

DATE	PRODUCTION	% BOX OFFICE	£ TAKEN
Easter	VERNON BIOSCOPE		
	OWEN MAGIVENEY		£14
	KYOTO		£10
	MAY GERALDINE		£14
	THREE SEABORASS		£20
June 8th - July 13th	H RALLANDS STOCK CO.	50%	
July 20th	THE PRODICAL SON	55%	£490
July 27th	MY MEMOSA MAID	60%	£675
August 3rd	GAY GORDONS	66.2/3%	£993
August 10th	MISS HOOK OF HOLLAND	60%	£760
August 17th	THE CHRISTIAN	50%	£647
August 24th	THE DAIRY MAIDS	62.5%	£945
August 31st	THE MERRY WIDOW	65%	£1210
September 7th	ARTHUR BUSHAY		
	LONDON COMPANY	65%	£445
September 14th	BREWSTER'S MILLIONS	57.5%	£405

1909

DATE	PRODUCTION	% BOX OFFICE	£ TAKEN
May 31st - July 12th	H RALLANDS STOCK CO.	50%	
July 19th	HIS HOUSE IN ORDER	40%	£291
July 26th	BREWSTER'S MILLIONS	55%	£483
August 2nd	THE ARCADIANS	62.5%	£297
August 9th	THE ARCADIANS	62.5%	£501
August 16th	THE MERRY WIDOW	65%	£117
August 23rd	PETE		£498
August 28th	MAUD ALLEN MATINEE	75%	£138

DATE	PRODUCTION	% BOX OFFICE	£ TAKEN
August 30th	THE KING OF CARDONIA	60%	£706
September 6th	AN ENGLISHMAN'S HOME	50%	£233
September 13th	THE FLAG LIEUTENANT	60%	£274

1910

DATE	PRODUCTION	% BOX OFFICE	£ TAKEN
May 16th	THE LADY OF OSTEND	52.5%	
May 23rd	THEATRE CLOSED		
May 30th	THEATRE CLOSED		
June 6th	THEATRE CLOSED		
June 13th	THEATRE CLOSED		
June 20th	MISS ELIZABETH INSOVER	50%	£120
June 27th	THE MARRIAGE OF		
	KITTY AND DAVID GARRICK	50%	£220
July 4th	THE LITTLE STRANGER	52.5%	£141
July 11th	THE LITTLE DAMOZEL	52.5%	£172
July 18th	DON	55%	£321
July 25th	THE DAIRY MAIDS	60%	£626
August 1st	THE DOLLAR PRINCESS	65%	£1061
August 8th	OUR MISS GIBBS	60%	£873
August 15th	THE MOUNTAINEERS	60%	£629
August 22nd	THE WHIP	60%	£1174
August 29th	THE MERRY WIDOW	65%	£863
September 5th	THE MERRY MONARCHS	60%	£491
September 12th	THE GIRL ON THE BOAT	55%	£243
September 19th	WHAT THE BUTLER SAW	55%	£254

1911

DATE	PRODUCTION	% BOX OFFICE	£ TAKEN
June 5th	THAT CHAFFEUR CHAP	60%	£132
June 12th	THEATRE CLOSED		
June 19th	THEATRE CLOSED		
June 26th	LUCKY MISS DARE		
	AND DAVID GARRICK	50%	£200
July 3rd	LUCKY MISS DARE		
	AND DAVID GARRICK	45%	£183
July 10th	MONEY	47.5%	£169
July 17th	WHAT THE BUTLER SAW	52.5%	£577
July 24th	THE CINGALEE	57.5%	£395
July 31st	BREWSTER'S MILLIONS	55%	£525
August 2nd	THE GIRL IN THE TRAIN	65%	£782
August 14th	THE ARCADIANS	62.5%	£653
August 23rd	PEGGY	60%	£542
August 28th	PEGGY	60%	£391
September 4th	THE WHIP	60%	£926
September 11th	ARSENE LUPIN	55%	£427
September 18th	THE GROTESQUES	55%	£267

1912

DATE	PRODUCTION	% BOX OFFICE	£ TAKEN
May 27th	JACK STRAW	47.5%	£166
June 3rd	THEATRE CLOSED		
June 10th	THEATRE CLOSED		
June 17th	THE MARCH HARES	55%	£128
June 24th	THE NOBODIES	£50 Fee	£134
July 1st	THE GAITORS	£52 Fee	£146
July 9th	LIGHTS OUT	50%	£285
July 15th	BUNTY PULLS THE STRINGS	57.5%	£504
July 22nd	A MEMBER OF TATTERSALLS	60%	£420
July 29th	COUNT OF LUXEMBOURG	65%	£898
August 5th	COUNT OF LUXEMBOURG	65%	£959
August 12th	THE CHOCOLATE SOLDIER	62.5%	£1157
August 19th	THE MEMOMSIE	60%	£798
August 26th	BABY MINE	50%	£683
September 2nd	THE QUAKER GIRL	65%	£1071
September 9th	OUR MISS GIBBS	60%	£475
September 16th	FANNY'S FIRST PLAY	57.5%	£290
September 23rd	*Illegible*	£50 Fee	£73

1913

DATE	PRODUCTION	% BOX OFFICE	£ TAKEN
May 12th	THE GAY LIEUTENANTS	55%	£195
June 23rd	THE GAITORS	52%	£159
June 30th	THE HONEYMOON	52.5%	£224
July 7th	HINDLE WAKES	55%	£375
July 14th	BUNTY PULLS THE STRINGS	57.5%	£372
July 21st	THE GLAD EYE	60%	£638
July 28th	GYPSY LOVE	65%	£701
August 4th	GYPSY LOVE	65%	£901
August 11th	BREWSTER'S MILLIONS	50%	£923
August 18th	PRINCESS CAPRICE	62.5%	£1067
August 25th	GIRL IN A TAXI	62.5%	£889
September 1st	DOLLAR PRINCESS & THE MERRY WIDOW	65%	£984
September 8th	THE CHOCOLATE SOLDIER	62.5%	£643
September 15th	OH I SAY	52.5%	£504
September 22nd	THE VAGABOND	55%	£79

1914

DATE	PRODUCTION	% BOX OFFICE	£ TAKEN
June 1st	THE NOBODIES	60%	£203
June 8th	THE METISANS	50%	£61
June 15th	THE QUAINTO	65%	£69
June 22nd	THE BROWNINGS	55%	£90
June 29th	THE LIEUTENANTS	55%	£120
July 6th	OFFICER 666	55%	£288
July 13th	DIPLOMACY	55%	£349
July 20th	OH I SAY	47.5%	£670
July 27th	THE MARRIAGE MARKET	65%	£914
August 3rd	THE MARRIAGE MARKET	65%	£753
August 10th	*War declared* - SEALED ORDERS	65%	£265

August 17th	BREWSTER'S MILLIONS	50%	£272
August 24th	THE BLUE MOUSE	50%	£314
August 31st	GYPSY LOVE	65%	£403
September 7th	WITHIN THE LAW	57.5%	£244
September 14th	WHO'S THE LADY	(CANCELLED - WAR)	
	Theatre open with pictures twice nightly		
September 21st	THE ROSARY	50%	£156

1915, 1916 and 1917

No records - Theatre presumed closed due to the War.

All bookings at other Island Theatres and Dance Halls were cancelled for this reason

1918

DATE	PRODUCTION	% BOX OFFICE	£ TAKEN

Theatre let to E Melton - 4 weeks August - Rent £200

Pictures September - receipts for month £574

1919

DATE	PRODUCTION	% BOX OFFICE	£ TAKEN
April 24th	K. C.	50%	£152
June 9th	COMEDY CADETS	£80 Fee	£266
June 16th	COMEDY CADETS	£80 Fee	£167
June 23rd	COMEDY CADETS	£70 Fee	£187
June 30th	SEVEN NOBODIES	£80 Fee	£478
July 7th	SEVEN NOBODIES	£70 Fee	£357
July 14th	CERTAINTY	£85 Fee	£417
July 21st	YOUNGER GENERATION	£50 Fee	£582
July 28th	NOTHING BUT THE TRUTH	55%	£905
August 4th	DADDY LONGLEGS	55%	£905
August 11th	OH JOY	65%	£969
August 18th	THE LILAC DOMINO	65%	£1078
August 25th	MAID OF THE MOUNTAINS	65%	£1118
September 1st	LUCK OF THE NAVY	52.5%	£743
September 8th	HINDLE WAKES	50%	£685
September 15th	DADDY LONGLEGS (FILM)	50%	£504
September 22nd	NORRIS REPORTOIRE COMPANY	£80 Fee	£305
September 29th	NORRIS REPORTOIRE COMPANY	£80 Fee	£136
October 6th	COMEDY CADETS		£61
October 13th	PICTURES		£27
October 20th	PICTURES		£36
October 27th	NORRIS REPORTOIRE COMPANY	£80 Fee	£85
November 3rd	NORRIS REPORTOIRE COMPANY	£80 Fee	£77
November 10th	BOXING 12th and 13th	331/3%	£159
November 17th	THE HUSTLERS	£65 Fee	£53
November 24th	MONTY'S FLAPPER	60%	£109
December 1st	ANN	60%	£48
December 8th	THE CHUMS		£43
December 15th	HILARITY		£53
December 22nd	DADDY LONGLEGS (FILM)		£67
December 29th	DOUGLAS CHORAL UNION	4 Nights - Rent £40	

1920

DATE	PRODUCTION	% BOX OFFICE	£ TAKEN
January 6th	THE MOUNTEBANKS	£45	
January 12th	NORRIS REPORTOIRE COMPANY		£111
January 19th	NORRIS REPORTOIRE COMPANY		£82
January 26th	NORRIS REPORTOIRE COMPANY		£73
February 2nd	NORRIS REPORTOIRE COMPANY		£84
February 9th	NORRIS REPORTOIRE COMPANY		£82
April 5th	NOTHING BUT THE TRUTH	55%	£310
May 24th	SEVEN NOBODIES	£80 Fee	£217
May 31st	SEVEN NOBODIES	£75 Fee	£133
June 7th	COMEDY CADETS	£75 Fee	£169
June 14th	COMEDY CADETS	£70 Fee	£181
June 21st	THE MOUNTEBANKS	60%	£239
June 28th	NORRIS REPORTORIE COMPANY	£80 Fee	£482
July 5th	NORRIS REPORTORIE COMPANY	£80 Fee	£584
July 12th	NORRIS REPORTORIE COMPANY	£80 Fee	£671
July 19th	PEG O'MY HEART	50%	£1409
July 26th	A SOUTHERN MAID	65%	£1533
August 2nd	A SOUTHERN MAID	65%	£1587
August 9th	CHU CHIN CHOW	65%	£1500
August 16th	CHU CHIN CHOW	65%	£1306
August 23rd	FAIR AND WARMER	45%	£1073
August 30th	TILLY OF BLOOMSBURY	55%	£1423
September 6th	CINDERELLA	50%	£991
September 13th	PAIR OF SILK STOCKINGS	45%	£714
September 20th	LADY WINDERMERE'S FAN	£90 Fee	£365
September 27th	BEAUTY AND THE BEAST	£90 Fee	£193
October 4th	SUMMIT'S CONCERT PARTY		£114

1921

DATE	PRODUCTION	% BOX OFFICE	£ TAKEN
March 24th	REX GERARD COMPANY	52.5%	£157
May 16th	THE NAUGHTY WIFE	£80 Fee	£153
May 23rd	THE SCARLET BAND	£80 Fee	£79
May 30th	TYRANNY OF TEARS	£80 Fee	£162
June 6th	DEAN LITTLE DEVIL	£80 Fee	£92
June 13th	NAUGHTY WIFE & SCARLET BAND	£80 Fee	£296
June 20th	THE SPORTSMAN	£80 Fee	£167
June 27th	THE JEFFERSONS	50%	£235
July 4th	THE PARTNERS	50%	£244
July 11th	IRENE	65%	£800
July 18th	BRAN PIE	60%	£1148
July 25th	PADDY THE NEXT BEST THING	55%	£1366
August 1st	FAIR AND WARMER	45%	£1182
August 8th	MAID OF THE MOUNTAINS	65%	£1290
August 15th	A NIGHT OUT	62.5%	£1233
August 22nd	PEG O'MY HEART	50%	£1251

August 29th	A LITTLE DUTCH GIRL	62.5%	£1195
September 5th	TILLY OF BLOOMSBURY	55%	£1001
September 12th	A PAIR OF SIXES	55%	£829
September 19th	BIFFY	55%	£552
September 26th	EIGHT COMEDY CADETS	£95 Fee	£184

1922

DATE	PRODUCTION	% BOX OFFICE	£ TAKEN
February 13th	PANTO - DICK WHITTINGTON	60%	£557
April 13th	THE YELLOW TICKET	50%	£148
May 29th	THE PARTNERS	45%	£127
June 5th	THE JEFFERSONS	45%	£171
June 12th	CASTE	45%	£200
June 19th	A SOCIAL CONVENIENCE	55%	£247
June 26th	IN THE NIGHT	45%	£269
July 3rd	A PAIR OF SIXES	62.5%	£545
July 10th	THE PEEP SHOW	60%	£1137
July 17th	THE PEEP SHOW	60%	£1061
July 24th	THE VIRGIN QUEEN	60%	£1031
July 31st	THE VIRGIN QUEEN	60%	£884
August 7th	WELCOME STRANGER	55%	£1177
August 14th	NIGHTIE NIGHT	52.5%	£1204
August 21st	BULLDOG DRUMMOND	52.5%	£1078
August 28th	SIGN ON THE DOOR	50%	£864
September 4th	BRAN PIE	60%	£1166
September 11th	BRAN PIE	60%	£897
September 18th	POLLY WITH A PAST	50%	£606
September 25th	HUNKY DORY	60%	£261

1923

DATE	PRODUCTION	% BOX OFFICE	£ TAKEN
May 21st	OTHER PEOPLE'S WORRIES	52.5%	£137
June 11th	DOUBLE OR QUIT	56%	£363
June 18th	SUCH A NICE YOUNG MAN	60%	£176
June 25th	THE WIDOW'S HUSBAND	50%	£213
July 2nd	ELISA COMES TO STAY	50%	£578
July 9th	BE MY FRIEND	60%	£274
July 16th	POT LUCK	60%	£767
July 23rd	CO-OPTIMISTS	65%	£1337
July 30th	COUSIN FROM NOWHERE	60%	£878
August 6th	WHEN KNIGHTS WERE BOLD	£450 Fee	£901
August 13th	THE LAST WALTZ	60%	£1166
August 20th	THE HAPPY ENDING	57.5%	£965
August 27th	DANCING MAD	60%	£1217
September 3rd	DANCING MAD	60%	£871
September 10th	POLLY	62.5%	£699
September 17th	BLUEBEARD'S EIGHTH WIFE	55%	£659
September 24th	WAY OF AN EAGLE	55%	£351

1924

DATE	PRODUCTION	% BOX OFFICE	£ TAKEN
April 21st	QUINNIES	55%	£110
June 9th	OCEANS OF JOY	60%	£338
June 16th	THE WIDOW'S HUSBAND	65%	£191
June 23rd	THE EDGE O'BEYOND	55%	£313
June 30th	A LITTLE BIT OF FLUFF	50%	£426
July 7th	OUR BETTERS	55%	£383
July 14th	MADAM POMPADOUR	65%	£624
July 21st	MADAM POMPADOUR	65%	£909
July 28th	BLUEBEARD'S EIGHTH WIFE	50%	£869
August 4th	IT PAYS TO ADVERTISE	50%	£644
August 11th	LITTLE NELLIE KELLY	60%	£1349
August 18th	LITTLE NELLIE KELLY	60%	£1178
August 25th	CATHERINE	60%	£966
September 1st	TONI	60%	£817
September 8th	TONS OF MONEY	60%	£925
September 15th	THE RISING GENERATION	50%	£525
September 22nd	PLUS FOURS	55%	£344
December 8th	SINBAD	60%	£793
December 15th	SINBAD		

1925

DATE	PRODUCTION	% BOX OFFICE	£ TAKEN
April 13th	CLOSED - REFURNISHING CARPETS		
June 1st	OCEANS OF NOTIONS	60%	£345
June 8th	THE OYSTER		
	AND THE MEDLER	50%	£103
June 15th	LITTLE BIT OF FLUFF	50%	£395
June 22nd	THE RISING GENERATION	50%	£244
June 29th	ISABELLE	55%	£239
July 6th	THE FARMER'S WIFE	50%	£620
July 13th	ADAM AND EVA	50%	£507
July 20th	KATINKA	60%	£977
July 27th	KATJA THE DANCER	65%	£1174
August 3rd	KATJA THE DANCER	60%	£1226
August 19th	POPPY	60%	£978
August 17th	JUST MARRIED	50%	£1387
August 24th	ALF'S BUTTON	50%	£1116
August 31st	THE STREET SINGER	60%	£1258
September 7th	IN THE NEXT ROOM	50%	£625
September 14th	BACHELOR HUSBANDS	50%	£553
September 21st	THE OPTIMIST	55%	£244
December 21st	LITTLE JACK HORNER	60%	£668

1926

DATE	PRODUCTION	% BOX OFFICE	£ TAKEN
May 24th	FLAMING FRONTIER (FILM)	50%	£164
June 14th	THE RIGHT AGE TO MARRY	55%	£358
June 21st	TONS OF MONEY	50%	£347
June 28th	NUMBER 17 COMPANY	55%	£140
July 5th	HOBSON'S CHOICE	52.5%	£310
July 12th	FARMER'S WIFE	50%	£398
July 19th	NO NO NANNETTE	60%	£1466
July 26th	NO NO NANNETTE	60%	£1256
August 2nd	KATJA THE DANCER	60%	£1017
August 9th	MERCENARY MARY	60%	£1376
August 16th	THE CAT'S CRADLE	50%	£851
August 23rd	THE UNFAIR SEX	50%	£749
August 30th	THE BEST PEOPLE	52.5%	£760
September 6th	JUST MARRIED	50%	£899
September 13th	THE GORILLA	50%	£388
September 20th	THE RESCUE PARTY	60%	£186

1927

DATE	PRODUCTION	% BOX OFFICE	£ TAKEN
June 6th	BROADWAY JONES	65%	£342
June 13th	THE NAUGHTY WIFE	50%	£528
June 20th	THE FANATICS	50%	£503
June 27th	ASK BECCLES	52.5%	£508
July 4th	THIS WOMAN'S BUSINESS	52.5%	£308
July 11th	TIP TOES	60%	£831
July 18th	NO NO NANETTE	60%	£1106
July 25th	THE STUDENT PRINCE	60%	£1309
August 1st	MY SON JOHN	60%	£952
August 8th	LADY LUCK	62.5%	£1179
August 15th	LIDO LADY	62.5%	£1136
August 26th	JUST A KISS	60%	£852
August 29th	LADY BE GOOD	60%	£1058
September 5th	ROSEMARIE	65%	£1187
September 12th	ROSEMARIE	65%	£1046
September 19th	FAIR AND WARMER	50%	£325

1928

DATE	PRODUCTION	% BOX OFFICE	£ TAKEN
May 28th	BIDDY	55%	£264
June 4th	MEET THE WIFE	50%	£457
June 11th	THE MONSTER	50%	£288
June 18th	THE CREAKING CHAIR	50%	£252
June 25th	PADDY THE NEXT		
	BEST THING	50%	£509
July 2nd	THE WRECKER	50%	£377
July 9th	THE PUNCH BOWL	60%	£464
July 16th	SUNNY	65%	£1244
July 23rd	LADY LUCK	60%	£1062
July 30th	MERCENARY MARY	60%	£925
August 6th	HIT THE DECK	60%	£1512
August 13th	THE GIRLFRIEND	60%	£1395
August 20th	THE DESERT SONG	65%	£1674
August 27th	THE STUDENT PRINCE	60%	£1322
September 3rd	LUMBER LOVE	60%	£836
September 10th	THE LETTER	60%	£406
September 17th	HUNDRETH CHANCE	50%	£373

1929

DATE	PRODUCTION	% BOX OFFICE	£ TAKEN
May 20th	GOOD MORNING BILL	50%	£250
June 10th	THE BURGLAR	50%	£516
June 17th	THE SEVENTH GUEST	50%	£247
June 24th	THE PERFECT WIFE	55%	£212
July 1st	GAY DOGS OF 1929	50%	£265
July 8th	YELLOW SANDS	55%	£473
July 15th	ROSEMARIE	65%	£1073
July 22nd	FAME	52.5%	£622
July 29th	THE VAGABOND KING	65%	£1240
August 5th	THE DESERT SONG	65%	£1253
August 12th	SO THIS IS LOVE	60%	£1368
August 19th	THE BURGLAR	£300	£921
August 26th	77 PARK LANE	50%	£813
September 2nd	GETTING MOTHER MARRIED	50%	£540
September 9th	PLUNDER	52.5%	£593
September 16th	ELISA COMES TO STAY	50%	£445
September 23rd	WHITE CARGO	65%	£432

1930

DATE	PRODUCTION	% BOX OFFICE	£ TAKEN
June 9th	BROWN SUGAR	50%	£192
June 16th	TELL ME THE TRUTH	50%	£181
June 23rd	BY CANDLELIGHT	50%	£180
June 30th	THE BURGLAR	52.5%	£143
July 7th	THIRD TIME LUCKY	55%	£310
July 14th	HOLD EVERYTHING	60%	£633
July 21st	LUCKY GIRL	60%	£819
July 28th	HERE COMES THE BRIDE	60%	£934
August 4th	LOVE LIES	60%	£807
August 11th	MR CINDERS	60%	£1297
August 18th	LILAC TIME	60%	£1056
August 25th	SILVER WINGS	60%	£876
September 1st	THE DESERT SONG	65%	£958
September 8th	THE FIVE O'CLOCK GIRL	60%	£775
September 16th	TRIAL OF MARY DUGGAN	52.5%	£224
September 22nd	SIMBA (FILM)	60%	£254

1931

DATE	PRODUCTION	% BOX OFFICE	£ TAKEN
May 25th	HE WALKED IN HER SLEEP	50%	£167
June 15th	NONE SO BLIND	52.5%	£289
June 22nd	THE YORKSHIRE PLAYERS	50%	£92
June 29th	THE YORKSHIRE PLAYERS	50%	£90
July 6th	JAMES LEGACY	52.5%	£162
July 13th	PRIVATE LIVES	50%	£295
July 20th	CYNARA	60%	£446
July 27th	THE LOVE RACE	60%	£746
August 3rd	FOLLOW A STAR	60%	£585
August 10th	THE STUDENT PRINCE	60%	£1112
August 17th	MR CINDERS	60%	£872
August 24th	LILAC TIME	57.5%	£538
August 31st	NIPPY	60%	£866
September 7th	AUTUMN CROCUS	57.5%	£376
September 14th	STRICTLY DISHONOURABLE	60%	£243

1932

DATE	PRODUCTION	% BOX OFFICE	£ TAKEN
May 16th	THERE'S ALWAYS JULIETTE	55%	£76
June 6th	LONDON WALL	55%	£113
June 27th	ROOKERY NOOK	55%	£180
July 4th	THE COLOUR BOX	60%	£110
July 11th	ITS A GIRL	55%	£422
July 18th	ALMOST A HONEYM00N	£25	£372
July 25th	LATE NIGHT FINAL	57.5%	£313
August 1st	FOR THE LOVE OF MIKE	60%	£713
August 8th	WONDER BAR	60%	£556
August 15th	MAID OF THE MOUNTAINS	60%	£758
August 22nd	THE MERRY WIDOW	70%	£1560
August 29th	THE MILLIONAIRE KID	60%	£601
September 5th	THE GREEN PACK	50%	£538
September 12th	TURKEY TIME	52.5%	£256

1933

DATE	PRODUCTION	% BOX OFFICE	£ TAKEN
June 5th	HALF A MILLION	50%	£121
June 12th	PLEASURE CRUISE	50%	£198
June 19th	THEATRE CLOSED		
June 26th	THEATRE CLOSED		
July 3rd	ITS A GIRL	£115	£163
July 10th	TEN MINUTE ALIBI	55%	£241
July 17th	NIGHT OF THE GARTER	55%	£436
July 24th	THE BEGGAR'S OPERA	50%	£274
July 31st	THE WANTED ADVENTURE	60%	£334
August 7th	HOLD MY HAND	60%	£579
August 14th	TELL HER THE TRUTH	60%	£757
August 21st	THE MERRY WIDOW	60%	£877
August 28th	THE DU BARRY	55%	£697
September 4th	THE HOLMES OF BAKER STREET	52%	£274
September 11th	ORDERS IS ORDERS (FILM)		£201

1934

DATE	PRODUCTION	% BOX OFFICE	£ TAKEN
June 11th	GOOD MORNING BILL	60%	£287
June 18th	THEATRE CLOSED		
June 25th	THEATRE CLOSED		
July 2nd	HIGH TEMPERATURE	52.5%	£114
July 9th	LABURNUM GROVE	55%	£210
July 16th	THE CHOCOLATE SOLDIER	62.5%	£484
July 23rd	FIRST EPISODE	55%	£451
July 30th	NICE GOINGS ON	60%	£537
August 6th	THE ARCADIANS	60%	£813
August 13th	THE WIND AND THE RAIN	52.5%	£520

1934 (continued)

DATE	PRODUCTION	% BOX OFFICE	£ TAKEN
August 20th	SPORTING LOVE	62.5%	£710
August 27th	THE LATE		
	CHRISTOPHER BEAN	57.5%	£294
September 3rd	LADY'S NIGHT	60%	£405
September 10th	WITHOUT WITNESS	50%	£162

1935

DATE	PRODUCTION	% BOX OFFICE	£ TAKEN
June 10th	BREWSTER'S MILLIONS (FILM)		£261
June 17th	KING OF PARIS (FILM)		£147
June 24th	THE MIGHTY BARNUM (FILM)		£98
July 1st	MATILDA GOES A CRUISING	50%	£184
July 8th	ELIZABETH SLEEPS OUT	55%	£108
July 15th	CHARLEY'S AUNT	50%	£356
July 22nd	LOVER'S LEAP	55%	£241
July 29th	MR TOWER OF LONDON	60%	£440
August 5th	THE SHINING HOUR	50%	£315
August 12th	THE GIRLFRIEND	60%	£774
August 19th	GILL DARLING	65%	£812
August 26th	YES MADAM	65%	£881
September 2nd	WALTZES FROM VIENNA	60%	£594
September 9th	NEW REELS ETC.		£74

1936

DATE	PRODUCTION	% BOX OFFICE	£ TAKEN
June 1st to July 13th	PICTURES		
July 20th	LOVE LAUGHS	60%	£688
July 27th	THE VAGABOND KING	60%	£568
August 3rd	THE MERRY WIDOW	60%	£841
August 10th	SEEING STARS	65%	£639
August 17th	ANYTHING GOES	65%	£737
August 24th	ANYTHING GOES	65%	£277
August 31st	LILAC TIME	60%	£435
September 7th	THE RIDGEWAY PARADE	55%	£312
September 14th	LOVE ON THE DOLE	57.5%	£252

1937

DATE	PRODUCTION	% BOX OFFICE	£ TAKEN
May 17th to July 5th	PICTURES		
July 12th	MR CINDERS	60%	£322
July 19th	GILL DARLING	62.5%	£646
July 26th	SANDY POWELL	60%	£941
August 2nd	SANDY POWELL	60%	£964
August 9th	SANDY POWELL	60%	£986
August 16th	SANDY POWELL	60%	£988
August 23rd	PLEASE TEACHER	65%	£725
August 30th	NO NO NANNETTE	65%	£449
September 6th	AREN'T MEN BEASTS	52.5%	£367

September 13th	DO YOU REMEMBER	55%	£144
December 16th	BABES IN THE WOOD	65%	

1938

DATE	PRODUCTION	% BOX OFFICE	£ TAKEN
June 27th	WINTER SPORTS ICE SHOW	65%	£549
July 4th	WINTER SPORTS ICE SHOW	65%	£525
July 11th	WINTER SPORTS ICE SHOW	65%	£502
July 18t	WINTER SPORTS ICE SHOW	65%	£830
July 25th	WINTER SPORTS ICE SHOW	65%	£983
August 1st	WINTER SPORTS ICE SHOW	65%	£889
August 8th	WINTER SPORTS ICE SHOW	65%	£793
August 15th	WINTER SPORTS ICE SHOW	65%	£943
August 22nd	WINTER SPORTS ICE SHOW	65%	£741
August 29th	WINTER SPORTS ICE SHOW	65%	£660
September 5th	PICTURES		£241
September 12th	PICTURES		£254

1939

DATE	PRODUCTION	% BOX OFFICE	£ TAKEN
May 29th	GEORGE AND MARGARET	50%	£125
June 5th	HINDLE WAKES	50%	£115
June 12th	WHILE PARENTS SLEEP	50%	£291
June 19th	PEG O'MY HEART	50%	£180
June 26th	THE ROTTERS	50%	£160
July 3rd	ALMOST A HONEYMOON	50%	£223
July 10th	NIGHT MUST FALL	50%	£257
July 17th	SANDY POWELL'S ROADSHOW	60%	£835
July 24th	SANDY POWELL'S ROADSHOW	60%	£699
July 31st	SANDY POWELL'S ROADSHOW	60%	£749
August 7th	SANDY POWELL'S ROADSHOW	60%	£879
August 14th	SANDY POWELL'S ROADSHOW	60%	£710
August 21st	DOUGLAS WAKEFIELD'S		
	ROADSHOW	60%	£948
August 28th	DOUGLAS WAKEFIELD'S		
	ROADSHOW	60%	£734

War declared on Germany September 3rd

October 30th	PYGMALION	50%	£108
November 6th	THE OUTSIDER	50%	£97
November 13th	GOODNESS HOW SAD	50%	£82
November 20th	BLACK LIMELIGHT	50%	£88
November 27th	AREN'T WE ALL	50%	£92
December 4th	COMMON SALARY	50%	£90
December 11th	LOOSE ENDS	50%	£99
December 18th	THE TWO MRS CARROLS	50%	£97
December 26th	ALF'S BUTTON	50%	£234

1940 - 1944

No records of professional shows during the war

1945

DATE	PRODUCTION	% BOX OFFICE	£ TAKEN
	Open all year to Sunday 16th December for Pictures		
December 24th to January 10th	CINDERELLA	60%	£1613

1946

DATE	PRODUCTION	% BOX OFFICE	£ TAKEN
June 8th - September 21st	TOM ARNOLD'S HAPPIDROME	65%	
October 14th	PINK STRING AND SEALING WAX	50%	£472-6-0
October 21st	REBECCA	50%	£528-8-3
October 28th	THIS HAPPY BREED	50%	£543-7-9
November 4th	JANE EYRE	50%	£530-14-6
November 11th	WHILE THE SUN SHINES	50%	£608-4-0
November 18th	SCHOOL FOR HUSBANDS	50%	£528-6-3
November 25th	THE CORN IS GREEN	50%	£633-19-6
December 2nd	LOVE IN A MIST	50%	£505-4-6
December 9th	BLITHE SPIRIT	50%	£520-5-3
December 23rd - January 10th	MOTHER GOOSE		£2,749

1947

DATE	PRODUCTION	% BOX OFFICE	£ TAKEN
January 16th	GIVE ME YESTERDAY		
January 20th	THE DUCHESS OF DANZIG		
January 27th	FLARE PATH	50%	£414-5-0
February 3rd	TEN LITTLE NIGGERS	50%	£391-11-9
February 10th	CLAUDIA	50%	£334-7-9
February 17th	QUALITY STREET	50%	£396-16-9
February 24th	DANGEROUS CORNER	50%	£351-5-3
March 3rd	FRENCH WITHOUT TEARS	50%	£407-14-6
March 10th	PYGMALION	50%	£425-10-3
March 17th	DADDY LONG LEGS	50%	£444-19-6
March 24th	MA'S BIT O'BRASS	50%	£467-14-0
March 31st	HAY FEVER	50%	£415-0-3
April 7th	MY WIFE'S FAMILY	50%	£622-17-3
April 14th	WIND OF HEAVEN	50%	£480-13-3
April 21st	PORTRAIT IN BLACK	50%	£388-15-0
April 28th	ARMS AND THE MAN	50%	£418-8-9
May 4th	MAN ABOUT THE HOUSE	50%	£526-15-6
May 11th	THE POLTERGEIST	50%	£437-1-0
May 18th	THE MAN WHO CAME TO DINNER	50%	£484-18-6
May 25th	IVANOVICH	50%	£433-1-0
June 7th - 13th September	HAPPIDROME	65%	£1,149
September 15th	WE PROUDLY PRESENT	60%	£691-5-6
September 22nd	ARSENIC AND OLD LACE	50%	£661-16-3
September 29th	IS YOUR HONEYMOON REALLY NECESSARY	50%	£641-7-6
October 6th	LOVE FROM A STRANGER	50%	£468-2-9
October 13th	SEE HOW THEY RUNG	50%	£534-2-9
October 20th	FREDA	50%	£501-17-9
October 27th	ONCE A CROOK	50%	£421-19-0
November 3rd	WHEN WE ARE MARRIED	50%	£488-5-3
November 10th	THE CASE OF THE FRIGHTENED LADY	50%	£482-16-0
November 17th	CURE FOR LOVE	50%	£472-5-3
November 24th	FOOLS RUSH IN	50%	£384-9-3
December 1st	THE EAGLE HAS TWO HEADS	50%	£457-18-9
December 8th	LADY FROM EDINBURGH	50%	£384-8-6
December 15th	A CHRISTMAS CAROL	50%	£505-0-6
December 24th - January 10th	BABES IN THE WOOD	55%	£2,750-6-6

1948

DATE	PRODUCTION	% BOX OFFICE	£ TAKEN
February 2nd	CANDIDA	50%	£512-6-3
February 9th	NIGHT MUST FALL	50%	£327-0-9
February 16th	ARTIFICIAL SILK	50%	£396-17-0
February 23rd	WUTHERING HEIGHTS	50%	£374-18-9
March 1st	LABURNUM GROVE	50%	£340-5-6
March 8th	THE WISHING WELL	50%	£364-19-6
March 15th	GRAND NATIONAL NIGHT	50%	£329-7-6
March 22nd	TOO YOUNG TO MARRY	50%	£436-19-3
March 29th	THE GUINEA PIG	50%	£702-6-6
April 5th	HOBSON'S CHOICE	50%	£444-10-6
April 12th	THE SHOP AT SLY CORNER	50%	£407-4-9
April 19th	MEET THE WIFE	50%	£387-8-3
April 26th	SMILING THRO'	50%	£367-19-0
May 3rd	DUET FOR TWO HANDS	50%	£380-0-0
May 10th	THE WINSLOW BOY	50%	£380-16-3
May 17th	MA'S BIT O'BRASS	50%	£556-10-0

Theatre Closed from 22nd May to 28th June 1948 for the installation of Delicolor Lighting Equipment.

DATE	PRODUCTION	% BOX OFFICE	£ TAKEN
June 28th - September 11th	LETS' GET ON WITH IT. WITH NAT MILLS AND BOBBY.		£1956 (Average per week).
September 13th	PRESENT LAUGHTER	50%	£842-17=0.
September 20th	MURDER ON THE NILE	50%	£670=15-0
September 27th	PEACE COMES TO PECKHAM	50%	£559-5-0
October 4th	THE HOUSEMASTER	50%	£491-13-6
October 11th	THE HASTY HEART	50%	£437-8-0
October 18th	LITTLE WOMEN	50%	£435-0-9
October 25th	PRIVATE LIVES	50%	£393-0-0
November 1st	IF FOUR WALLS TOLD	50%	£396-4-6
November 8th	PADDY THE NEXT BEST THING	50%	£460-5-3
November 15th	THE GHOST TRAIN	50%	£414-10-3
November 22nd	THE IMPORTANCE OF BEING EARNEST	50%	£372-19-6
November 29th	AN INSPECTOR CALLS	50%	£338-0-0
December 6th	THE POTTERS	50%	£347-19-6
December 13th	GEORGE AND MARGARET	50%	£338-0-0
December 24th - January 15th	JACK AND THE BEANSTALK	55%	£2,573-19-0

1949

DATE	PRODUCTION	% BOX OFFICE	£ TAKEN
February 28th - June 11th	*Theatre closed for decoration and re-seating*		
June 11th - September 17th	TOO FUNNY FOR WORDS		£1,577 (Average per week).

1949 (continued)

DATE	PRODUCTION	% BOX OFFICE	£ TAKEN
September 19th	ON MONDAY NEXT	50%	£569-9-3
September 26th	EASY MONEY	50%	£460-16-0
October 3rd	LITTLE LAMBS EAT IVY	50%	£421-10-3
October 10th	PAYMENT DEFERRED	50%	£370-19-6
October 17th	MIRANDA	50%	£342-15-0
October 24th	MURDER WITHOUT CRIME	50%	£311-15-9
October 31st	THE BRONTES	50%	£320-14-9
November 7th	HIGH TEMPERATURE	50%	£360-11-6
November 14th	DEEP ARE THE ROOTS	50%	£487-11-0
November 21st	CHARLEY'S AUNT	50%	£437-8-9
November 28th	THE GISCONDA SMILE	50%	£301-3-3
December 5th	GOODBYE MR CHIPS	50%	£334-5-9
December 12th	THE GIRL WHO JUST COULD'NT	50%	£256-1-6
December 19th	A CHRISTMAS CAROL	50%	£203-2-3
December 26th - January 7th	ALADDIN	55%	£2,181-18-0

1950

DATE	PRODUCTION	% BOX OFFICE	£ TAKEN
March 6th	IT'S A BOY	50%	£258-12-0
March 13th	GRANITE	50%	£228-1-3
March 20th	HE WALKED IN HER SLEEP	50%	£239-7-6
March 27th	HEAVEN & CHARING CROSS	50%	£226-9-9
April 3rd	NOAH	50%	£321-6-3
April 10th	FLY AWAY PETER	50%	£326-0-3
April 17th	ROPE	50%	£218-9-3
April 24th	MOUNTAIN AIR	50%	£264-0-0
May 1st	THE PARAGON	50%	£216-15-0
May 8th	ACACIA AVENUE	50%	£432-18-9
May 15th	THE CAT AND CANARY	50%	£318-10-9
May 22nd	THIRD TIME LUCKY	50%	£325-17-3
June 5th	BORN YESTERDAY	50%	£526-1-0
June 12th	WHILE PARENTS SLEEP	50%	£581-16-0
June 19th	LIGHT OF HEART	50%	£538-4-9
June 26th	THE HAPPIEST DAYS OF YOUR LIFE	50%	£631-3-9
July 2nd	SEE HOW THEY RUN	40%	£692-12-6
July 9th	SEE HOW THEY RUN	40%	£801-18-0
July 16th	THE CHILTERN HUNDREDS	40%	£1028-12-0
July 23rd	THE CHILTERN HUNDREDS	40%	£659-9-0
August 31st	ONE WILD OAT	40%	£1236-12-6
August 7th	ONE WILD OAT	40%	£1108-6-0
August 14th	OFF THE RECORD	40%	£1285-14-6
August 21st	OFF THE RECORD	40%	£1113-15-0
August 28th	FLY AWAY PETER	40%	£613-0-0
September 4th	FLY AWAY PETER	40%	£496-10-6
September 11th	BED, BOARD AND ROMANCE	50%	£653-17-3
September 18th	THE BARRATTS OF WIMPOLE STREET	50%	£381-18-3
September 25th	THEY WALKED ALONE	50%	£313-4-0
October 2nd	EDWARD MY SON	50%	£262-4-0
October 9th	BLACK CHIFFON	50%	£269-15-6

October 16th	YOUNG WIVES TALE	50%	£266-10-3
October 23rd	DEAR MURDERER	50%	£210-8-0
October 30th	BABY MINE	50%	£197-17-0
November 6th	CRIME PASSIONEL	50%	£189-6-0
November 13th	MADAME LOUISE	50%	£189-18-0
November 20th	WOMEN ARE MURDER	50%	£215-17-6
November 27th	RANDOM HARVEST	50%	£199-3-3
December 4th	GLASS MENAGARIE	50%	£16-11-9
December 11th	GATHER NO MORE	50%	£148-4-3
December 26th - January 6th	LITTLE RED RIDING HOOD	55%	£1767-4-9

1951

DATE	PRODUCTION	% BOX OFFICE	£ TAKEN
May 13th - 19th	TIDE	60%	£560-9-0
June 23rd- September 15th	SOLDIERS IN SKIRTS	55%	£23,298

1952

DATE	PRODUCTION	% BOX OFFICE	£ TAKEN
June 21st - 13th September	SOLDIERS IN SKIRTS	55 % Receipts	£18,423

1953

DATE	PRODUCTION	% BOX OFFICE	£ TAKEN
June 20th - 12th September	RIDERS OF THE RANGE	55%	£19,376

1954

DATE	PRODUCTION
June - August	WOULD YOU BELIEVE IT
September	DIAL M FOR MURDER

1955

DATE	PRODUCTION
June 20th	THE LITTLE HUT
June 27th	THE HOLLOW
July 9th	ME AND MY GIRL
July 11th	THE AFFAIRS OF STATE
July 18th	RELUCTANT HEROES
August 6th	IT WON'T BE A STYLISH MARRIAGE
August 20th	FOR BETTER FOR WORSE
August 27th	A WORMS EYE VIEW
August 29th	DEAR CHARLES
September 5th	MY WIFE'S LODGER

1956 - 1959

The Gaiety was used principally as a Cinema with only occasional theatre use for amateur dramatic societies

1960

DATE	PRODUCTION
July 4th	PEEPING TOM
June - September	THE HAPPY HOLIDAY SHOW

1961

DATE	PRODUCTION
June - September	THE HAPPY HOLIDAY SHOW

1962

DATE	PRODUCTION
June - September	THE HAPPY HOLIDAY SHOW

1963

DATE	PRODUCTION
June - September	THE HAPPY HOLIDAY SHOW

1964

DATE	PRODUCTION
June - September	THE HAPPY HOLIDAY SHOW

1965

DATE	PRODUCTION
June - September	THE HAPPY HOLIDAY SHOW

1966

DATE	PRODUCTION
	The Seamen's strike of this year curtailed the season's programme
June - September	SHOWTIME 66
18th - 24th September	THE HUGHIE GREEN SHOW

1967

DATE	PRODUCTION
May - June	PALACE OF VARIETIES
June - September	SHOWTIME 67

1968

DATE	PRODUCTION
June	THE HOLIDAY SHOW

1969

DATE	PRODUCTION
May - September	THE SEVEN-FORTY-FIVE-SHOW AND SUNDAY SPECTACULARS

1970

DATE	PRODUCTION
May - September	THE GAIETY SHOW

1971

DATE	PRODUCTION
June	SHOWTIME 71
August - September	OLD TYME MUSIC HALL

1972

DATE	PRODUCTION
May - July	THOSE WERE THE DAYS
July - September	SUMMER SHOWTIME
	THE SUNDAY SHOW ALTERNATED WITH
	THE REGINALD DIXON SHOW

1973

DATE	PRODUCTION
June - September	HOLIDAY SHOWTIME

1974

DATE	PRODUCTION
June - September	STARTIME 74

1975

DATE	PRODUCTION
June - September	THE TOM O'CONNOR SHOW
Sundays	KARMA, THE LIGHTNING HYPNOTIST

1976

DATE	PRODUCTION
June - September	HOLIDAY SHOWTIME
Sundays	KARMA, THE LIGHTNING HYPNOTIST

1977

DATE	PRODUCTION
June - September	THE JUBILEE SHOW
Sundays	KARMA THE LIGHTNING HYPNOTIST
September	THE GOLDEN YEARS OF MUSIC HALL
Sundays	KARMA, THE LIGHTING HYPNOTIST

1978

DATE	PRODUCTION
May - July	THE AL JOLSON MINSTREL SHOW
July - August	AN EVENING WITH DES O'CONNOR
August - September	SHOWTIME 78

1979

DATE	PRODUCTION
May	COUNTRY SPECTACULAR
June	MANANAN FESTIVAL MUSIC AND ARTS

1979 (continued)

DATE	PRODUCTION
July	MARY O'HARA STARTED CELTIC WEEK
July - August	ONE THOUSAND YEARS OF FUN
	RONNIE DUKES, RICKI LEE AND FAMILY
September	THE JIMMY LOGAN LAUGHTER SHOW

1980

DATE	PRODUCTION
May - June	MOTOR CYCLE NEWS CINEMA SHOW
June - September	SEEING STARS STARRING BOBBY KNUTT

1981

DATE	PRODUCTION
May to June	HELLO LOFTY STARRING DON ESTELLE
June	MOTOR CYCLE NEWS CINEMA SHOW
June - September	VARIETY STARTIME
July - August	ONE MAN AND HIS SHOW STARRING DES O'CONNOR

1982

DATE	PRODUCTION
June	MOTOR CYCLE NEWS CINEMA
June - July	THE HILLSIDERS
July - August	STARTIME 82
September	VARIETY SHOWTIME

1983

DATE	PRODUCTION
May - June	COUNTRY MUSIC JAMBOREE
June	MOTOR CYCLE NEWS FILM SHOW
June - July	WHITE HEATHER SHOW
July - September	SHOWTIME 83
October	A MAN FOR ALL SEASONS

1984

DATE	PRODUCTION
April	THE MANTIDS OF NEM
May	REBECCA
May	BOEING BOEING
May - June	THE CHARLIE WILLIAMS SHOW
July - September	PYJAMA TOPS STARRING JOHN INMAN
September	THE GOOD OLDE DAYS

1985

DATE	PRODUCTION
June	A TOUCH OF TARTAN STARRING ANDY STEWART
July - September	THE MATING GAME STARRING ROBIN NEDWELL
September	BEDROOM FARCE
September	GILBERT AND SULLIVAN, D'OYLY CARTE OPERA CO.

1986

DATE	PRODUCTION
April	THE LION, THE WITCH AND THE WARDROBE
May - June	MOTOR CYCLE NEWS CINEMA
June	LAST OF THE RED HOT LOVERS
June	JESUS CHRIST SUPERSTAR
June - September	A BIT ON THE SIDE STARRING LIONEL BLAIR
September	THE BRONTE STORY

1987

DATE	PRODUCTION
April	TALES OF TOAD HALL
April	THE RIVALS
May	ANY QUESTIONS' BBC RADIO 4 LIVE BROADCAST
	with John Timpson (Chairman), Magnus Magnusson, Austin Mitchell MP, Norman St John-Stevas MP and Baroness Seear
May - June	MOTOR CYCLE NEWS CINEMA
June	MURDER BY SEX
June - September	MY GIDDY AUNT STARRING MOLLY SUGDEN
September	THE TART AND THE VICARS WIFE
October	ROUGH CROSSING

1988

DATE	PRODUCTION
March	FUNNY PECULIAR
April	STEPPING OUT
May - June	THE TART AND THE VICARS WIFE
June - July	DON'T MISUNDERSTAND ME
August - September	TOUCH AND GO
September - October	FUR COAT AND NO KNICKERS
October	THE HUNCHBACK OF NOTRE DAME
October	RICHARD BAKER'S GRAND TOUR OF MELODY
October	WINNIE THE POOH
November	AN IDEAL HUSBAND

1989

DATE	PRODUCTION
May - June	NOT WITH A BANG
June - July	SUMMER SONGS AT THE GAIETY
July - August	BEDSIDE MANNERS / MORNING MATINEES: THE CARE BEARS
August	ROBIN HOOD AND HIS MUCKY MEN
September	THE LIVER BIRDS
September	RUN FOR YOUR WIFE
September	THE PIRATES OF PENZANCE
October	HOLD TIGHT! IT'S 60'S NIGHT
October	THE MAGICIAN'S NEPHEW
October	MOVE OVER MRS MARKHAM STARRING PEGGY MOUNT
October	UNDERNEATH THE ARCHES
	STARRING BERNIE WINTERS AND RICHARD WHITMORE
October - November	JOSEPH AND THE AMAZING TECHNICOLOR DREAMCOAT
November	THE RAILWAY CHILDREN

1990

DATE	PRODUCTION
March	TONS OF MONEY
March	SHIRLEY VALENTINE
March	A VERY PRIVATE DIARY STARRING VICTOR SPINETTI
May	LADIES NIGHT
May	FIND THE LADY
May - June	LITTLE SHOP OF HORRORS
June	HOLD TIGHT! IT'S 60s NIGHT
July	SEASIDE ROMP STARRING JACK DOUGLAS
July	TRINIDAD CARNIVAL SPECTACULAR
August	ON THE PISTE
August	CANTERBURY TALES
August	A TALE OF TWO CITIES
August - September	HENCEFORWARD
September	THE WOMAN IN BLACK
October	THE MERCHANT OF VENICE

1991

DATE	PRODUCTION
April	LETTICE AND LOVEAGE
May	THE GILBERT AND SULLIVAN STORY
June	PRIVATES ON PARADE
August	WAYNE SLEEP
October	GASLIGHT
November	LAST TANGO IN WHITBY

1992

DATE	PRODUCTION
May	AN EVENING WITH SIR HARRY SECOMBE
May	THE FANCY MAN
June	STAGELAND
July	FLABBERGHASTED
August	EDUCATING RITA
August - September	DEAD OF NIGHT
September	ABILGAIL'S PARTY
September	DIAL 'M' FOR MURDER
October	DON'T DRESS FOR DINNER
October	MACBETH

1993

DATE	PRODUCTION
May	AS YOU LIKE IT
May	SPRING AND PORT WINE
June	HAVING A BALL
REPERTORY:	
July	DANGEROUS OBSESSION
July	ONE FOR THE ROAD
July	IRA LEVIN'S DEATH TRAP
August	ROUND AND ROUND THE GARDEN
August	DOUBLE TROUBLE
August	THE SECRETARY BIRD
August	BLITHE SPIRIT
August - September	THE BUSINESS OF MURDER
September	DRY ROT
September	HABEAS CORPUS
September	REBECCA

1994

DATE	PRODUCTION
June	SATURDAY NIGHT
July	SAILOR BEWARE
REPERTORY:	
July	REVENGE
July	THE MAINTENANCE MAN
August	THE LATE EDWINA BLACK
August	GOOSE PIMPLES
August	OUR DAY OUT
August	AN EVENING WITH GARY LINEKER
August - September	IT MUST HAVE BEEN MURDER
September	HOW THE OTHER HALF LOVES
September	THE UNEXPECTED GUEST
September	HAY FEVER
September - October	WIFE BEGINS AT FORTY
October	TRAP FOR A LONELY MAN
October	LOOK NO HANS
October	CHARLEY'S AUNT

1995

DATE	PRODUCTION
June	CHRIS BLACK EXPERIENCE
June	BOYZONE
July	LA TRAVIATTA
REPERTORY:	
July	OLD TYME MUSIC HALL
August	WAIT UNTIL DARK
August	WIND IN THE WILLOWS
August	FISH OUT OF WATER
August	JOSEPH AND THE AMAZING TECHNICOLOR DREAMCOAT
August - September	MY GIDDY AUNT
September	MURDER BY MISADVENTURE
September	84 CHARING CROSS ROAD
September	SHIRLEY VALENTINE
September	BEST OF BRITISH

1996

DATE	PRODUCTION
April	I HAVE BEEN HERE BEFORE
May	THE JUNGLE BOOK
June	PATSY CLINE, THE MUSICAL
July	PATRICK MOORE, SPACE LECTURE
July	KEN DODD LAUGHTER SHOW
July	LITTLE SHOP OF HORRORS
REPERTORY:	
July - August	GODSPELL

1996 (continued)

DATE	PRODUCTION
August	ROCK HARD 60s NIGHT
August	HAPPY AS A SANDBAG
August	I'M GETTING MY ACT TOGETHER & TAKING IT ON THE ROAD
August	YOU'RE A GOOD MAN CHARLIE BROWN
September	THE FANTASTICKS
October	THE PHANTOM OF THE OPERA ON ICE

1997

DATE	PRODUCTION
April	A MIDSUMMER NIGHT'S DREAM
April	THE ARCHERS
	Actors reminiscences of BBC Radio 4's long-running farming soap
April	SNOW WHITE AND THE SEVEN DWARFS
July - August	JOSEPH AND THE AMAZING TECHNICOLOR DREAMCOAT

1998

DATE	PRODUCTION
April	GLEN MILLER BAND
April	PHIL COOL
April	EMMA CHRISTIAN
May	ERROL BROWN
May	CLEO LAINE
July	THE DUBLINERS
July	AS ACCORDING TO KOSSOFF STARRING DAVID KOSSOFF
July	KENNY BALL AND HIS JAZZMEN
August	PAUL DANIELS MAGIC SHOW
August	CHAS AND DAVE
August	QUIMANTU MUSIC OF THE ANDES
August	KEN DODD
August	SYD LAWRENCE ORCHESTRA
August	HINGE AND BRACKET
August	RHYTHMS OF AFRICA
August	THE RUSSIAN FOLK ENSEMBLE
September	CHRIS BARBER JAZZ BAND
September	LAST NIGHT OF THE PROMS
November	CLAIRE AND ANTOINETTE CANN PIANO DUET
November	THE NASH ENSEMBLE

1999

DATE	PRODUCTION
March	PATRICK MOORE
March	JOHN HEGLEY
March	THE ROYAL FAMILY: A TRIBUTE TO QUEEN
March	JACQUES LOUSSIER TRIO
April	PENDYRUS MALE CHOIR
April	MAGIC OF THE MUSICALS
April	RICHARD DIGANCE
April	ERROL BROWN
May	RICHARD STILGOE AND PETER SKELLERN
June	ROCKIN' ON HEAVEN'S DOOR

June	BERNARD MANNING
June	THE CANTERVILLE GHOST
July	THE REDUCED SHAKESPEARE COMPANY
July	AN EVENING WITH TOM O'CONNOR
July	THE DUBLINERS
July	THE MIKADO
July	PAUL DANIELS MAGIC SHOW
July	BRENDAN SHINE
July	KIT AND THE WIDOW
August	FIVEPENNY PIECE
August	HONOR BLACKMAN
August	VOULEZ VOUZ: A TRIBUTE TO ABBA
August	LA TRAVIATTA
August	LA BOHEME
August	FINBAR FUREY
August	KEN DODD LAUGHTER SHOW
August	JAMES BYRNE
September	AN EVENING WITH SIR JOHN MILLS
September	A DISAGREEABLE MAN
September	THE THREE TENORS
September	THE HOUGHTON WEAVERS
October	LONDON CITY BALLET
October	JALEO
October	LELAND CHEN
November	THE KING'S SINGERS
December	EMMA CHRISTIAN

2000

DATE	PRODUCTION
March	TOM O'CONNOR
March	BEYOND THE BARRICADE
April	THE ROYAL SHAKESPEARE COMPANY
May	THE ROYAL FAMILY: A TRIBUTE TO QUEEN
May	TOSCA
May	CARMEN
May	A POLICEMAN'S LOT
June	BERNARD MANNING
June	KEN DODD
July	JOSEPH AND THE AMAZING TECHNICOLOR DREAMCOAT
July	THE CORSICAN BROTHERS
July 16th 2000	**THE TELEPHONE GIRL - CENTENARY PERFORMANCE**

This list comprises professional companies only. Tribute is paid to the many amateur companies that have kept The Gaiety Theatre alive during the course of its history. Their work is not included here because consistent and continuous records were unavailable.

TECHNICAL SPECIFICATION

Get In Access

Via door at rear of stage; 2.14 x 3.05m

then down 10 steps. (Awkward for very heavy

items)

Stage

Proscenium Arch: 8.68 x 9.4m

Performance Space: 8.68 x 12.2m

Wing Width: SR 1.5m; SL 3.96m

Height to Grid: 14.63m

Rake: 1 in 36

29 Double Purchase Counterweights, all at 1ft.

spacing Fly Floor on SR.

Flying Bars

Bar 30

Bar 29

Bar 28

Bar 27

Bar 26

Bar 25 LX 5

   Beam (2' Spacing)

Bar 24

Bar 23

Bar 22

Bar 21

Bar 20 LX 4

Bar 19

Bar 18

Bar 17

Bar 16

Bar 15

Bar 14

Bar 13 LX 3

   Beam (2' Spacing)

Bar 12

   (2' Spacing)

Bar 11

Bar 10

Bar 9 LX 2

Bar 8

Bar 7

Bar 6

Bar 5

Bar 4

   (Crossover Bridge) LX 1 (On Hand Winch)

Bar 2 (House Tabs) Fixed

Bar 1 (Act Drop) Fixed

All bars are at 1' spacing except where stated.

1 X Tab Track

8 X Dressing Rooms
2 X Shower Rooms
No Wardrobe Facilities (Washing Facilities at
discretion of House Keeping)

Staff

Stage Manager and Assistant Stage Manager
Chief Technician and Assistant Technician
Follow Spots & Casuals available
No security personnel on site.

Not accessible to the disabled.
Smoking not permitted anywhere in the theatre.
Pyrotechnics/naked flames and smoking etc. as
part of the plot by approval from Resident Fire
Officer only.

FLATS

The Following are in width

16' 6" high solid

18' X 2

2' X 2

3'3" X 1

3'6" X 2 (windows)

4' X 4

4' X 2 (doors)

4' X 2 (windows)

5' x 2

5'8" x 2

5'9" X 1(door)

6' X 2

6' X 2 (doors)

6' X 4 (window)

7'9" X 1(double door)

8' X 1 (french window)

Full set of stage braces and weights to match
flats supplied.

Rostrum

36 4'x4'x1' rostra (steel frame) Property of IoM
Arts Council, availability not guaranteed

Cloths

1 set of house tabs (blue)
1 Cyclorama
1 set of blacks tabs
1 set of red tabs
1 set of white tabs

1 blue tab (no split)
1 gathered gauze
1 cinema silver tab

Entire set of Black Box masking both hard and
soft legs and soft borders, with conduit available.
Stage covering is black dance floor or original
wood finish. (No fixing to stage allowed)

Orchestra Pit

Access under stage
Accommodates 15 comfortably, RAT© lit music
stands supplied.

Lighting

Strand 520i Control Console,

120 Dimmers.

40 x Cantatta Fresnels.

30 x 1k Par Cans. (24 Full and 6 Floor)

18 x E.T.C. Source 4 Zoom Profile Lanterns

10 x Strand SL Zoom Profile 15-32 600 w

8 x 1k Harmony P.C.

4 x Alto F 2000/2500 w Fresnals.

16 x 4 Circuit 300 Watt Codas.

(Inter-Changeable)

2 x Korrigan 1200w Follow Spots

18 x Chroma Q 'CQ1' Colour Scrollers

6 x P16 Birdies

5 Fixed lighting bars in rig .

Can be brought to stage level for rigging.

Sound

Soundcraft K2 32 channel desk.
Peavey Miniframe 208 Media Matrix 2.3.
Mini disk.
Compact Disk.
Cassette Player/recorder.
Revox.
SPX990 & REV 7.
FOH System,
EAW JF 80's Pros Speakers. SB250 Sub Bass,
RCF PL81 Delay System
On stage, 4 X EV System 200 stage monitors.

Mic List

6 x SM58
4 x SM57
7 x Audio Technica "AT815R" Electret
Condenser (Rifle)
1 x D112 (egg)
2 x AKG CK91 Condenser
2 x AKG CK98 Shotgun
6 x D.I. (Passive)
3 x Crown Boundary Mics
Also including AKG D190(X3) D310(X2)
D330(X2) D130(X2)

Facilities for recording & editing.
Acoustics suitable for music and spoken word.

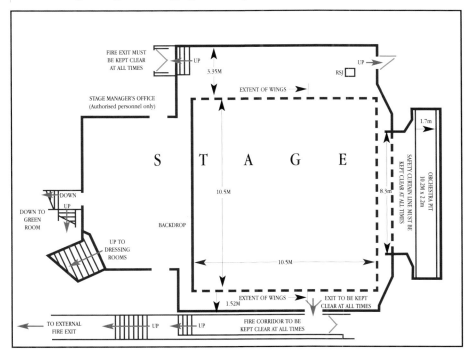

BIBLIOGRAPHY

BOOKS, ARTICLES & REPORTS

CHAPPELL, Connery, 'Island of Barbed Wire' (London, 1984)

CONNOLLY, Paul (Ed), 'The Theatres Trust Newsletter, December 1999

CRESSWELL, Yvonne (Ed), 'Living With the Wire: Civilian Internment in the Isle of Man during the two World Wars' (Douglas, 1994)

CRINGLE, Terry, 'Here is the News - An Illustrated Manx History' (Douglas, 1992)

DAY BOOK OF THE GAIETY THEATRE, 1905 - 1953

EARL, John, 'The Gaiety Theatre and Opera House, Douglas, Isle of Man', report for The Theatres Trust, 1996

EARL, John, 'Why Historians Get All The Best Seats', Theatres Trust Friends Newsletter, Issue 25, September 1992

FRIENDS OF THE GAIETY (Eds), 'The Gaiety Theatre', Brochure (Douglas, 1984)

FRIENDS OF THE GAIETY, Restoration Sub-committee Reports, 1990 - 1998

GALLAGHER, Lyn, 'The Grand Opera House, Belfast' (Belfast, 1995)

GLASSTONE, Victor, 'Victorian and Edwardian Theatres: An Architectural and Social Survey' (London, 1975)

GLASSTONE, Victor, ' Recommendations for Restoration and Renovation, Gaiety Theatre, Douglas, Isle of Man', report to the Manx Government, April 1978

HALLIWELL, Leslie, 'Seats in All Parts: Half a Lifetime at the Movies' (London, 1985)

IMPERIAL WAR MUSEUM, interviews with Dr Hans Gal and Hugh Eric Rank in the 1980s, for the Department of Sound Records, 'Civilian Internment in Britain 1939 - 1945' (Manx Museum)

ISLE OF MAN EXAMINER ANNUALS

ISLE OF MAN NATURAL HISTORY AND ANTIQUARIAN SOCIETY, 'Architectural and Social Aspects of Douglas', pp 168 - 171

ISLE OF MAN YEAR BOOK, Norris Modern Press, 1906

LEWIN, T. A., 'Films Shown at Gaiety (sic) Theatre Douglas, Isle of Man between 1956 and 1961' (Personal notebook)

KELLY, Peter, ' Creating The Gaiety and The Grand', Manx Life, November / December 1977; also notes for this article

KELLY, Peter, 'The Gaiety - A Technical Look',

booklet (Douglas, 1984, in the Manx Collection at the Manx Museum)

KELLY, Robert, 'With a Song in Their Hearts' (Douglas, 1995)

KELSEY, Jacqui, 'The Gaiety Theatre' in 'Home from Home' magazine, Spring 1999

KINVIG, R. H., 'The Isle of Man: A Social, Cultural and Political History' (Liverpool, 1975)

KNIVETON, Gordon (Ed), 'Douglas Centenary, 1896 - 1996' (Douglas, 1996)

McCARTHY, Sean, 'Frank Matcham's Early Career', published in 'Theatre Notebook', vol. XXV, nos. 3 and 4, and vol. XXVI, no. 2

McCARTHY, Sean & CHESHIRE, D. F, (Eds), 'Theatrephile', Vol. 1, no. 2, March 1984

MACKINTOSH, Iain & SELL, Michael (Eds), 'Curtains !!! or A New Life for Old Theatres' (Eastbourne, 1982)

MOORE, Arthur, 'Fifty Years of Manx Amusements', series in Mona's Herald

THE PALACE AND DERBY CASTLE COMPANY:
    Letting Books, 1899, 1917-18, 1934, 1943
    Company Balance Sheet, 31 December 1900
    Board minutes 1948, 1949, 1954
    Statement of Accounts, 1955

PATENT APPLICATIONS:
1894, No. 4407, 2 March 1894. A. R. Dean's application for a self-folding seat, and a seat with a self-straightening back
1902, No. 27,146, 9 December. Frank Matcham and Robert Briggs' application for the construction of circles in theatres

PEARSON, Lynn, 'The People's Palaces': The Story of the Seaside Pleasure Buildings of 1870 - 1914' (Buckingham, 1991)

PENDLETON, Cliff, 'The Theatre, The Music Hall, and Douglas in the Isle of Man' (Personal memoir, unpublished, written in late 1980s)

PERTWEE, Jon, 'Moon Boots and Dinner Suits' (1984)

READ, Jack, 'Empires, Hippodromes & Palaces' (London, 1985)

ROBERTS, Arthur, 'Fifty Years of Spoof' (London, year unknown)

ROBINSON, Vaughan & McCARROLL, Danny (Eds), 'The Isle of Man: Celebrating a Sense of Place' (Liverpool, 1990)

RODGERS, Kate, 'Our Heritage - Did You Know? Facts and Stories from the Past' (Isle of Man, 1992)

SLACK, Stuart, 'Streets of Douglas - Old and New' (Douglas, 1996)

SNOW, Miranda, 'The Gaiety Theatre', thesis, unpublished, written c. 1979

SOUTHERN, Richard, 'The Victorian Theatre: A Pictorial Survey' (Newton Abbott, 1970)

SPENCELEY, Bob, 'Modernisation at The Gaiety' Antiquarian Corner, 1987

STANDEN, Frieda, 'Trivial Tales of Music and Mann' (Douglas, 1990)

STANDEN, Frieda, 'Those Were The Days', (Douglas 1992)

STENNING, Canon E. H., 'Portrait of the Isle of Man' (London, 1958)

STOKES, Mervin, 'From Rags to Riches', lecture notes and script

SYKES, Frank, 'A Nostalgic History of Isle of Man Theatres' (Unpublished, compiled 1982, in the Manx Collection in the Manx Museum)

TYNWALD COURT, Hansard, 16 February 1971, 17 February 1976, 18 October 1976, 15 March 1977, 6 July 1977

WALKER, Brian (Ed), 'Frank Matcham: Theatre Architect' (Belfast, 1980)

WATSON, Ernest B., 'Notes on Theatre-going', extracted from 'A Study of the Nineteenth-Century London Stage' (Harvard, 1926)

WEBBER, David T., 'Illustrated Encyclopaedia of the Isle of Man' (Douglas, 1997)

WEST, Margery, 'Island at War' (Isle of Man, 1986)

WILMORE, David, 'The Historical Stage Equipment at The Gaiety Theatre', report presented to the Manx Government (1988)

WOOD, Haydn, 'A Cavalcade of Music, 1888 - 1938' (Personal memoir, unpublished)

NEWSPAPERS & JOURNALS

MANX SUN
8 July 1893 (The Palace Opera House)
15 July 1893 (The Palace Opera House)
23 April 1898 (Winding up The Pavilion)
6 August 1898 (Development of the Palace & Derby Castle Company)
8 July 1899 (Trades exhibition at The Pavilion)
15 July 1899 (Trades exhibition at The Pavilion)
9 September 1899 (End of trades exhibition)
16 December 1899 (P. & D. C. Co. a.g.m.)
21 July 1900 (Opening of Gaiety)
21 July 1900 (What's on)

MONA'S HERALD
1 July 1947 (Review)

16 September 1947 (Review)
7 October 1947 (Review)
16 December 1947 (Review)

ISLE OF MAN EXAMINER
1 July 1893 (The Marina)
2 April 1898 (Formation of the P. & D. C. Co.)
31 December 1898 (P. & D. C. Co. a.g.m.)
July 1900 (Opening of Gaiety)
1938 passim, (Reviews)
23 February 1951 (Review)
14 September 1951 (Indecency charge, 'Soldiers in Skirts')
9 April 1970 (Future of Gaiety)
16 July 1976 (Mannin Entertainments ends lease)
7 January 1977 (Summer leasing available)
4 March 1977 (£150,000 needed for repairs)
18 March 1977 (£200,000 needed for repairs)

ISLE OF MAN COURIER
20 March 1970 (Future of Gaiety)
25 June 1971 (Licence owners)
1 October 1971 (Leased by consortium)
30 November 1973 (Possible structural weakness)
13 October 1978 (Second phase of restoration)

ISLE OF MAN WEEKLY TIMES
3 April 1970 (Rumours of alterations)
4 February 1971(Government to buy Gaiety)
18 February 1971 (Government to buy Gaiety)
25 February 1971 (Future of Gaiety)
1 July 1971 (Future plans of Ken Daly)
6 December 1973 (Officially pronounced safe)
12 October 1976 (£50,000 needed for repair)
7 March 1978 (New equipment installed)

TABS
Vol. 14, no. 3, December 1956 (Strand Electric and Engineering Co., London)

THE MANXMAN
3 February 1900 (The new theatre)
21 July 1900 (Opening of Gaiety)

THE STAGE
19 July 1900 (Opening of Gaiety)

THE ERA
21 July 1900 (Opening of Gaiety)

ISLE OF MAN TIMES
January 1901 (Death of Queen Victoria)

GREEN FINAL
15 February 1971 (Government plans to purchase)

HALIFAX EVENING COURIER
16 May 1904 (Death of Jonas Binns)

VANITY FAIR
5 July 1911 (Matcham profiled)

There were copies of articles and features in magazines and papers available to the author from various private sources where there was no firm evidence of the title, date or some other defining feature. It has proved impossible to determine the precise provenance of these items although there is little doubt of their legitimacy. These have largely been included in this bibliography where it was felt possible to adequately describe them. Many articles that have appeared in the Island's more recent publications (such as Manx Life, Manx Life Style, Manx Tails, the Isle of Man Victorian Society's Newsletters, Money Media, Island Life as well as the regular papers, The Isle of Man Examiner, The Manx Independent and The Isle of Man Courier) have, however, been omitted. This is because of the sheer volume involved, and also because most of the relevant material came from other sources quoted, or the private collections of those who have contributed to the book, either directly to the author or in letters to other contributors.

PUBLISHER'S PRESENTATION COPIES

The following list includes names of those who kindly supported this edition of 'A Full Circle. 100 Years of The Gaiety Theatre', by subscribing for copies prior to its publication. The list also includes names of those who have contributed to the regeneration of the Gaiety Theatre as recommended by the Theatre Management.

The publisher is most grateful to all those listed below whose kind consideration in so many different capacities has combined to help make this book possible.

Adams, Charlotte

Adlard, Janet Wendy

Anderson, Janet and Michael

Barton, Amanda

Barton, Andrew

Barwell, Doreen

Brooksbank, Sandra

Butterworth, The family of the late David L., Gaiety Senior Tour Guide.

Callister, Helen

Clark, Ian and Monica

Clowser, Andrew

Cretney, The Hon. David MHK

Danielson, R. G.

Davison, Margaret

Dixon, Clive

Earl, John

Falconer, John

Forward, Fay

Gawne, Kit

Gelling, The Hon. Donald MHK

Guthrie, The Rev'd J. L.

Groenewald, R. and D.

Daunt, Sir Timothy, KCMG, His Excellency the Lieutenant Governor, and Lady Daunt

Harrison, Stephen

Harrocks, David

Henry, Joan

Hibbert, Derek

Holt, Richard and Juliet.

Jones, Gwen

Jones, Noel Debroy, Lord Bishop of Sodor and Man

Leece, Mr and Mrs E.

Lewthwaite, P. A. and P. M.

Lowey, The Hon. Eddie MLC

Longman, Peter

Moore, S. L.

New, Major General Sir Laurence CB CBE, and Lady New

Nivison, The Hon. J. A. C. K.

Partington, The Ven. Brian, Archdeacon of Sodor and Man

Quayle, Chadena

Roe, Ken

Roney, Lilian

Sentance, Charles

Sheppard, Merlin

Sidebotham, Beryl

Sims, Roger

Smith The Rev'd Alec

Sparks, Hammy

Taylor, A.

Tours (IOM)

Turner, Fred and Carolyn

Uren, Lennie and Freda

Wilmore, Dr David

A CELEBRATION IN THANKSGIVING

The following is the order of service to be held on Sunday 23rd July 2000 at St Thomas' Church, Douglas, to mark the centenary of the Gaiety Theatre and Opera House.

The service follows similar lines of that which was held to launch the restoration project ten years earlier.

A Celebration in Thanksgiving for the Restoration
of
The Gaiety Theatre
In its Centenary Year
Sunday 23rd July 2000
at 3.0pm

As the congregation assembles, the orchestra will play the Overture to 'The Telephone Girl' which was the first production to be staged at the Gaiety Theatre on the 16th July 1900.

After words of welcome by the Reverend Alec Smith (Actors' Church Union Chaplain to the Gaiety), a brief account of the Theatre's history and recent restoration will be given by Mervin Stokes (Manager), Séamus Shea (Production Manager) and Charles Sentance (Chairman of the Restoration Sub Committee).

Then in Thanksgiving will be sung the hymn;
Tune: Praxis Pletatis

Praise to the Lord! the Almighty, the King of Creation!
Oh my Soul, Praise Him, for he is thy health and salvation,
All ye who hear,
Now to his temple draw near,
Joining in glad adoration.

Praise to the Lord! who doth prosper thy work and defend thee
Surely his goodness and mercy here daily attend thee;
Ponder anew
What the Almighty can do,
If with his love he befriend thee.

Praise to the Lord! O let all that is in me adore him!
All that hath life and breath, come now with praises before him.
Let the Amen
Sound from his people again;
Gladly for aye we adore him!

A reading from The Apocrypha
Ecclesiasticus Chapter 38 vv 24-end

The Venerable Brian Partington (Archdeacon of Sodor and Mann) representing the Department of Tourism and Leisure.

A MUSICAL INTERLUDE
Eleanor Shimmin (Mezzo-Soprano),
Alan Wilcocks (Bass)

CHAPLAIN
Acknowledging that all our abilities are the gifts of a gracious God, let us give Him our most hearty thanks for all that has been achieved throughout the past 100 years.

LET US PRAY: Prayer

Let us thank God for the manifold gifts he has given to men and women,
especially for those displayed in the life of the theatre;
For the talents of acting and singing, mime and dancing:
For the arts of writing and composing, directing and producing.

Response: WE GIVE THANKS

For the great and honourable traditions of the Theatre and Stage;
For those who have served our own Gaiety Theatre with such distinction in the past and for those who succeed them today;
For actors and actresses, dancers and singers,
comedians and all variety artists;
For musicians, directors and producers;
For scenic artists, electricians, stage hands, dressers and callers;
For Theatre Managers and their staffs, attendants, administrators, cleaners and commissionaires.

Response: WE GIVE THANKS

For those whose vision and generosity have made possible
the restoration of our Theatre;
For the Isle of Man Government, The Friends of the Gaiety
and our many benefactors;
For the consultants, artists and craftsman who have brought us
their skills of design and construction.
For all who have given of themselves, their time and their abilities
for our continuing entertainment and enlightenment.
For our own Manager, Mervin Stokes - and his loyal, dedicated staff.

Response: WE GIVE THANKS

Hymn (Tune: Angel Voices)

Come to us Creative Spirit,
In our Father's House,
Every Natural Talent Foster,
Hidden Skills Arouse,
That within your earthly temple
Wise and simple
May rejoice.

Poet, Painter Music Maker
All your treasures bring;
Craftsmen, Actor, Graceful Dancer,
Make your offering;
Join your hands in celebration!
Let Creation
Shout and sing!

Word from God eternal springing,
Fill our minds, we pray,
And in all Artistic Vision
give integrity.
May the flame within us burning
Kindle yearning
Day by Day.

In all places and forever
Glory be expressed
To the Son, with God the Father,
and the Spirit blessed.
In our worship and our living,
Keep us striving
Towards the best

(David Mowbray with permission)

Please sit for
A READING FROM THE NEW TESTAMENT
St Matthew Chapter 25 vv 14-29
(Major General Sir Laurence New CB CBE,
President of the Friends of the Gaiety)

A MUSICAL INTERLUDE
Songs and Duets
with Eleanor Shimmin and Alan Wilcocks

THE SERMON
(The Reverend Canon Bill Hall,
General Secretary of the Actors' Church Union)

Hymn: Nun Danket

Now Thank we all our God,
With heart and hands and voices,
Who wondrous things hath done,
In whom His world rejoices;
Who from our mother's arms

Hath blessed us on our way
With countless gifts of love,
And still is our today.

O may this bounteous God
Through all our life be near us,
With ever joyful hearts
And blessed peace to cheer us;
And keep us in His grace
And guide us when perplexed,
And free us from all ills
In this world and the next.

All praise and thanks to God
The Father now be given,
The Son, and Him who reigns
With them in highest heaven,
The one eternal God
Whom earth and heaven adore,
For thus it as, is now,
And shall be evermore.

THE BLESSING
(The Right Reverend Noel Debroy Jones CB BA
Lord Bishop of Sodor and Man)

As the congregation disperses the Orchestra will play a selection from Lloyd Webber's 'Joseph and the Amazing Technicolor Dreamcoat', one of the current Gaiety Theatre centenary productions.

We are grateful to those who have contributed so significantly to the Service:
Eleanor Shimmin
Alan Wilcocks
John Riley (organ)
Mr Dick Ray and his Resident Cast and Orchestra
The Friends of the Gaiety Theatre
Red Cross

PROMOTIONAL TOUR ITINERARY

The following is a list of venues visited on a promotional centenary tour for the Gaiety Theatre, by Mervin Stokes and Séamus Shea.

1997
Monday September 8
The Wimbledon Theatre, **London**
Thursday September 11
The Theatres Trust, **London**
Monday October 13
The Theatre Royal, **Newcastle**
Tuesday October 14
The Empire Theatre, **Sunderland**

1998
Thursday February 12
English Heritage, **London**
Monday April 27
The Royal Lyceum Theatre, **Edinburgh**
Wednesday April 29
The Citizens Theatre, **Glasgow**
Friday May 1
His Majesty's Theatre, **Aberdeen**
Sunday May 3
The Gaiety Theatre, **Ayr**
Sunday May 31
Theatre Museum, **Covent Garden**
Sunday September 6
The Theatre Royal, **Margate**
Tuesday September 8
The Medway Arts Centre, **Chatham**
Wednesday September 9
The Cinema & Theatres Assoc., **London**
Thursday September 24
Guernsey, Channel Islands.
Friday September 25
Alderney, Channel Islands.
Saturday September 26
Sark, Channel Islands
Monday September 28,
Jersey, Channel Islands

Sunday October 4
The Coronation Hall Theatre, **Ulverston**
Wednesday October 7
The Opera House, **Buxton**
Saturday October 10
The Grand Theatre, **Blackpool**

1999
Thursday January 28
Manx Museum, **Isle Of Man**
Saturday January 30
Santa Cruz, **California**, USA
Sunday January 31
Gilroy, **California**, USA
Wednesday February 3
San Diego, **California**, USA
Friday February 5
Stubenville University, **Ohio**, USA
Monday February 8
Theatre Studies O.U., **Ohio**, USA
Tuesday February 9
History Dpt. O.U., **Ohio**, USA
Wednesday February 10
Opera House, Nelsonville, **Ohio**, USA
Saturday February 13
Washington Manx Assoc.,
Washington DC, USA
Tuesday March 16
Mount Murray Country Club,
Isle Of Man
Sunday April 11
The Theatre Royal, **York**
Tuesday April 13
The Opera House, **Wakefield**
Thursday April 15
The International Conference Centre,
Harrogate

Monday May 10
The Connaught Theatre, **Worthing**
Wednesday May 12
The International Centre, **Bournemouth**
Thursday May 13
The Tivoli Theatre, **Wimbourne**
Saturday July 03
Erin Arts Centre, **Isle Of Man**
Tuesday July 28
Stakis Hotel, **Isle Of Man**
Saturday September 4
The Theatre Royal, **Lincoln**
Monday September 6
The Birmingham and Midland Institute,
Birmingham
Wednesday September 8
The Key Theatre, **Peterborough**
Friday September 10
The Theatre Royal, **Bury St Edmunds**
Sunday October 3
The Arts Theatre, **Cambridge**
Monday October 4
The Wyvern Theatre, **Swindon**
Tuesday October 5
The Playhouse Theatre, **Salisbury**
Thursday October 7
The Theatre Royal, **Bath**
Thursday October 21
Manx Museum, **Isle Of Man**

ROLL CALL

Management and staff of the Gaiety Theatre as at July 16th 2000

Top row, from left: Eddie Lowey MLC, Chairman of the Leisure Division, Isle of Man Department of Tourism and Leisure; Mervin Russell Stokes, General Manager; Séamus Shea, Production Manager; Annette Christian, House Manager; June Kirby, Assistant House Manager.
Middle row: Margaret Davison, Acting Head Housekeeper; Elaine McLaren, Box Office; Graham Bayliss, Stage Manager.
Bottom row: Alex Davidson, Chief Technician, Light and Sound; Carl Crellin, Assistant Technician, Light and Sound; Neill Cowin, Box Office.

INDEX

A

ABC, Blackpool; 85
Act Drop; 31, 33-4, 44-6, 69-71, 79-81, 85-6, 106
Actors; 29, 32, 37-8, 40, 42, 46, 49, 53, 55, 57, 108
Actors' Church Union; 79
Alhambra, London; 31
Amadeus String Quartet; 55
Amphitheatre; 36-7, 42-4, 48, 66-7, 69, 71, 80-2, 85, 87-8, 102, 106-8
Anderson Sawmills; 103
Arminson, Iris; 66
Association of British Theatre Technicians (ABTT); 97

B

Babbacombe School; 18
Baillie-Scott, McKay Hugh; 48
Banks' Dining Rooms and Playhouse; 49
Barrier; 37, 42-3, 66-7, 80-1, 85, 102, 106-8
Barton, Amanda; 108
Barwell, Doreen; ix, xiii
Barwell, Fred; 84-5, 107
Beauchamp, Alexander; 91
Beerbohm, Max; 52
Belfast Roof Principle; 34
Bethel, Dr. John; 60
Betjeman, Sir John; 73
Bingo; 59, 62, 69
Binns, Jonas and Sons, Halifax; 45, 85
Blackburn and Starling; 42
Blackpool Tower; 16
Blanche, Ada; 52
Bond, Len; 60
Box Offices; 56, 62, 65, 70, 74, 77, 82-3, 107
Boxes; 24, 37, 48, 51, 57, 89
Boyzone; 78
Bridges; 38, 74, 94, 103
Bridgeman, George; 18
Bridgeman, Mary; 18
Bridson, Jimmy; 55
Briggs' Patent Panic Bolt; 41
Broadbent, Leonard; 26
Brown, John Archibald; 24, 26-7, 50-1
Brown, Tony, M.H.K.; 91, 101
Burnand, Frank; 52
Butterworth, David; 89
Buttimore, Simon; 87

C

Caine, Hall; 52-3
Callister, Helen; 89

Cambridge Music Hall, London; 19
Campbell, Harry; 56
Canopy; 40, 64-5, 76, 86-90
Canova; 44
Captain Barton Tennison's Assembly Rooms, Douglas; 49
Carine, Mark; 24
Carpets; 37, 68, 72, 88
Carpet cut; 37
Cast Iron Workshop, Wakefield; 86
Castle Mona Estate; 24
Castle, Roy; 78
Castle Rushen; 103
Charmer Builders; 103
Cinematographs; 26
Cinema Usage; 55, 71, 80
Circuses; 19, 22
Cirques, Grand; 19
Citizen's, Glasgow; 95
Clague, Ian; 100
Clague, Stuart, Services; 88
Class system; 41-3, 48, 104, 107-8
Cleator, Eric; 89
Clifton Suspension Bridge; 16
Clough and Shepherd; 61
Coffee Palace, Douglas; 49
Coliseum, London; 18, 20-1, 32-3, 71
Commissioners, Douglas; 24, 26
Cookson, Mona; 27
Co-operative Society, Douglas; 62
Compton Organ; 56
Corbett, Ronnie; 59
Corkill, Arthur; 59
Corkill, Denis; 89
Corkhill, Jackie; 97
Corner Trap; 37
Corsican Trap; 38, 93, 95-7
Corsican Brothers, The; 38, 53, 95-6
Counterweights; 37-40, 69, 85, 104
Cowin, Katie; 60
Cranbourne Mansions; 48
Creasey's; 104, 106
Crellin, Major Geoff; 60
Crescent Cinema, Douglas; 55, 61-2
Cretney, Jack; 74
Crockford's; 59
Cunliffe-Owen, Sir Dudley; 59-60

D

Daly, Dawn; 66
Daly, Ken; 60, 63, 66

Danta; 103
Davies, Michael; 89
Dean, A.R and Co.; 43, 46, 48
Dent, Fred; 33
Denville Stock Company; 54
Derby Castle, Douglas; 23, 54, 56
Derby, James, Seventh Earl of; 29
Derby, The; 29
Devereaux, Alf; 60
Dixon, Clive; 100
Dixon, Jack; 74
Dixon's Assembly Rooms, Douglas; 49
Dodd, Ken; 78
Dorsey, Gerry; 59
Douglas Choral Union; 50, 74
Douglas Corporation; 26, 49, 51, 57
Douglas Harbour; 16-7
Douglas Head; 28-9, 49
Douglas, Jack; 78-9
Douglas Round Table; 88
Dress Circle; 31, 34, 37, 64, 66, 69, 71-2, 85, 91-2, 99, 102
Dress Circle Bar; 60, 72, 82, 106
Drunkenness; 31, 43
Dumbell's Bank; 50
Duncan Peter; 56-7

E

Earl, John; 97
Early Doors; 40, 42
Edward VII; 21
Electric Light; 31-2, 40, 42
Elephant and Castle, London; 19, 32
Elliston James F.; 20
Empire, Birmingham; 44
Empire, Hackney; 18
Empire, Douglas; 23
Empire, Longton; 59
Empire, Shepherds Bush; 18
English Heritage; 79
Everyman, Cheltenham; 75
Eyre manuscript; 95

F

Falcon Cliff, Douglas; 23, 27
Family Circle; 37, 42
Fauteuils; 37, 41-3, 45, 106-8
Finchley, London; 19
Fine Art International Consultancy of; 79, 81, 87, 91, 104
Fire alarm system; 102-3

First World War; 32, 54, 58, 85
Fishing Industry; 16, 49, 58-9
Flats; 39-40, 94
Fly Tower; 38-40, 78
Ford, Clinton; 68
Forde, Florrie; 54-5
Formby, George; 53
Forrest, Edward; 24
Foster, Norman; 22
Foyer; 31, 40-4, 46, 51, 65-6, 70-1, 83, 86, 88, 91-2, 99, 106-8
Frescoes; 46, 64, 85, 104
Friends of The Gaiety; 74, 77-9, 88-9, 94, 98-101, 109
Fry, Stephen; 58
'Funny Peculiar'; 56
Furse lighting board; 101

G
Galbraith, Harry; 74, 79
Gale, Barbara; 100
Gallery; 34, 36-9, 40, 42-3, 45, 64, 66-9, 71-2, 80, 85, 87, 91, 98-9, 102, 104, 106-8
Gas; 19, 24, 31-2, 37, 41-3, 45, 83, 87, 92, 99
Gastelle, Stella; 53
Gelling, Donald, M.H.K.; 109
Ghosts; 102
Gilbey Horse Carriages; 62
Gill, Alex; 36
Glasstone, Victor; 71-2, 77
Globe, London; 108
Glover, J. M.; 52
Gough Ritchie Trust; 89
Government, Isle of Man; 16, 24, 58-60, 62-3, 66, 68-78, 86-7, 89, 91, 98, 103-4, 106, 109
Governor's Circle; 37, 42
Grand, Douglas; 21-4, 26-7, 33, 49-50
Grand, Islington; 20-1
Grave Trap; 37, 68, 93
Green, A. S. and Co; 85

H
Hann, Walter; 85
Happy Holland Minstrels; 60
Harker, Joseph; 45
Hartley, Stella; 59
Harris, Sir Augustus; 51
Haven, Steve de; 77
Hemming, Alfred; 22
Hemsley, William T.; 45
Hengler, Charles; 19, 22
Henniker, Lord; 50
Her Majesty's, London; 75
Highgate Cemetery; 54
Hillary, Sir William; 16
Hippodrome, Bolton

Hippodrome, Brighton; 19
Hippodrome, Hulme; 59
Hippodrome, London; 17-9, 21, 33, 48
Hippodrome, Manchester; 19
Hitchcock, Alfred; 53
Holtham, Dick; 89
Howerd, Frankie; 59
Hull, Alan; 75
Hull, Lionel; xiii
Humperdinck, Englebert; 59

I
Ibsen, Henrik; 52
Industrialisation; 16
Inman, John; 77
Isle of Man Bank; 78
Isle of Man Times; 54

J
Jacobi, Derek; 94
Johnson, Dr Samuel; 30
Jong, Felix de; 21

K
Kean, Charles; 38
Kelly, Jimmy; 103
Killip, J. L. and Collister; 37
"King Gobnegeay"; 53
Kneen, Deemster; 50

L
'La Poupée'; 53
Laxey Glen Gardens; 34
Leigh, Mike; 75
Lieutenant Governor; 24, 37, 74, 77, 98
Lightfoot, Thomas; 22
Livery Yard, Douglas; 49
Lloyd Webber, Andrew; 22
Lough, John Graham; 45
Levilly, Peter; 53
Lowenfeld, Henry; 53
Lowey, Eddie, M.L.C.; 60, 109
Lyceum, Edinburgh; 78, 93-4
Lyceum, Sheffield; 93
Lyric, Hammersmith; 18

M
MacHarrie, Coll; 76
McCammon, G. A.; 51
McEvoy, Tony; 68-70
McGarvey, Gerry; 89
Mackintosh, Charles Rennie; 48
Mannanan; 16
Mannin Entertainments; 60, 66, 71-2
Manx American Association; 98
Manx Heritage Foundation; 98

Manxman, The; 63
'Manx Last Night of the Proms, The'; 100
Manx Lottery; 62, 75
Manx Motor Museum; 62
Manx Museum; 72, 86
Manx Radio; 77
Manx Telecom; 98
Manx Youth Band, The; 100
Marsden, Gordon and Co.; 61-2
Margate Free Press
Marina, Douglas; 23-5, 27
Marsland, John; 66
Martin, C. J.; 79
Matcham, Brian; 97-8
Matcham, Constance Amy; 19
Matcham, Evelyn; 19
Matcham, Frank; 16-22, 27, 29, 32-3, 35-7, 39-41, 43-46, 48, 54, 61, 66, 70-3, 75, 77-8, 80-2, 85-6, 88, 91-2, 97, 99, 106, 108
Matcham, Maria; 19-20, 22
Matcham Suite; 87-89
May, Phil; 45
May, Fanny Harriet; 45
Media Matrix; 101
Metropolitan Music Hall, London; 21
Mining industry; 24
'Minstrels From Amsterdam'; 60
Moody Manners Opera Company; 52
Moore Stephens; 100
Morris, William; 48
Moss, H. E.; 21-2, 45
Movietone News; 55
Music Hall; 27, 29-33, 43, 49
Myers, Sidney; 59

N
National Portrait Gallery; 86
National Trust; 79, 86, 93-4
Newton Abbot, Devon; 18
New, Lady; 74
New, Sir Laurence; 74, 77
New, Douglas; 49
Niblick, Drummond; 86
Nivison, Jack; 60
'No Limit'; 53

O
Odeon, Leicester Square; 31
Old Vic, London; 18
Old Vic, Bristol; 78
Opera; 29-30, 32-3, 51-3
Opera House, Buxton; 91
Opera House, Bury; 20
Opera House, Douglas; 23
Opera House Dunfermline; 75
Opera House, London; 46

Opera House, Wakefield; 21, 59, 85, 98
Orientalism; 31, 45
Otto Gas Engine; 42

P

Paddle; 38
Paignton, Devon; 18
Paint Frame; 39-40
Palace Coliseum, Douglas; 60
Palace and Derby Castle Company, The; 18,
22-4, 26-7, 35-6, 50, 52, 55-7, 59-61, 63, 85,
106
Palace Pavilion, Douglas; 23-4, 33-5, 37, 42-44
Palladium, London; 18
Panopticon of Science and Art; 31
Paragon, Mile End Road; 20
Pascoe, Alan; 56
Pathè News; 55
Patent Theatres; 30
Pavilion, Douglas; 18, 23, 24, 26-7, 50, 101,
104
Pertwee, Jon; 55
Philips, Mr; 36
Phipps, C. J.; 32
Picture House Cinema, Douglas; 55
Pit stalls; 34, 37, 40, 42, 51, 64-6, 81, 83, 88-9,
102, 104-5, 107
Plasterwork; 35, 37, 43-4, 48, 64, 70, 72, 83-4,
107
Plastic Decoration and Papier Machè Co.; 44
Playhouse, London; 75
Poulter, F. C.; 50
Prince of Wales, Douglas; 49
Prologues; 20
Proscenium; 31, 33-5, 37, 39, 44-6, 48, 62, 64,
68-9, 83, 87, 105
Projection suite; 55
Prostitutes; 31
Purcell family; 20,21

Q

Quayle, Dan; 98
Quayle, Thomas; 40
Queen's, Keighley; 48

R

Radcliffe, Percy; 60
'Rags to Riches' tour; 97
Raymond, Paul; 59
Regal Cinema, Douglas; 55-6
Rennison, William J.; 24
Revill family; 20-1
Richmond, London; 18
Riley, John; 79
Ring, Attorney General; 50
Robinson, Jethro T.; 18-9, 21

Robinson, John; 22
Rose Window; 44, 64, 82-4, 86, 89
Royal Hall, Harrogate; 75, 87, 104
Royal National Lifeboat Institution; 16
Royal Opera House, Covent Garden; 30, 106
Royal Theatre, Douglas; 49
Royalty Cinema, Douglas; 55
Royalty, Glasgow; 19
Rules Restaurant; 54
Ruskin, Thomas; 48
Russell, Ken; 75
Rutland, Duke of; 49

S

Sachs, Edwin; 20
Safety Curtain; 41, 69-70, 75, 86, 104
San Francisco; 16
Savage, Canon Ernest; 54
Savoy, London; 32
Scott, Clement; 54
Second World War; 18
Serpette, Gaston; 52
Sefton Hotel; 40
Sentance, Charles; 77, 79, 89
Service Players; 55
Shaftesbury, London; 52
Shakespeare, William; 30, 108
Shaw, George Bernard; 54
Shea, Séamus; 97-99, 101, 103-4
Shimmin, Marion; 79
Sieferts Demolition; 60
Slips, 37, 43-5, 64, 66
Sloats; 38, 74
Smith, Dr Angus; 31
Smith, Rev'd Alec; 79
Smuggling; 59
'Soldiers in Skirts'; 56
Stage, The; 49-50, 68
Stage curtains; 45-6, 62, 64, 69, 72, 80-7, 89,
91-2
Stage machinery; 37-43
Stencil work; 44, 91
St Paul's Church, Halifax; 45
St Thomas' Church; 54, 79
Standish, Myles; 98
'Steaming'; 56
Stevenson, Sir Ralph; 60
Stoll, Oswald; 21
Stoll Moss Empires; 21, 45
Stokes, Mervin Russell; 61-2, 77-9, 82, 96-103,
106-9
Strand Cinema, Douglas; 55
Sturgess, Arthur; 52
Sugden, Molly; 78-9
Sugg Lighting Co.; 83, 89
Sun-burner; 19, 37, 42, 82-3

Surrey Zoological Gardens, Southwark; 30
T
'The Telephone Girl'; 51-2, 98
Tussauds, Louis, Waxworks; 62
Telestage; 70
Theatre Museum, Covent Garden; 98
Theatre Royal, Bath; 95
Theatre Royal, Blackburn; 20
Theatre Royal, Douglas; 23
Theatre Royal, Drury Lane; 30
Theatre Royal, Hanley; 32
Theatre Royal, Ipswich; 95
Theatre Royal, Ramsey; 49
Theatre Royal, Stockport; 20
Theatres Trust; 97
Tollerton, Leeds; 83
Tourism; 16, 24, 58-9
Tourism, Department of; 60, 71, 73
T.T. Races; 53
Trades Exhibition (1899); 26-7
Tree, Sir Herbert Beerbohm; 45
Turner Son and Walker, Liverpool; 44
Tyne Theatre and Opera House, Newcastle;
38, 74, 94-5
Tynwald; 24, 60

U
Uren, Lenny; 56

V
Vanity Fair; 86
Variety; 23-4, 27, 33, 44, 51-3, 56, 59-60
Ventilation system (grilles); 70
Victoria, Douglas; 49
Victoria Hall, Halifax; 45
Victorian Stained Glass Company; 82, 87
Villa Marina; 59, 70, 109
Villa Marina Arcade; 70

W
Wakeman, Rick; 99
Wallpaper; 43-4, 57, 64-5, 72, 88, 91-2, 99,
106-7
Waterloo, Douglas; 49
Watterson, Linda; 79
Webb, Alderman; 50
Wilde, Oscar; 32
Wilkinson, Bob; 60
Wilmore, Dr David; 70, 72, 74, 76, 78-80, 82-3,
88-9, 93-7, 99, 103
Wilmot, Charles; 45
Windsor Castle; 102
Winter Garden, Douglas; 29
Wing forks; 39-40, 104
Wood, Michael; 74
Wren, Sir Christopher; 51